Women of the Homefront

Women of the Homefront

World War II Recollections of 55 Americans

Edited by Pauline E. Parker

McFarland & Company, Inc., Publishers
Jefferson, North Carolina, and London

Library of Congress Cataloguing-in-Publication Data

Women of the homefront : World War II recollections of 55
Americans / edited by Pauline E. Parker.
    p.   cm.
Includes bibliographical references and index.

ISBN 0-7864-1346-8 (softcover binding : 50# alkaline paper)

    1. World War, 1939–1945 — Women — United States—
Biography.   2. World War, 1939–1945 — Personal narratives,
American.   I. Parker, Pauline E.
D810.W7 W657 2002
940.53'082 — dc21   2002009232

British Library cataloguing data are available

Cover photograph: The Putnam women, circa 1942

Manufactured in the United States of America

McFarland & Company, Inc., Publishers
  Box 611, Jefferson, North Carolina 28640
  www.mcfarlandpub.com

Acknowledgments

To the members of the writing class at the Beatitudes retirement campus in Phoenix who taught me that writing can improve with age; to Louise de Wald, the longtime teacher who knew it all the time; to the women who offered their stories and proved it; to Carol Waters for her persistence in acquiring difficult interviews and recording them; to Margaret and Christian Freer for their determination in recruiting authors for four years; to Lunette Mulkey for recruiting more authors; to the families whose enthusiasm provided assurance that such a book was a worthwhile effort; to Susan Walsh and Janet Putnam for their assistance in typing and proofreading; to the special medical staffs at Oregon Health Science University who gave far more than medical aid to keep me going, insisting that "we have to get that book published"; to my agent, Elizabet McHugh; to Pam, for providing the right words and phrases, and for her unfailing insistence that the book will be a winner; to Nancy, whose drive and commitment broadened the scope of the book; to Bill, my husand, who kept the records straight and for his unflagging support; to my extended family, who helped keep both the book and me alive until the dream became a reality; and to Ann, who always makes it happen; I acknowledge my great indebtedness and extend my deepest gratitude.

Contents

Voices from the Services and Military Hospitals

Voices from Military Dependents

Voices from Daily Life

Voices from Abroad

A Lonely Voice for Peace

Voices of Grief

Preface

Women of the Homefront captures the experiences and feelings of young women living through the turmoil and upheaval of World War II before our stories are lost forever. These personal recollections recall not only a dramatic period in our history, but also a period before the feminist movement came into its own, before young women became convinced they could aspire to the same opportunities and rights as their brothers.

We are the first to say that we American wives and sweethearts fared far better than civilians in other countries caught up in the conflict. Our experiences cannot be compared with those of men and women on the front lines or captured by the enemy. Women on the American homefront carried the war in our minds and imaginations, without much fear of being thrust far from homes or going without food, without having to face the dangers of armed conflict. War's reality came home when the dreaded telegram was delivered or a wounded loved one returned. Perhaps that is why so little has been written about us. Still, what happened to us on the day-to-day level required patience, endurance and a stout heart and influenced our futures far more than we realized at the time.

For many of us, our men were taken away at the most crucial time of our lives—the mating and procreating period—as happens in all wars. We ventured out of protective homes, took over men's jobs to feed the war machine, learned haphazardly to drive cars in order to venture into strange and lonely country to be near our loved ones as long as possible, struggled with parenting alone in difficult situations, and found the courage, somehow, to keep a "stiff upper lip" for four or more years of waiting. And there

1

was no military structure to order our lives or to create the close *esprit de corps* available to our men.

The original intent of this book was to restrict its boundaries to women in the United States. It didn't even occur to me to do otherwise, until unsolicited manuscripts came in, written of young women's experiences in other countries, both allied and enemy. These women, who married American men as a result of the war, brought their own histories with them from their homelands. I had to include them. They stand alone to remind us of the grimness of the struggle elsewhere.

We read and listen to today's women explaining our experiences, desires and outlook upon our world and want to say to them, "It wasn't quite like that. All we wanted at the time was to do our best in getting through the war so that we could acquire or resume our traditional roles of homemaker and mother. The shift in expectations came later."

We gave little thought to the budding change in women's roles. Our lives at that wartime moment took center stage. Most would feel uncomfortable or deny vehemently the suggestion that we were part of a feminist movement. Yet many of us returned to or entered the work force within a few years after our children were in school, many in positions not imagined as available to women before World War II.

Age and marital status had much to do with women's wartime experiences. Teenage girls were expected to help with recycling materials at school, folding bandages and entertaining the troops before they left for the war and when they were brought back to hospitals. These young ladies were indispensable to the United Services Organization (USO) and to the local efforts to make life more bearable for the young men stranded on bases far from home and recreational resources and for those in hospitals for long periods. As the war progressed, the girls filled many of the routine, paper-shuffling local jobs, as well.

Older single women had the freedom to venture into other worlds and a large number of them did. The adventurous entered the newly developed women's military services. The federal government held examinations in regions and cities to select young women to travel to Washington, D.C., and other places to be trained as secretaries and clerks, often referred to as G.G.s, government girls. Many took the exams. Others heeded the call of the factories. Most spent many hours in volunteer work.

Married women without children were most likely to follow their husbands until the men were shipped overseas. They rented rooms in private homes, or set up makeshift homes off bases. Many sought war jobs, however temporary, wherever their husbands were stationed. When their spouses shipped out, they often settled into jobs to wait out the war. Some returned to their parents' homes.

Wives with children, particularly those married to enlisted men with limited incomes, often stayed with parents or other family members. If the camps where their husbands were stationed afforded housing for married military personnel, and the commanding officer allowed, they usually remained on base until their husbands were sent overseas. Then, they frequently returned to their families or joined other military wives with children to share expenses and their loneliness. Older parents throughout the war provided shelter, food, and reassurance for many young daughters and grandchildren, as well as for camp-following wives before their men went to sea or overseas.

The relationship between the sexes changed some during this period. Barriers were eased, although not to the extent they were in the sixties. Before Pearl Harbor, young men in uniform were often shunned by young women, on advice of parents. Military men were an unknown quantity. Soon after Pearl Harbor, everybody had brothers or friends in uniform. The assumption quickly developed that cheering up a stranger would be repaid by some other young woman somewhere cheering up a brother. Flirting was handled easily and "sexual harassment" was not yet a household phrase.

Fear of strangers was much less intense than today. If a car broke down, a young woman would turn to a man in uniform for assistance. It was a wartime duty to pick up hitch-hiking men in uniform thumbing their way into town from an out-of-the-way base. One well-known poster proclaimed, "When you ride alone, you ride with Hitler." Even in Los Angeles, women thought little of walking home from the Palladium Ballroom in pairs after a dance.

We worked at all sorts of jobs. Teachers continued to teach. Others went into the war industries and government. Almost anywhere, a young woman could find employment, often dull paper-shuffling work resulting from the vast governmental demand for forms. Yet most would walk away in an instant if it meant they could follow their fiancé, boyfriend, or husband for even a single week. They could find work somewhere else when their men were shipped out. This lack of commitment to a particular job was soon accepted as routine and employers became resigned.

When it was all over, the nation settled down into the seemingly traditional norm. When the baby boom began overwhelming the educational system, the call went out for more teachers. Some mothers who had taught before the war returned to their profession. They were praised by society. Other mothers went back to school. The campus environment was much more accepting of older students because of the influx of veterans taking advantage of the G.I. Bill. As time went on, more and more women became working mothers, and money was not necessarily the driving force. It wasn't easy. We struggled with a free-floating sense of guilt that we were abandoning our children. Society of the '50's nourished that guilt. But we persevered.

With a few exceptions, we writers of these memoirs are in our seventies and eighties. Our contributions have mainly been written within the past four years. We are living examples of the advances in the medical and pharmaceutical technologies of the past fifty years. Heart bypasses, pacemakers, hip replacements, oncology operations, radiation treatments and drug therapies abound among us. Canes, walkers and wheelchairs keep a number of us mobile. Some of us are widows and others still have our husbands at hand. Most have celebrated 50th wedding anniversaries. We carry on — a habit probably picked up long ago, after Pearl Harbor.

This book is a small tribute to those women who by themselves raised the children, kept their families together, kept industry going, served in the military and kept alive the faith and hope of those abroad in war.

For over a decade I have carried the dream of gathering women's World War II experiences into a book for those who lived them, for their children and grandchildren and for posterity. These are the true voices of some of the women from that period, voices that will not be heard again. This is our gift to the future.

Pauline E. Parker
Portland, Oregon
Summer 2002

Voices from
Pearl Harbor

Paradise Destroyed

Pauline B. Hurlbut
(as told to Christian Freer)

Ah, Hawaii! Oahu...Diamond Head...Waikiki...tropical breezes, sandy beaches, curling surf...what a great place for a junior Army officer, recently out of West Point, to begin his Army career.

My first lieutenant husband and I arrived in 1940. We moved into Army quarters adjacent to Hickam Army Air Base, where he had been assigned as ordnance officer. We enjoyed the pleasant living, with Japanese or Chinese servants to look after the house and garden, and the relaxed atmosphere of a peacetime Army base. I was beginning to feel comfortable as the wife of an officer. We made friends, not only among our Army associates, but with Navy people and civilians, as well. Life was sweet until...

On that quiet, sunny Sunday morning we were still asleep when the first bombs were dropped. "Oh, my God, it's the Japanese!" my husband exclaimed as he struggled into his uniform. He was out the door in no time, headed for his duty post at the ordnance depot. That was the last I saw or heard of him for four long and anxious days until he got a message to me that he was alive and well.

From our quarters I could not see Pearl Harbor, but the explosions and smoke from Battleship Row gave evidence of the violence of the attack. Later we learned that at our nearby airfield most of the planes were sitting ducks for enemy bombing and strafing runs; only a couple managed to get into the air.

That morning runners appeared with orders for us dependents to evacuate our quarters and head for the mountains. There was no way of knowing if there might be a follow-up Japanese air strike. Hickam Airfield and the surrounding area where we were quartered would be a primary target. I left with the clothes on my back, and with several other young wives, drove up into the hills, where there were many beautiful places owned by wealthy island families. I went to the home of friends; but whether we were friends or not even acquaintances, the people up there took us all in and put us up until other arrangements could be made for us. I was particularly thankful for any help I could get, for I was eight months pregnant with my first child.

For some time there had been an underlying, mostly unspoken, feeling that war with Japan was bound to come sooner or later. Now it was sooner. Although we had never been warned of possible hostilities, much less had any drills or alerts or even instructions, the discipline of military life we had absorbed stood us in good stead. Despite intense anxiety and great confusion, there was no panic among us and we were pretty well prepared to accept the situation as it was.

After Pearl Harbor things were pretty tense, with so many Japanese on the islands and nobody knowing for sure where their loyalties lay. It must have been terribly difficult for them too.

After a couple of weeks I, along with a lot of other dependents, got my shipping orders. Of course we were limited to what we could take with us. I packed only a suitcase with summer clothing. I was somewhat surprised to see a few women scurrying about trying to take their silverware with them.

We sailed around Christmas time (it may even have been on Christmas Day, I'm not sure) on the SS *Mariposa*. The ship was crowded with evacuees, some of whom had already suffered grievous losses and others who would lose dear ones in the coming months and years of the war. At our departure many of us tried to hold back our tears, some more successfully than others.

The crossing was uneventful. Even though it was mid-winter, the Pacific Ocean lived up to its name and the seas were smooth. That was fortunate for me, my pregnancy by now almost full-term, but maybe it wouldn't have made any difference in the end.

When we landed at San Francisco after several days, I was lucky enough to stay with a friend of my family. I stayed with her until arrangements could be made for me to travel to my family home in St. Louis, Missouri.

Soon after my arrival, I was delivered of my baby…stillborn. I have often wondered whether things might have been different for the baby and me were it not for December 7, 1941, or if my baby was a casualty of Pearl Harbor.

December 7, 1941— Honolulu, Territory of Hawaii

Barbara M. McLaren

My two little sons and I were living at my parents' home in Honolulu. My Navy husband was aboard a ship stationed at Cavite, Manila's Naval Station, Philippine Islands. He had left Pearl Harbor exactly one year previously, December 6, 1940. The few ship's wives who were still in Honolulu had just celebrated the day — one year gone, two more to go.

On December 7, I awoke to much commotion in the house beyond the hedge at the back of our yard. Something was amiss. My mother turned on the radio and we all gathered to listen to Webley Edwards announcing that the Japanese were bombing Pearl Harbor; we were at war with Japan! In an agitated voice, he kept telling us to "Keep calm! Keep calm!"

My dad, district manager of Mackay Radio and Telegraph, went down to his office immediately. During the day he phoned home occasionally with descriptions of what was going on. One dreadful message was that at Pearl Harbor the bodies were being piled up like cordwood.

It wasn't long before we heard "Extra! Extra!" being shouted on a street two blocks away, so I ran to get a newspaper. The second headline was that Cavite was also under attack. I pictured everything my dad described happening at Pearl Harbor also happening in Cavite and was sick with worry about Ken. Would I ever see him again?

With Oahu dependent on shipping for most of our staples, I was very much concerned about baby foods for my two-and-a-half and one-and-a-half year old sons. Monday morning, I went shopping at the neighborhood stores, one Chinese and one Japanese. It seemed strange to be buying from a Japanese at that time. Although I had shopped there many times over the years, I felt uncomfortable.

That afternoon my dad and I were standing on the sidewalk leading to our house when we became aware of a plane flying, and it flew directly over us, showing its rising sun emblem on the wings. It continued on and soon we saw a column of smoke rising. It was one of several fire bombings of Japanese stores in retaliation for their ceasing to send money home to Japan. Apparently when the local Japanese had gotten wind of what was to happen or might happen, their loyalties were with America.

During that night, as I got up to tend my children, there was an explosion at Punahou School a block away and shrapnel peppered our roof. Punctured it, too. My parents had a leaky roof all through the war. My two-and-a-half year old, Jim, said, "Airplane, boom!"

We lived at the foot of Manoa Valley and all night on both December 7 and 8 we could hear sirens going up the road to the valley. It turned out that at the head of the valley there were encampments of Filipinos and Japanese and they were having their own little war. The sirens we heard were those of ambulances as well as police cars.

During that first week, a classmate of my husband phoned to say he was in Waikiki and wanted me to come see him. I did and he said he'd been on the *Oklahoma* on December 7 and woke up as he flew through the air and landed in the oily water. Flaming oil on the water became a great concern but he was rescued fairly quickly. Like many, the only clothes he had were what he'd worn to bed the night before.

During the next few weeks we all had to register at stations set up all over the island. Then we had to go to assigned places to be fitted with gas masks which we were to carry every time we left the house. Blackouts were in effect and Mother had sewn black curtains for one room in which we sat every evening, listening to the radio or playing cards or reading. Before we went to bed we always listened at a certain time to learn if there were any instructions for the night. Now and then they'd expect a raid and would advise keeping any important papers and our gas masks at bedside.

There were no masks for small children. We were to soak towels in the bathtub for them. We had been instructed to put our gas masks on first, then wrap a wet towel around the face of a child. I could just picture the reaction if I were to approach either of my children wearing a gas mask with grasshopper eyes and hose snout and try to put a wet towel over his face!

The warning came often enough that I tried to evacuate — that is, to leave for the United States mainland. Then things quieted down for a while and I took my name off the list. A friend who also had two little boys was doing the same thing. We shopped together for pants to wear on the ship, in case we did go, and decided bright yellow would be a good color to wear if the ship should sink and we'd be in the water! I put my name on and off the list several times and, finally, in April I put it on and kept it on. I had become very adept at taking apart tricycles and packing them in a trunk, then reassembling them each time I decided I'd stay in Hawaii instead of leaving.

Finally the boys and I evacuated on Easter Sunday, April 5, 1942, on the *S.S. Lurline*, much changed from its life as a luxury liner. There were six of us in a cabin originally designed for two. It had two tiers of three bunks each — another lady with her two children on one side, and my two boys and me on the other. The *Lurline* was escorted by a Navy ship and we made it safely to San Francisco.

A Navy Teenager at Pearl Harbor

Virginia B. Scrymgeour

It was Sunday morning and there was no sign of either of the two local newspapers, so we turned on the radio and learned that Pearl Harbor was being bombed — that this was the real thing, not a "drill."

My father was a lieutenant commander in the Navy and we lived in Honolulu in December 1941. Father had just assumed a new command and had gone to sea on maneuvers on Friday, December 5. My mother, 8-year-old brother and I, 13 going on 14, were at home in the residential area of Kahala which is on the far side of Diamond Head from Waikiki, very near the U.S. Army base Fort Ruger and about two blocks away from the waterfront.

My mother had recently taken a first aid course, so she ordered us to bathe and put on clean clothes! Under her calm instruction, we taped and rigged blankets over windows and listened to both radio stations and also monitored the police calls. There were reports of sightings of parachutes, none of which turned out to be true. Trucks from Fort Ruger rumbled by on Kahala Avenue and we could hear anti-aircraft guns in Diamond Head in occasional bursts of fire.

We noticed that the neighbor who lived in the house behind us was washing his car and we assumed he knew nothing of the raid, so my mother and I walked up to tell him what had happened. Later, he told us that he had thought we were sorority girls told to tell an outrageous story to someone as part of our initiation!

Air raid alerts were sounded several times during the day and we climbed between two double-bed mattresses until the "all clear" sounded. We had been under the mattresses so long that we really were very tired of the weight when the "all clear" sounded. We had missed an earlier signal and been there through two alerts.

We finally learned that Dad was safe and he finally found out that we were safe as well. Assuming that we would be evacuated eventually, we started sorting and throwing away personal and household items toward packing up. Of course, there was no way to know how long things would be in storage, so Mom held a garage sale to peel down. She parted with most of her kitchen pots and pans, not realizing how many years it would be before she would be able to replace them.

I carried thermoses of coffee to the soldiers at the machine gun post which was set up on the beach behind much barbed wire. Christmas came and went. I dug up a mock orange bush for our Christmas tree. I decorated the bush and we opened a few presents. My father was there.

After packing our household effects, we moved out of the house into a family-style hotel to be ready for evacuation to the mainland. Other Navy wives and children were there. By now, we had all been finger-printed and issued gas masks. Alerts sounded on and off. I was close enough to my school to run to the hotel when an alert sounded, which they did all the time we remained in Honolulu. Our apartment was screened and had very little window glass, so many of the families gathered at our place during alerts.

Dad showed up occasionally for short visits—usually only overnight. He insisted that we finally put our name on the evacuation list and, so it was on Good Friday, 1942, we left Dad on the pier as we sailed out of Honolulu on the *Aquitania*—a handsome Cunard passenger liner which had been converted into a troop ship and had been carrying troops from Australia to the Pacific war zones. It was now repositioning itself to the Atlantic and, thus, had room to pick up evacuees in Hawaii. My father had assured us that we would be escorted by Navy ships as we sailed to California, but the first morning at sea there were no other ships in sight. We were told the *Aquitania* was fast enough to go it alone, zigzagging all the way to San Pedro. Adults may have been concerned but we teenagers spent the time as one would usually spend time on an ocean liner — eating, sleeping, looking at the sea, walking the decks and chatting.

Our cabin was originally designed for one or two passengers, but three rows of bunk beds in tiers of three now filled the room and the elegant tapestry covering the ceiling showed boot prints! But only Mom, my brother and I occupied it. Bunks had also been installed along the decks—canvas lashed to pipe frames in tiers of four. These were raised to a vertical position as there were no troops aboard. We would lower one or two to sit on when we were on deck.

The *Aquitania* was too big to dock in San Pedro, so she anchored out in the harbor and we were transferred to shore in ferry boats from Catalina Island. One passenger went to a telephone booth as soon as we got ashore to let her family members know she had arrived and was told by a telephone operator that it was a military secret that the *Aquitania* was in port and "don't you know there's a war on?"

Eventually we returned to the eastern United States, settling in Arlington, Virginia, just across the Potomac River from Washington, D. C. Mom volunteered at the ration board. I worked at a civilian hospital in D. C. as a JANGO (Junior Army Navy Guild Organization)—a candy-striper type volunteer.

My father was trapped in a desk job in Washington for a while, but finally got back to the war in the Pacific. Mom re-upholstered a living room chair while he was in the fighting at Iwo Jima to keep from worrying too much about him.

The summer of 1944 I was 16 and able to take a government job as a file clerk, which paid $1260 per annum. On VE Day we danced in Pennsylvania Avenue in front of the White House.

I entered the freshman class at the College of William and Mary in September 1946. We were 100 women and 300 men in the class. Of that 300 men, 275 were veterans who had returned from war and were taking advantage of the G.I. Bill. A serious group indeed.

Voices from Relocation Camps

When I Lost
My Liberty

Kiyoka Kurumada

I recall that fateful day, December 7, 1941, as if it were yesterday, for that was the day we lost our civil rights, liberty and protection of the Constitution. The day following the attack on Pearl Harbor, I was peremptorily discharged from the Security First National Bank of Seattle, a coveted position that I had gotten after graduation from a business college and one I held with so much pride, as I was but one of a chosen few among Japanese Americans to get a white-collar job. As with the African-Americans before the Watts riot, because of our all too obvious features, no Japanese American was able to get a "decent" position. I hurried home, hurt, angry and ashamed that I could be summarily fired from a job simply because of my ancestry.

Those were frightening days; the *Post Intelligencer* Hearst newspaper was whipping the public into a frenzy with their insinuations of spies and fifth-column activities (undercover anti-American activities) amongst the Japanese population (all disproved in later years), and the pervasive air of distrust emanating from the public in general was overwhelming, disquieting, a premonition of impending disaster.

A curfew was enacted affecting only the people of Japanese ancestry and daily, we huddled by our radio, listening to news of the war, its ramifications and consequences as regarding our status. Other Asians began wearing tags stating, "I am Chinese," anything to avoid being picked up by the police or attacked by the hysterical and panicked populace, a witch-hunt mentality in those days.

Comic books depicting Japanese atrocities by comedic Japanese men with buck teeth and horned rim glasses all added to the hysteria and bigotry that ran rampant. Dad came running home from work one evening, completely out of breath, and collapsed. He gasped out that a man had apparently waited for him to walk out from his work place and as he approached the parking lot, attempted to attack him with a butcher knife. Of course, this incident was never reported to the police because we knew only too well that the perpetrator of the crime would become a hero and the victim, my father, the villain. Dad, too, lost his job in the ensuing days, as did Mama and my brother.

A feeling of impending disaster hung over the very air we breathed and permeated our every thought in those days, and finally, the ax fell. We were all told to be ready for evacuation from the West Coast and given a few days to rid ourselves of our worldly possessions. Our homes, furniture, pets, cherished belongings, all must be discarded. One suitcase was allowed for each individual. My parents had to pack the necessities in their suitcases— sheets, pillows, pots, pans, iron, needles, thread, all the accouterments necessary for living. In the children's suitcases we stuffed as much clothing as we could.

I remember seeing the scavengers with trucks in front of every Japanese American house, taking advantage of our predicament and buying at a fraction of the value our treasures: piano, refrigerator, washing machine, etc. Our new refrigerator sold for $20 and the rest, likewise. Dad and Mom were busy burning anything Japanese because to be caught with them in our homes was to bring on imprisonment. Many were incarcerated immediately when the police burst into homes and literally pulled people into jail, all because of a bit of inconsequential Japanese literature that they had in their possession.

A few days later, my family, Dad, Mamma, brother, sister and I joined with others of Japanese ancestry in a long queue, waiting for the numbers assigned to us to be called so that we could board the bus that was to take us, no one knew where. Pervading us all was the fright, the lonesome, forlorn and agonizing feelings of citizens who have lost their civil rights, which are supposedly guaranteed under the Constitution of the United States of America. We were packed like homeless refugees with our only worldly belonging, a suitcase; a lifetime packed into one suitcase. We were the Isseis, first-generation Americans; Niseis, second-generation Americans; and a few Sanseis, third-generation Americans.

On the bus, not a word was spoken, each in his own thoughts; tears suppressed, sometimes spilling out and trickling down a cheek but never a sound, all the while knowing that if but one broke out into a sob, the pain would become too unbearable, unquenchable.

The stoicism of the Japanese, inherent even amongst the Niseis, was perceptible in their every action. We were taught as children, no, not taught per se, but made very aware that we must not make waves, never bring shame by action or words, as it would reflect upon the family and the entire Japanese community.

We were driven to our so-called assembly center, the Puyallup Fairgrounds. Soldiers with rifles guarded our every movement. Like sheep being herded to slaughter, we meekly obeyed, and with our meager belongings, were assigned our homes for the next three months. The horse stables had been readied, one for each family, whether one child or eight, a family per stable. A lucky few got one of the rooms in a barrack. We were one of the fortunate ones to be assigned a 10'x10' room with bare wooden walls and a couple of windows with a foot-wide opening on top, running the entire width of the wall on each side. So much for any privacy.

Mama went to work immediately, filling bags with straw for our mattresses and Dad scrounged and pilfered odds and ends of lumber with which to make a crude table and stools. Amazingly, Mamma made our quarters quite livable with curtains and government issue, drab, olive green blankets. From our former three-story home in Seattle, with the amenities of a lifetime, a collection of Japanese art and furniture, to subsistence within four bare walls is irreconcilable, but of necessity was endured. Philosopher Neitzsche said, "That which does not kill me makes me stronger," and this was proven to us over and over. Amazingly too, my parents never, ever complained and, to this day, I marvel at their stoicism, "Bushido spirit," in accepting with so much grace what had been forced upon them.

Because we were teenagers, Nisei teenagers, taught never to rebel against those in authority, we meekly accepted, no, endured too, the outside toilets located about a half block away and learned to await the call from the "shower master" to take our showers. The hot water was for the lucky few who got there first.

I had a few loyal Caucasian boyfriends who were kind enough to visit me with chocolates and food items, but always there was the barbed wire fence between us, soldiers on either end of the fence, looking on and I always felt a regrettably disturbed and ashamed feeling to be on the wrong side of the barbed wire.

The food in those first few weeks (although called basic Army food) was intolerable and all of us lived with constant diarrhea and upset stomachs. Canned wieners and bread puddings are the two culprits that remain in my memory as "gross" and which were served with such frequency that to this day, I cannot bear the very sight of them.

For those of us who worked, and all of us did, we earned $16 or $19 (for supervisors, and I was one of the lucky ones) per month, which bought necessities or luxuries, whichever was prioritized as important for each of us. In those drab surroundings, "hyacinths for my soul" became of utmost importance to me and I promptly joined three book clubs which helped to "take me miles away."

There were brighter moments for the young and I had many new friends, socializing with more Japanese Americans than I had ever seen. As our cameras and radios had been confiscated, another enjoyment was learning to play cards, pinochle. The dances provided another diversion, and after tables and benches had been cleared in the mess hall, the camp band played Glenn Miller music. To us it was as lovely as Miller's own band and for a short respite, we forgot the barbed wires and soldiers guarding us.

The three months, in spite of hardships encountered, lack of privacy, etc. went quickly, and one day, I found myself volunteering to be the first to go to our permanent camp, lay the groundwork and prepare the camp for the rest of the evacuees.

Once again, we were riding to an unknown destination on a darkened, vintage train that poured smoke into our car. The shades had been drawn so that we could not see or be seen, and when the train stopped in a deserted area, we were once again loaded into the backs of open Army trucks and again driven elsewhere. The exuberance of youth in a new and otherwise exciting experience was entirely missing and so, if the Army had known of our cultural background, they would not have been as concerned in their guarded stance.

The desolate landscape that greeted our eyes was beyond any expectations: arid sand dunes and cactuses, obscenely surrounded by tall, barbed wire fences. The new camp was named Minidoka and was located near Hunt, Idaho. This unfriendly land, with the ingenuity of the Issei farmers, hard working men of the soil, would be turned into a fertile land that provided us with our fresh vegetables, a feat unbelievable to those of us who had been city dwellers.

Soldiers at the ready in strategically placed towers greeted us. Rows upon rows of barracks, one room as before for an entire family, this time, however, without any toilet facilities. We were told upon arrival to dig holes and that facilities would be installed as soon as possible. This brings to mind the first evening when I had to go to the toilet. I ventured outside the door of my barracks, the enveloping black of the desert night engulfed me and as my eyes adjusted to the darkness, the shadows cast by the empty barracks lurked menacingly. Without any lights and with just a few stars shining, the desert loomed threateningly and the sounds made my very skin crawl. I returned to my barracks and asked a friend to accompany me. As we traversed the dusty, virgin grounds, a moth flew into my hair, frightening me to such an extreme state that I am certain my friend was more frightened than I by my actions. I survived this night without visiting the "hole" and decided that I would somehow manage to contain myself at night until such time as proper facilities were built and lights placed outside.

The people arrived and were assigned their rooms. In our otherwise bare room was a small pot-bellied stove to warm us against the bitter cold of an Idaho winter, but no coal to burn, only the scavenged bits of wood. The crevices

Residents of block seven at Camp Minidoka, including the family of Kiyoka Kumagai.

between the boards of our walls allowed the cold winds of winter and the sand to infiltrate through every space and cranny, covering everything in our room with a fine coating of sand. In spite of this travail, Mamma would clean with resignation, completely reconciled to her fate and the fact of injustice that this incarceration and evacuation was indeed a travesty that must be endured. After the sand storm, she would have our room sparking clean before we all came home from the camp offices and always somehow managed to have treats of rice and sometimes accompaniments for the rice, which she managed to "acquire" through her endeavors working in the mess hall. I do recall also, that she managed to keep all of us clean and our clothes neatly ironed, our sheets and pillowcases fresh and clean, all through her efforts with the washboard and some running cold water in the trough outside and a distance away. As I think back, I wonder how Mamma had the foresight to bring an iron, enough linens, a few pots and pans, etc. when we were allowed such a limited amount of luggage. The longer I live, my admiration for her grows and I regret forever that I never thanked her for all she did.

In retrospect, I compare the pioneers of yesteryears and their hardships with those of us who carved out niches in that barren land. All sought freedom, those pioneers who had it and wanted more, as well as the Japanese Americans who were incarcerated and were working to become free. And, in the meantime, our hearts were determined to survive our imprisonment as best we could.

We, as Niseis, never spoke of our incarceration through all these many years, as if there were a stigma attached to it, and I doubt if our children ever gave much thought to what had transpired so many years ago. As I began to write this story, many, many thoughts surfaced which had lain dormant for lo, these 60 years. I had never spoken to my four children or to anyone else regarding the foregoing, as if by not letting it cross my memory, this part of my life never happened. Yes, I have only recently told them a little of what transpired in those days, how my husband, who had a pilot's license, volunteered for the U.S. Air Force immediately upon hearing of Pearl Harbor and how he was rejected because of his ethnic background. How he volunteered once again for the Army after being evacuated from California because of his Japanese heritage and upon return to his native state, Utah, where they once again rejected him. He was a homegrown son of Utah, well known through much publicized reports of his prowess in swimming, football, baseball, which brought him much acclaim and to his high school and the University of Utah, where he graduated with honors. But for his birth to Japanese parents, and the calumny of wartime hysteria, there were no jobs for him and the Army and Air Force rejected him only because of his Japanese heritage.

Ten days after I gave birth to our first son, my husband was finally drafted and served in Germany. I spent the rest of the war years waiting for him to come home, happy with the love of my son and family, but the target of many prejudicial and bigoted actions. When the West Coast was once again opened to us, we went to Los Angeles as did so many Japanese Americans, and faced more countless acts of bigotry: doors slammed in our faces when asking about rentals, real estate agents informing us that they could not sell any homes to us because of our ancestry, signs in shop windows stating "no Japs."

I have asked my children whether they had been taught about World War II and its ramifications regarding the Japanese Americans and learned that it was mentioned as if in afterthought and not in any great detail. To me, this important, historical data affecting a segment of American citizens warrants at least a chapter in all American history books.

Thank God for the few activist Sansei who have brought this to the fore. It is because of them that we can now talk amongst ourselves and our children about what was, and not feel the "shame?" or whatever caused us to never mention "those days." It is to the Watts riots, too, that we as Japanese Americans owe much of the civil rights that we have gained. To the blacks who brought the inequities of unequal opportunities to light go my thanks. Because of their fearless fight for their own civil rights, we have been emboldened to speak out as never before. Our inherited inhibitions are gone by the wayside and truly with each passing generation, I see a brighter future for all of our children.

Being Professional

Helen Rurup

There were seven siblings in my family and they were all born in Bakersfield, California. We all went to elementary and high school with friendly and very smart Japanese kids. We never thought of the differences. That was the way it was—until Pearl Harbor. Lots of Bakersfield boys were stationed with the Navy in Hawaii.

At that time, my older brother, Bill Baldwin, was in the California National Guard at Ft. Lewis, Washington. Our first thought was, "What will happen to him?" He later was assigned to an armored division and was sent to France for landing on D-Day plus one. While returning in his tank from battles in Germany on the road in France, he unexpectedly met up with our younger brother, Burr, in the infantry walking up to the front. It was winter time and Bill took off his overcoat and gave it to his brother, saying, "You will need this." Fortunately, they both came home.

I was twenty-one years old in August, 1941, and had graduated from UC Berkeley in June. I had taken the Civil Service test for Social Worker 1 at the Kern County Welfare Department and passed. The Department hired me in November for a respectable monthly salary of $120. I rode a bicycle eight miles round trip to work. With so many family members, we had to sign up and wait our turn for the family car.

I was very "green," still learning the job, when I was issued a gas mask early in February, 1942. We were told we might be attacked. The next day I was told I would be assigned with three other social workers for a week out at the county fairgrounds to interview Japanese persons and complete their referrals of to Relocation Centers in Idaho or Arizona. The people I was to interview were either Japanese-born adults or United States-born Japanese including students and small children. This last group were U.S. citizens.

I don't remember what the actual temperature was but the large barn-like building was cold, physically and emotionally. Still intimidated by any kind of one-on-one interview, I tackled the job. I knew several of the families well who stood in line waiting for the next interviews. I also knew that these owners of small and large vegetable gardens, small corner stores, service providers, etc. had already sold their properties and possessions well below market value. I wanted to smile in recognition but didn't. It was misery.

I told each person I was sorry that they had to take certain actions by a certain date soon. The Japanese government and our government were at war. To safeguard all others required that persons of Japanese background be moved to a different location. It was hard and I hated to do it. It was embarrassing when I talked to the many people that I knew, but as a professional, I had been assigned to make sure they all knew what was expected of them.

One young lady, Oshi, had been a very special friend in high school. We had eaten lunch together often. I knew her sister slightly and her two brothers who played on our high school football team. The whole family was in the line. Their father owned a vegetable garden and I knew in elementary school the kids had all gone to Japanese church-school after our daily school classes. While I talked to them I remember trying to be so hard and unemotional, and being ashamed for being that way.

I also interviewed, through family interpreters, many older adults who had come to Kern County in 1918 and 1919. I remember being so angry that almost all of these older persons who had lived here so long could not, or would not, speak a word of English. Why not?

I didn't really feel guilty, but confused during this interview time. I knew the US government was doing what they thought was right to protect all the rest of us. Who was to know whether any of the local Japanese had had covert contact with the Japanese government? Adding to my feelings of unrest, I was remembering a beautiful white house near my family's home, owned by a Japanese couple, that burned to the ground in the middle of the night, a few months before the war started. The story in the neighborhood was that the couple had burned their own home and returned to Japan. We hadn't thought of war at that time.

During the war years, because of my still confused and somewhat guilty feelings, I purposely didn't want to read about or hear anything about the Kern Japanese in their relocation centers. When many years later our President and Congress decided to give each citizen who had been relocated a cash settlement, I disagreed. The relocation action had been taken while we were at war. The government thought it had to be done to protect our lives. The relocation was right for that time, February, 1942. But I was still confused.

While working at the Welfare Department, single and dating, I also belonged to a social sorority in Bakersfield. One of our activities was attending and arranging parties for the cadets stationed at a brand new training center at Minter Field about 16 miles from town. In the fall of 1942 at one of these small parties in the Coca Cola Community Center, I met a 26-year old cadet from Wisconsin. I married him in August, 1943 in Roswell, New Mexico, after he graduated as a pilot. He had previously been in the US Air Force Bombardment Unit at Hickam Field on December 7, 1941. He survived and remembered but never talked about the Japanese bombing, other than to say he wished he could have jumped inside his helmet at the time. He participated in the battle of Midway, became a pilot instructor in B-17's and, later, transported B-29's until the end of the war. He died in January, 2001, after 57 years of marriage.

We always thought it ironic that I was interviewing Japanese people, even though many were US citizens, just days after he had gone through a horrendous attack by people from their homeland.

Teaching at Manzanar

Lois A. Ferguson

My husband's master's thesis was on the subject of the Oriental community in Los Angeles. His research had led him to downtown "Little Tokyo" and other Oriental communities where he became closely involved in the people and made many good friends; hence, when American Japanese were abruptly and unjustly evacuated to relocation centers in the desert, he got a job with the government at Manzanar where he set up a junior college and night school program. I, too, was hired, as a training teacher for the many Japanese college graduates who had not been hired in schools because of racial prejudice.

On September 19th and December 29th, 1942, I sent the following two open letters to family, friends and colleagues describing our experiences.

September 19, 1942

You don't have to live here long to discover that something you strongly suspicioned is true — only the rosier side of our treatment of the Japanese goes out to the press. Articles such as Jim Marshall's in an August issue of Collier's *in which he ends up by saying Americans need feel nothing but pride over the Japanese Relocation Camps, are definitely misleading, to say the least. True, we don't beat them physically or starve them or anything as obviously brutal as all that, but Manzanar is no Utopia, and it is supposed to be one of the best of the camps.*

Row after row of black barracks surrounded by fine tan dust is not very aesthetic. The beautiful, jagged, snow-covered mountains on either side of the valley here are the saving grace. Each barrack is divided into four "apartments" in each of which live from five to ten people. This means room for Army cots and not much else. If your family consists of five to ten people you are lucky; otherwise, no telling who else will share your room with you.

A young minister and his wife share a room with an old Japanese couple and their 28 year old son. The minister and his wife are completely American and can hardly communicate with the old couple, who speak only Japanese and who love squeaky Japanese music which they play on their phonograph day and night, much to the distraction of the minister unit. All of their ideas and customs clash; the only escape for the young couple is to stay away from their home as much as possible. This is only one example from a community of 10,000 souls.

The apartment is just a bare room; so far, the floor consists only of boards with large cracks in between, and two-inch knot holes dotting the surface frequently. The fine dust here revels in such entrances. The walls are just widely spaced boards too. An attempt is being made to cover the floors with linoleum and the walls with plaster board before winter sets in. The one oil stove in each "apartment" is hardly adequate to cope with such competition from the cracks.

For each row of houses in a block, there is a men's bath house and a women's bath house. Nothing is partitioned off in either. One of the teachers who came into camp raised such a fuss over this lack of privacy (saying she roomed with her two sisters all her life and had never seen more than their arms and legs) that a shower and some toilets were partitioned off in the block in which the teachers are staying.

The older Japanese, especially those born and raised in Japan, don't mind this phase of community living, as public baths and rest rooms for both men and women together are the custom in Japan. The younger, Americanized people have as many varied opinions on this matter as any cross section of public opinion anywhere in America would show.

A large mess hall is located in each block. The people have to line up outside and stand in the sun for 15-20 minutes until the cafeteria-style serving progresses sufficiently so they get into the hall. They get as much as they want to eat. The food is pretty heavy — rice and many other starchy foods three times per day. Only very young children get milk at each meal. Other children and adults get milk only once in awhile. More fresh fruits and vegetables should be served. Perhaps this will be taken care of as the truck garden and fruit orchards here "get going."

There is a special mess hall for the Caucasian personnel. The meals here are well-balanced, more than you can possibly eat, all the milk you can drink and only 35 cents a meal. I think it would be much better for us to eat with the Japanese and to have the same food, but we aren't allowed to go to their mess even if we prefer, and we can't bring Japanese guests into ours.

Administrative orders from San Francisco told us to open elementary schools September 15. With less than half the teachers here and no books or supplies, we opened school on September 15. The Japanese set a great store by school. Children arrived hours early, scrubbed and shining, delighted to think they were going back to school at last. They entered messy recreation barracks with one or possibly two teachers per 100-200 students. The teachers had just arrived, hadn't had time to put up pictures or even know what it was all about themselves. The children sat on the dirty, cracky floor. There was nothing for them to do. Only the *teachers' ingenuity at telling stories, playing games, etc., provided any kind of activity.*

The second day of school was no better and the wind blew all the night before and that morning besides, which brought dust and drafts through the boards on which the children sat. The caretakers in some buildings had hosed the floors off that morning, so they were wet besides. The Project Director here finally decided that he couldn't be responsible for an epidemic no matter what the regional office ordered, so he wired San Francisco that the elementary schools were closed until the regional office saw that the buildings were lined with linoleum and plaster board, that partitions were made in the long barracks for individual classrooms (there had been four classes of 30–50 children each in one long room), that regular text books and other supplies were provided, and that we had sufficient teachers.

The main thing that has tied the older Japanese to America is the fine school opportunities for their children here. When construction was begun on an open air theater in the camp, the people protested loudly and long, saying, "Schools first, then recreational facilities." So far, they have neither.

The government is having great difficulty getting a sufficient number of teachers in these camps. There is a teacher shortage all over the country right now, because of higher salaries in defense industries. Comparatively few are interested in coming into these camps in the first place. Many who sign up and come, take one look at the place and resign. It's no place for a sissy.

So far, we are living the same way the Japanese are expected to, except we have a little more space per person in the barracks, and our rooms were the first to get linoleum and plaster board. There aren't enough beds to go around for us, so two people sleep on a mattress on the floor, while two more sleep on the box springs on the floor. Others use cots. We all use the public facilities.

Salaries for teachers are not very big, especially when you consider that we are working for Civil Service, which means Civil Service hours — no teacher's usual long vacations, etc. We work in the school room from 8–5 daily with children present from 8:30–4:00 with one and a half hours at noon. We work from 8:00 to 12:00 on Saturdays and there are no Christmas or summer vacations like other teachers get. We are hoping Manzanar can be taken into the State setup, which would change all this and benefit the children greatly.

One thing which drives the teachers away from here and which would drive the Japanese away too, if they could go, is the dust. Dust in itself is not so bad, but when it's in a climate that includes a good strong wind storm at least once a week, it's not so funny. During these storms, you eat, smell and see nothing but dust. Everything you possess is thick with the stuff. When you wake up in the morning, the only white place on your pillow is right where your head has been. The other night, one of these storms raged all night long; everything in and on the building rattled and whistled; the beacon light from the airport flashed through the room every few seconds, and my husband and I felt as though we were in a hotel on

Fifth and Broadway in New York. The first thing Fergie said the next morning was, as he shoveled the dirt off his face, "Hand me a piece of toilet paper; I want to write out my resignation."

The Japanese and American-Japanese here all seem so cheerful, despite their depressing circumstances. They are always good-natured and polite and accommodating. The Nisei are just like any group of healthy young American people — very good sense of humor, etc. On the whole, smart and intellectual. They realize the situation they are in and likely to be up against after the war, and are doing exceedingly intelligent thinking about it. Most of the Nisei feel that the evacuation had to be, and are as anxious to have the Allied Nations win the war as any good American. About 60 percent of the Japanese here are Nisei; they are the ones who are holding most of the jobs and doing most of the self-governing here; hence, we come in contact with them more than with the Issei and Kibei. The last two groups are ones I would like to know more about. There are many Issei vs. Nisei problems, as well as Kibei vs. Nisei problems. Issei were born in Japan and cannot become American citizens. Nisei are American-born and are American citizens. Kibei were born in America but educated in Japan.

Docile, quiet and humble as the members of this camp are, the two tiny towns near here, Independence, six miles from here and Lone Pine, 10 miles, are getting out petitions to have an eight-foot wall put around Manzanar, have the Army guard doubled, and eventually have Manzanar moved away altogether. That gives you a good idea how the residents of the valley regard this camp.

One hundred twenty-one privates, one corporal, two lieutenants and one captain are stationed within a few feet of camp. The M.P.'s hate guard duty out here on the desert. They claim they're going nuts from boredom and from the climate. Twenty-three of them went AWOL in one week. One of the 23 ended up at an embarkation point in San Francisco and was shipped abroad. These fellows claim they'd rather be in the thick of battle than stuck out here.

There are many Quakers here and a finer people I never hope to see. This place has more intellectuals and liberals than most communities do, but still there are a few petty, stuffed shirts here, too. I guess you can never escape from them altogether. The administrative staff on the whole is pretty good, especially in the Education Department where there is a great sprinkling of Ph.D's and M.A's.

Fergie is Principal of Adult Education, including setting up a junior college program here. He has lots of plans and is very interested in his work. Now, if Government red tape won't be too confining, he can really go to town.

I had a demonstration fourth grade for one week for 60 Japanese-American college graduates. Now I am to be a training teacher with three Japanese-American student teachers under me in the fifth and sixth grades. The student teachers are so eager to do a good job that it's really inspiring.

Despite the way this letter may sound, Fergie and I are very happy here. It is intensely interesting, stimulating and fascinating. It offers a real

*challenge, and I hope we can do some good, both along the lines of help-
ing prepare these people for the post-war world and helping prepare the
outside world toward accepting and rehabilitating these people intelli-
gently after the war. Another important point is that Fergie and I can be
together in our war time barracks.*

I hope everybody writes us, as it's so much fun to receive mail here.

So long, Lois

December 29, 1942

*I should have written a dozen logs between the last one and this in order
to keep you up with the progress of events in Manzanar, but we've been
so busy living the material for the logs we haven't had time to stop and
write them.*

*Starting with the latest first is more to the point this time, as everyone
is now interested in the December 7 demonstration at Manzanar. We
helped get the day of Sunday, December 6 started right for the M.P.'s next
door to the camp by escorting 150 high school seniors on an all day hike
and inadvertently passing the outside boundary line with them, necessi-
tating the M.P.s' coming after us in jeeps and chasing us back where we
belonged. We didn't mind, as it gave some of us our first chance to ride
in a jeep, and we bounced along over the desert terrain — sage brush and
all — at a terrific speed. It was rather disappointing to some of the students, though, as this was the first time in nine months they had been
outside the barbed wire boundary. It gave them a happy feeling of freedom, only to be frustrated a little further on.*

*We finished our hike and picnic in a different direction and returned
to camp in the late afternoon. We saw a large crowd around the police
station. As we walked down that way, the crowd dispersed and we learned
that they had gathered to demand the release of a man they felt had been
unjustly imprisoned for the beating up of a J.A.C.L. (Japanese American Citizen League) officer the night before. Ralph Merritt, the new project director, addressed the crowd and told them if they would disperse,
the man would be brought back to Manzanar from the Independence jail
and given a fair trial. This seemed to satisfy the crowd for the nonce and
they went home.*

*That evening at about 7 o'clock (after dark) a girl friend and I were
walking over to the latrine when we looked up at the end of the block and
saw a vast stream of dark figures walking determinedly and silently toward
the police station. They kept coming endlessly and looked so ominous that
Libby and I turned and ran back to our room, where we fastened the door,
turned out the lights, and with Fergie, looked out the windows to see what
was going on. We saw men in dark coats distributed around all of our
buildings and a little group of them was gathered right before our door.
We saw jeep-load after jeep-load of armed M.P.s unloaded at the lighted
entrance to the camp. By this time, it was 7:30 and time for an open forum
Fergie was to conduct, so the three of us ventured out and walked to the
mess hall in which the meeting was to be held.*

There was quite a goodly audience — albeit a frightened and nervous looking group — gathered there. The Nisei who had been helping Fergie on the meeting said it should be called off. Fergie agreed with him and sent the people home. This move later proved to be the correct one as a meeting just a block away (a P.T.A. picture show) was broken up by the mob and one very prominent pro-American beaten and left for dead.

We returned to our vigil at the window of our darkened room and watched figures running around, some even trying to crawl under the barracks. Then we heard beautifully terrifying singing from the mob in front of the police station. They were singing songs in Japanese, one of them the Japanese National Anthem. This mob, contrary to their agreement of the afternoon to disperse, had come back to again demand the release of their man. (It later developed that their interpreter had betrayed them, and had told them to return, that justice would not be accorded the prisoner.) Then we heard explosions and machine guns. Men began running away from the police station. Two truck-loads of soldiers were unloaded before our door, formed a big circle with their bayonets pointing outward and came and searched the block, asking all the Caucasian teachers if any of them had been bothered. Now, it was after 10 o'clock; we were exhausted, so Libby went home with a friend who stopped by, and into bed we crawled. Shortly thereafter, we heard gongs and tin pans being beaten all over camp, obviously the call to meetings.

The next morning, receiving instructions to hold school as usual, off I trudged to my building up in the middle of camp. A young Kibei boy who is a friend of ours walked a little way with me and three Issei men whom I had never seen before accosted me at different times en route. All had practically the same thing to say, "We are so sorry for what happened last night; there are a few bad people in camp who are making things much harder for all of us. This was nothing directed against you Caucasian teachers. We appreciate what you are doing for us."

Upon reaching school, I found one little boy sitting in front of the locked building. I scurried around and found the custodian, who came and opened the building and lit the ovens. Only about 25 children arrived all day. All but one of the student teachers arrived, and we carried on as best we could. It seemed that at the meetings in camp the previous night, it had been decided to have a general strike in camp and not to send the children to school.

Tuesday, we tried to hold school again. The custodian had my building open and the fires lit. Seventeen children arrived and one student teacher. The custodian told us that a group of men had already visited the school to see that none of the children from their block were attending and had threatened the other children to be careful. About half an hour late, the rest of the student teachers scuttled in, looking frightened. They said they had been stopped on the way and told not to come. They had received threatening letters for teaching the previous day. They had come under risk to tell me they were not trying to shirk, but that it just wasn't wise for them to teach. I replied that I understood, that I appreciated their coming, and for them to go home, that I could handle all the children that were there.

First, I asked them to tell the custodian — a dear, helpful, eager little lady who doesn't speak English — that if there was any danger to her in being there that I wanted her to go home, too. The teachers said she refused to go and leave me there all alone. I was touched by her loyalty and she and I carried on until I heard a knocking at the front door. When I went to open it, I found that the custodian had boarded it up. It was the principal, saying there was no use trying to hold school under these conditions, so home we all went. The children who had come to school had been amazingly unconcerned; they just went on with their school work quietly.

For two days, the tension in camp had been thick enough to cut with a knife. The usually bustling place looked deserted except for occasional small clusters of men. The only people working were the cooks in the mess halls. In the personnel mess hall, we were taking turns waiting on table and doing dishes ourselves. The few people who had dared to report for work the first day had received threatening letters. Over 300 M.P.s had been added to the regular guard and patrolled camp with machine guns set up on jeeps. There was a guard thrown all around the administration office and residences. The place was under martial law on the one hand and under the complete intimidation of a small under-cover group of pro-Axis leaders using gangster methods on the other.

By now, we had learned more definitely what had taken place in front of the police station Sunday night. There was no doubt but that it was a pro-Axis demonstration, using the pretext of a man unjustly imprisoned for the immediate excuse. It completed the pattern of scattered beatings of Nisei who were leaders of the American democratic way of life. The J.A.C.L. leaders were often the targets, as they had urged and aided the evacuation in the first place.

Sunday night, the military captain had ordered the mob to disperse. When they did not, tear gas bombs were thrown in their midst. The wind blew the gas away and one Japanese started to grab a nearby car. Somehow, some machine guns were let off a bit and one 17 year old boy was killed and about a dozen other people were injured. Unfortunately, the boy who was killed was only an innocent on-looker (with many other high school students who had come to watch the first excitement they've had in camp). He was a fine boy who had two brothers in the US Army. His parents were quite wonderful about it and said it was the price of the sins of the camp.

The only two teachers who dared venture forth into the mob that night were Janet (who is afraid to go to the latrine by herself after dark and who awakens one of her room mates at two or three in the morning to walk over with her) and Louis. Janet has been having discussions of minorities and mob violence in her high school classes, and that night in the mob as she saw various of her high school students, she would go up to them, shaking her finger and say, "Joe, what are you doing here? Haven't we talked about mob violence in class? Now, you go right on home." The kids would grin sheepishly and shuffle off (only out of Janet's sight, no doubt.)

Various mothers and children from the Caucasian staff had been removed from camp at once. Tuesday afternoon at 3 o'clock, Mr. Merritt gave orders that all teachers were to be packed to leave and come to a meeting within the hour. At the meeting, Mr. Merritt said we could consider this an American experiment which had blown up in our hands. He said that we would do what scientists usually do when a test tube blows up in their hands; we will reach for another test tube and try again. Further, he said, the reasons for this episode went way back in the historical past of a suppressed American minority people, and he hoped America would learn a lesson from this experience about the treatment of minorities.

Thus, we left camp for a hotel in Lone Pine for a few days. Some of the men went back to camp each day to do what work they could. Fergie said that Wednesday every person in camp had on a black arm band in mourning for the boy who was killed Sunday night. Even tiny babies wore tiny black bands. Thursday afternoon, I received word that Fergie had gone with an Army convoy to Death Valley taking a group of about 80 Japanese-Americans to safety after having been beaten or threatened. There they set up camp in an old C.C.C. camp to await assignment to a new camp.

Fergie had several exciting stories to tell upon his return from Death Valley. Characteristically, he had "pumped" the evacuees. Togo Tanaka, editor of a newspaper, and prominent in J.A.C.L., a U.C.L.A Phi Beta Kappa, said he had not slept a night through in two months. He knew this pro-Axis element was gunning for him; he had been threatened repeatedly. The night of the demonstration, hearing one mob was coming to kill him, he put on a disguise of towels to pad his slight build to a husky one, a cap low over his face, a coat collar turned high, and a meat cleaver in his hand, he got into the mob coming after him, and went with them to his own door. There they yelled for Togo. His wife came to the door with their small baby and said Togo was not there. Someone grabbed at her; someone else said, "Leave her alone; we will get his father." One man got up and made a horrible speech about Togo, calling him a yellow-bellied traitor, disloyal to the Emperor, etc. Togo, the most mild of individuals, said that guy doesn't know how close he came to having a meat cleaver sunk in his head.

Another mob went up to the hospital to kill the boy who had been badly beaten the night before. The doctors and nurses went to hide him and he couldn't be found. The mob couldn't find him either. Later, we learned that he had hidden himself in the contraptions of a traction bed. That same night, one of the men who had helped beat this boy so badly was brought up to the hospital with a couple of bullets in him and laid on a bed right next to his victim, where they lay glowering at each other. Mobs were in several other places that night, too, and similar happenstances took place.

As things stand now, martial law has been released, although the additional guard is still there. They are trying to weed out as much of the pro-Axis element as has exposed itself and they will relocate the loyal Americans as fast as they can to jobs or schools in the mid-west and east. If in the first place Americans and aliens had been segregated, this would have been avoided. Of course, many of the aliens who are denied American citizenship are loyal to America too, and they should have been put in the American camp as fast as they were determined.

The pro-Axis group has been saying to the Americans, "Ah, ha, what does your American citizenship mean now? Here you are right with the rest of us." I am convinced that the vast majority of Japanese, both American citizens and alien, are still decidedly loyal to the U.S., even in spite of being denied all their rights of life, liberty and the pursuit of happiness, and this has been a severe trial of their devotion too. I am wondering how the rest of us could have stood the test under similar circumstances. This wholesale evacuation of one minority group has set a dangerous precedent for America which I hope she will never repeat with another minority group that happens to be in particular disfavor for some reason or other.

Those Japanese born and raised in America, going to American schools, theatres, baseball games, etc. are completely representative of Americans. In Manzanar we have our jitterbugs, our high school romeos in "zoot suit" attire — long hair, collegiate hats, huge coats, tapering pants, and flashy colors. We have strong Y.M.C.A. organizations, hundreds of loyal Boy Scouts, P.T.A.'s, food sales, swing music concerts, classical music concerts, and anything else you can think of that's typically American. To think America was the great melting pot was a source of great satisfaction to me, and the fine thing we have would be lost the day we begin to segregate minority groups and fence them off or return them to their native lands. Our whole strength would be lost, and I would want to leave America then, too.

We have returned to Manzanar after our respite in the hotel at Lone Pine and the camp is returning slowly to normal. As we arise each morning and look out the window, we see all the teachers streaming toward the latrine in vari-colored pajamas and robes, clutching tooth brushes in one hand and towels in the other, hair akimbo and sleep in their eyes. No secrets from anyone here.

The last log left the schools in pretty bad condition too, and I'm glad to say that, despite much confusion, gradually this situation has improved to the place where the school room floors are linoleum-covered now, the walls and ceilings are covered with plasterboard and we are getting some books and a few supplies, as well as a few benches and tables, with prospects of more. The children are very delighted with all these improvements and say it really looks like a school now. The improvement in their attitude, respect, and discipline has advanced noticeably as the school improves and order and learning are coming out of chaos. They need the normalcy of regular school in their lives and schools are the best medium for making more and better Americans. Then, they missed all the Christmas fun that comes at school this time of year, too.

Someone asked what the people do here — that is, the Japanese. A town of 10,000 people is quite a community. Just think of all the processes it takes to maintain a town that size, and you know what the people here do. There is a $250,000 Army 250-bed hospital with another $250,000 worth of equipment in it. This is staffed with excellent Japanese doctors, *nurses, dieticians, chemists, etc. that are needed for any hospital. It's an excellently run affair that grew out of a barracks where the doctors had to run outside to wash their hands.*

There is a dental clinic, a fire department, a police department, a garbage crew, an electricians crew, a carpentry crew, stenographers, cooks, potential teachers in training, adult school teachers, clerks and managers in the dry goods store and the canteen, wonderful art departments, a visual aids department run by a man formerly in charge of the geological displays at the Chicago Museum of Natural History and on ad infinitum. Also, there is a large camouflage net factory in which American citizens are employed. For several months 1,000 men were out in the beet fields of Montana, Utah, Wyoming, and Idaho saving the crops from ruin. They have a big truck garden and fruit orchard here.

There is a children's village containing over 60 orphans that receive beautiful training and care from a college-trained couple that ran the Japanese children's orphanage in Los Angeles. They have a big hot house where they are experimenting in the raising of Guayule, the rubber substitute. There is a camp newspaper, etc., etc. There are trained technicians and professionals in every line imaginable among the evacuees here.

Another 5,000 of the Nisei boys are soldiers in the Armed Forces of the U.S.A. Over 300 Nisei are in eastern and mid-western universities.

Whew! That's all I can bat out this round, and I'll bet it's more than anyone can take, provided there's anyone still with me.

Lois

In 1943, after a year at Manzanar, Fergie was drafted into the Army and we left.

Voices from
School

College Days Without Men

Ruth D. Balcomb

During the war years of 1941-1945 I was between the ages of 15 and 19. I was Ruth McCord Dewar and I grew up in East Orange, New Jersey. My father was first vice president of National City Bank on Wall Street, New York City, the bank now known as Citicorp. When he retired he was making the good salary of $25,000 a year. Then, bread was ten cents a loaf. In wartime we all grew vegetables in our small backyards for the first time in our lives and they were called Victory gardens. Deliveries of food were not dependable because of the gas rationing. Door to door milk delivery went back to horse-drawn carriages.

Neighborhoods started preparing for bombing attacks at the beginning of the war. Each street had an appointed monitor to be sure everyone blocked all light from inside the houses. We all bought dark green shades and lowered them each evening. Air raid sirens were installed for the first time and practice drills occurred once a month. Each street was patrolled by a warden looking for lights showing or people on the street. My father was the warden in charge of our street and the neighboring block. The street lights had the top half covered with black paint and all headlights of the cars were partially blacked out. It sounds funny now, but we were petrified that the war would come to the East Coast.

We didn't drive much anywhere because gasoline was then rationed, so we rode the trolleys or trains when needed. We weren't such a mobile society as we are today. Our family Buick sat months in the garage without being started. Then came rationing of shoes, sugar, meats. We were allowed two pairs of shoes a year. Sneakers and some sandals not made from leather did not require coupons. I worked at the high school each Saturday where people registered for their coupons. When I entered college, my mother had to give up my year's ration of meat and sugar to the university.

I gave up two evenings a week to the Red Cross where, for three hours, we folded bandages for different purposes to be sent overseas. Knitting socks and scarves for soldiers was all the rage and we all carried our knitting with us everywhere we went. The wool was dull khaki yarn, not too appetizing a color.

When the 1943 school prom and graduation came, there were more girls than boys. As half of my class did, I sat out the prom at home for the lack of a date. The next year, at Miami University in Oxford, Ohio, the only non-military men were guys who were rated 4-F and non-draftable, which was a terrible stigma put upon them, as three-fourths of them had only minor deficiencies like low weight, hearing loss, flat feet, etc. So, the population of the school of non-military was 500 men to 4,000 women. One didn't date. One wrote letters to G.I.s and looked forward daily to mail from overseas.

Then the military arrived on campus. Men in the V-5, V-12 programs of the Navy were being trained and we had one batch of Women Marines. [V-5 was the U.S. naval aviation cadet program that trained officer pilots. V-12 was a Naval Reserve officer training program; volunteers received military training while completing their bachelor's degrees.] When they changed classes, of course, they marched. They got the sidewalks and we all had to walk on the grass around them. No ifs, ands or buts about it! When these men got leave, we had some chances for a date or two before they were shipped out and another batch was brought in for training.

Some of the girl dorms were given to the military and we were housed in the empty fraternity houses. What an experience! Men shower in one great big stall. The first week or two, we women were all trying to get to the shower when no one else was around. We were used to privacy. The four johns had no walls around them. That was a new experience, too, while changing pads, etc. and talking to your next seated neighbor. In three weeks, all embarrassment and privacy needs were gone and we had a ball showering three to eight at a time and scrubbing each other's backs while talking about our past day's experiences.

Cigarettes were in short supply. Most were given free to soldiers. If you smoked, you watched the stores to see when shipments came in and then everyone raced to stand in line for the two packs rationed to a customer — and never enough for all. I started smoking in college, as all the fun was with everyone in the smokers. If inhaling others' smoke, you might as well smoke yourself. What a terrible time to start. Aha! I had a wonderful father! He had a charge account at Macy's. Macy's allotted a carton to every charge account customer twice a month and my father mailed half to me and the other half to my sister. I bargained and exchanged them sometimes for other necessities.

Travel for any reason was not easy. On my way to and from college in the fall and at Christmas time, I traveled from Newark, New Jersey, to Xenia, Ohio, and bussed to Miami University. Often our train would be sidetracked for troop trains going to the East Coast and then overseas. Once we waited 18 hours on the sidetrack. There were no diners on the train and we ran out of water. I arrived home 26 hours late, and that was not unusual. I only got home for Christmas and summer vacations. The normal Pennsylvania Railroad train ride was 16-18 hours each way. Nowadays that would seem awful, then it was the usual.

Every time we girls left the dormitory after seven at night, we had to sign a book and state where we were going and we had to be back by ten o'clock on weekdays, eleven on Fridays and twelve on Saturdays. Doors were locked on all women's dorms at those hours and if you were locked out, you were in dire trouble. One of us hung around the smoker if someone was missing and waited for a signal and then opened the windows and let her in — with a struggle. Then someone got caught and that system was no longer available.

We were not allowed to ride in anyone's car without a specific permit from our parents for each trip we wished to take. We cheated some on this, though students' cars not being allowed on campus, there weren't too many possibilities for breaking the rules.

The tragic times were the days letters arrived notifying students that boyfriends or brothers were wounded or killed in battle. In 1944 and 1945, there was an average of one a week to some girlfriend or sister at the university.

But then the war ended and the men returned my senior year and suddenly the ratio was four men to one woman. It was heyday, except the boys were now men and wanted all or nothing on the first date and many girls had trouble resisting. I had four friends kicked out of college two months before graduation because they were pregnant. Many men dropped out as they couldn't settle down to studies, war nerves still making them edgy.

And then the world quieted down for a bit and we faced the adjustments to a new life of peace.

Small Town Girl

Barbara J. Sloan

I was sixteen years old and a senior in Albany (Oregon) High School on December 7, 1941. Most people remember exactly where they were and what they were doing when they heard on the radio of the attack on Pearl Harbor. I have no clear memory of it. I do remember Mom being very anxious about my two brothers having to go to war. My big concern was graduating. As time went on and some of my classmates were enlisting, it became real to me. As I remember, we always stayed away from military men because they were "wild" and not to be trusted. How soon all of that changed when the boys I knew were being called to duty.

The first time I came in contact with the military was in February of 1942. A group of soldiers was being transferred from a camp in Washington to one in California. It was a weekend and they had a layover in the Albany National Guard building. Some of the mothers got together and thought it would be nice to have a dance for the boys. The call went out for young ladies to attend. They appealed to our sense of duty for the boys and the country. It worked. It turned out to be a wonderful evening and all of the fellas were well-behaved and fun so I changed my ideas about soldiers.

Our school was getting into the war effort. There were contests to see which class could collect the most scrap materials. And the boys were anxious to enlist and go off to war. We graduated in May, 1942. It wasn't long before the fellas started leaving for the service. One or two of the girls joined also. One or two others married their high school sweethearts and started the trials of trying to follow their husbands. The girls who stayed home filled the need of entertaining the boys at the USO.

Albany was a small town of 7,000 or so people. There were two movie theaters and one bowling alley. That was the extent of our entertainment. When Camp Adair was built between Albany and Corvallis, a place was needed to entertain the boys. It wasn't long before the townspeople found a building on Main Street for the USO. It included a nice dance floor upstairs and a snack bar with a sitting area downstairs. The few parents who volunteered to help run the place had to find a dance band and any other entertainment they could.

Mom and Dad became involved, so my older sister Helen and I were called on to fill in for the snackbar and for the dances. Almost every Friday and Saturday night a five-piece band made up of the townspeople would come and play for the dances. The camp furnished buses to bring the fellas to town. They also would bus the girls to the camp for dances out there. The dances seemed to be a highlight for the boys. I can't say the girls didn't look forward to them, too.

Almost every Sunday Mom would be cooking a big dinner for the boys we knew and some we didn't. The boys seemed to really enjoy it after the Army food. So many young, homesick boys came looking for someone to talk to. We met many nice boys from all over the US. Some had never been away from their hometown, let alone their relatives. The USOs and local townspeople filled a big need for them.

One night the call came from Mom that they needed girls to go to the base for a noncom dance for the 91st Quartermasters. For some reason, we were not too anxious to go. Mom wouldn't let us get out of it. It turned out to be a fateful evening for Helen and me. When we walked into the hall, two second lieutenants were running the dance. Apparently, we caught their eye, so they told us later. They had flipped a coin to see who got the brown head and who got the red head. As it turned out, Helen, the brunette, married Jack after the war, and I was engaged to Buck for two years during the war.

Ration tickets were given to each family for different foods, gas, tires, etc. I remember one incident. My sister Polly had come home from college with coupons she had saved and had her mouth set for steak. She gave the coupons to Dad, asking him to bring home the steaks that night for dinner. Lo and behold, when she opened the package, there were steaks, all right, but they were ling cod steaks. Needless to say, there were some unhappy campers at dinner.

Nylons were just coming on the market when the war started. They would last you a good long time. Somebody invented a little gadget that you could buy which would, more or less, knit the run. You slipped the stocking over a glass where the run was and pushed the gadget up and down. It was tricky to work, mind you, but those were desperate times and called for desperate deeds.

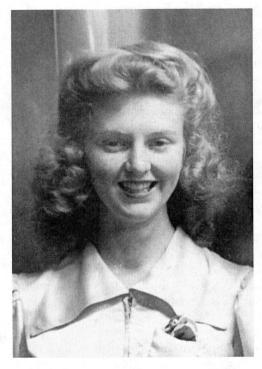

Barbara Putnam Sloan, Albany, Oregon, July 1942.

Silk stockings were impossible to buy and nylons were hard to find, so the cosmetic companies came to the rescue by making leg makeup. It was very similar to the liquid face makeup of today. It did not stay on well. If you were too tired after a dance to wash it off, the sheets would be a mess. That didn't make for a happy mother, I can tell you.

Jobs were not hard to find. The jobs that I had were simply offered to me. One was working with Helen at the draft board. We had the place pretty much to ourselves, as the woman who ran the office was involved with a major at Camp Adair, so we didn't see much of her. It was our job to get information on the boys being drafted so the board could make judgments as to how they would be classified — A-1, 4-F, etc.

The job became boring, so four of us girls decided to go to Los Angeles. Helen had been offered a job with Gladden McBean, a pottery making company, as a key punch operator. She helped my friend Pat and me get jobs as painters of the Desert Rose pattern of Franciscan Ware. We sat at a potter's wheel with our three colors of paint. A table was in front of the wheel with slots in it where the greenware was stacked. We would take the green color on our brushes first to color the rim of the dish. We had to do the whole stack so we wouldn't mix the pink color with the green. After we finished the green rim and leaves, we would change color and do the roses. Took a lot of brain power for this! When we were too bored and hot, we would fill a bucket with cold water and put our feet in it. Somehow, our Scottish boss didn't approve of this when he finally caught us.

Pat and I had found a room for rent on LaBrea Street, in Hollywood. We had two good-looking Canadian fellas who lived upstairs. They became good friends—so good, in fact, that at Christmas they gave us a bottle of bourbon. It was the first time that Pat or I had ever been away from home on Christmas, so we were feeling very low. Here we had this bottle and neither of us knew what to do with it. We had never had a drink before, so we thought we would try it. After all, it was Christmas Eve. It tasted so awful we decided to put it in the grapefruit juice that we had. We found that it tasted pretty good that way, so drink we did! It wasn't long before Pat got sick and the landlady knocked on the door, wanting to know what was going on. We lied! Said it was the flu. I think she believed us, but who knows? We didn't try that again. I made it to work the next day but poor ole Pat didn't.

One month, we spent way too much on clothes and stuff, and we were relying on crackers and peanut butter way too soon. After a few days of this we felt desperate. To get food off our minds we decided to go to town and window shop. It was a Sunday and not much else to do. As we were looking, a captain and a first lieutenant approached us and asked if they could join us. We looked at each other, both having the same thought. Here could be a dinner! As luck would have it, they were hungry and invited us to eat with them. Do I need to say we accepted and had a delightful dinner at the Palladium? It shows you how innocent those times were. Being naive helped, too. But the fellas of those days never assumed that you had to pay for your date by going to bed with them.

The Palladium was a very popular night club in Hollywood. Every Saturday night, one of the big bands would play there. The place was always packed. We met some very nice fellas that we dated briefly and kept in touch with throughout the war. It was like being in a candy store, you could pick and choose the fella you wanted. Talk about spoiled girls!

It was so different in those times. We girls had no fear of walking home after a dance or of ever being molested. Even in Los Angeles, we would walk home about a mile from the Palladium, never thinking that something could happen to us. We never had a problem of any kind, unless you consider the guys flirting with us a problem, which we didn't.

Taking the train used to be the way to travel. You always wore your best dress and ate in the dining car. The tables had white linen cloths, cloth napkins and flowers. The waiters were usually black and took good care of you. That all came to a halt after the war started. We were lucky to even get on a train, as there were so many military men and dependents moving from one place to another or going home on leave.

My sister Polly and I went to Los Angeles for a visit when I was seventeen years old. At each station, as we went along the way, we picked up more passengers. By the time we reached Fresno, the train was full but they let more soldiers on and the next thing I knew, a sergeant picked me up, took my seat, sat me on his lap and announced that he wasn't about to stand all the way to Los Angeles. He was an older fellow and seemed to be nice, so Polly didn't fuss, nor did I. The atmosphere on the trains was always light-hearted and fun.

The last train trip I took was after the war ended. Buck, my fiancé, had come home from Italy and was discharged. He asked me to go to Huron, South Dakota, to meet him and become acquainted with his family. The trains I took going and coming home were loaded with the happiest fellas you ever want to see. The war was over and they were heading home. It was one big party.

Buck and I met, almost like strangers, in the Omaha, Nebraska, train depot. That was the closest station to his home town. After spending two weeks with his family and friends, I found that we had grown apart and I wasn't ready to settle down just yet, so the engagement was broken. We did stay in touch until I finally married in 1949.

Growing Up in Wartime

Anona Stoetzl Kuehne

1938: "Peace for our time." I was 13 years old, living with my family in Madera, California, when Neville Chamberlain met with Hitler and returned to Britain with that assurance. Even at that age, I had an uneasy feeling about what was going on in the world. The newsreels were showing Hitler's troops goose-stepping and the masses of people saluting and chanting "Sieg Heil!" It looked like mass hysteria to my young eyes and I felt very uneasy about it.

In 1939, I was visiting my great aunt who had just moved to California from Alaska. She and her husband had built a cozy cabin in the mountains near Grass Valley. We brought a radio to them and the first thing we heard on it was that Germany had invaded Poland, without the rest of the world able or willing to do much about it.

As the drums of war kept pounding away and territory kept being gobbled up by the tyrants of the Axis, the voices at home got louder and louder. I listened to incessant arguments about what, if anything, the United States should do. Lend lease, and what Congress should do about it, was a big issue.

Soon we were losing merchant ships at an alarming rate and that probably started people thinking that Europe wasn't so far away after all. Some young American men joined the armed forces and some went to England in hopes that they could join the Royal Air Force.

War bond rallies were held in the local theater between the double-feature movies and it became a contest to see who would buy the most bonds. It added to the small-town gossip: who bought how many bonds and for how much? Rumors of hoarding started drifting through the air. Where did so-and-so get those new tires? Someone installed a gasoline tank on his property. Sugar and soap could be had at some special place — and on and on. We finally had ration stamps for food, clothing, gasoline and tires.

We were far better off in the country towns than the folks in the cities. In Madera, we grew most of our vegetables and had chickens and eggs. The city folk dug up their lawns and planted Victory gardens.

My family also had lots of rabbits. It was my job to butcher the rabbits and stretch the pelts in the sun. I later used the fur to line mittens. They were great to ward off the freezing fog when I rode my bike to school.

We saved all of the lard and cooking fat. My mother made soap with it, which turned out pretty well. What lard was left was taken to the butcher shop and collected for the government. I guess they made soap out of it, too.

There were drives for rubber and metal. We saw newsreels of women donating their girdles. I thought that was a great idea. We were also asked to toss in our pots and pans for the good of the war effort. They needed aluminum to make airplanes.

I worked in the local movie theater after school and on weekends and got to see all of the newsreels. It was the only way to see what was going on in motion. Our local paper left a lot to be desired. I think the news and cartoons were what people came to see at the movies. There was always applause when the "shorts" came on.

The farmers needed workers, so high school kids were bussed to the jobs in the fields. I worked picking tomatoes, olives and cotton. Picking cotton wrecks the hands and my boyfriend at the time was very upset that I would ruin my hands. I was surprised that the truckers for the tomatoes wanted only perfect tomatoes. I fretted about the waste of tomatoes that were left. I learned that it takes a lot of olives to fill a box and that I'd never get rich picking olives.

I didn't have any close Oriental friends, but I remember going to gym class one day and the teacher telling us that the Japanese girls were gone. They had been taken away by the government. This was soon after Pearl Harbor and people were afraid the Japanese were helping the armed forces of Japan. A small Japanese submarine was found swept up on the California coast, which didn't help our loyal Japanese citizens. Our teacher asked us to write to internees in the camps. The girls were also asked to knit squares which were collected to make blankets for the camps.

Most of the male students in my high school class joined the armed forces unless they had to farm the land. These "farm kids" were turned into fighter pilots in a very short time. I'm sure most had never been in an airplane before. Most of them returned home, but some didn't. I was lucky. No one in my family was lost in the war.

I was asked to help at the local USO. We had a small facility near the highway, so soldiers and sailors who were going through California on the bus or hitchhiking would drop in for a rest or food and drink. Cookies and coffee or some kind of refreshments were always served. Sometimes we played records and danced. They were mostly very young and very homesick young men.

Anona Kuehne in her high school graduation picture.

I had been in a dancing school since the age of four and was still dancing at 17 and 18. We had a very good drama teacher and had done some good light comedy and short skits. We were asked to go to Lemore Air Base and entertain the troops and I was to do a solo ballet. We were to perform in a huge hangar which was filled to capacity, about 4,000 people. I had never seen so many people in one place before. I saw women in uniform for the first time. My costume was black tights and multicolored gathered silk long sleeves—all in all, a dramatic look. As I leapt onto the stage, a deafening roar of cheering and whistling met me — and I hadn't even started dancing yet. It was an astounding sensation that every young woman should experience once in a life time. I worried all through the dance that the cheering would stop or turn to boos when I finished, but not to worry. These people were really starved for entertainment.

I received a scholarship to Mills College in Oakland in 1943. My father had a truck so he helped three of us girls move — tires and gasoline were a problem so we pooled our resources for transportation.

I baby-sat to earn money, and I had all the jobs I could handle. A lot of young wives moved to this area to be near their husbands, so they were without family to watch their children when they went out. The war caused many people to get "out and about" who probably wouldn't have gone very far otherwise.

By this time the shipyards were turning out one Liberty ship a week and each ship had to be christened. Mills College was invited to a ship christening in Richmond, California. By the time the buses got organized and everyone arrived at the pier, it was later than expected and dark, so they rushed the ceremony a bit and the ship started down the ramp and almost missed getting hit by the champagne bottle. As soon as the ship was in the water, the workmen started on a new ship. They were building them 24 hours a day.

In the summer of 1944 I met Bill, my husband-to-be. He had been in Africa and Ireland as a civilian with Douglas Aircraft, keeping the planes flying during the African campaign. He came home in 1944 to join the Navy. We announced our engagement just before he left for San Diego. From there, he was sent to Chicago for more schooling and eventually ordered to Monterey, California, for more schooling. We made plans to get married before he was sent overseas.

I had to get permission from the president of the college to get married, since married students were frowned upon in those days. I then had to find fabric for a wedding dress. None was available. A clerk in a San Francisco department store said she would save something for me if it came in, which she did. It wasn't satin, but it worked. The fabric cost $4 but I had fifty-year old lace that my great aunt gave to me to embellish the dress. My wedding dress didn't last, but I used the lace later for one of our daughters' wedding dress.

Bill had to pass all of his tests on Friday to get leave for the weekend, so we were all set to get married on the only three-day weekend he had — if he got all A's on the tests. The best man had to get leave from the Air Corps. We had purchased the train tickets for my friends from school to attend. I went to the infirmary to pick up the required health certificate and the doctor took one look at me and put me in the hospital because I had broken out with the measles! We postponed the wedding for a week and scrambled around making new arrangements. We were married March 10, 1945. My aunt had collected gas stamps and loaned us her car to drive from my parents' home to Carmel for a two-day honeymoon. (She said that every time she cleaned the car for the next 10 years, there was rice in it.) After the honeymoon, I dropped my new husband in nearby Monterey on Monday morning, drove back alone to Madera and took the train back to school.

Houses were unavailable so I looked at rooms to rent for the few weekends we could be together. I found a room and kitchen near campus. Our apartment was $25 a month and had a large hole in the wall. We shared the bathroom down the hall with two other apartments. I patched the hole with wallpaper and made an ice box *sans* ice from an orange crate which sat outside the window. It worked pretty well until the earwigs discovered the lettuce. We finally found a real ice box that the ice man furnished with ice.

At school I regularly rolled bandages. The field hospitals needed specially folded gauze for sponges. They had to be done just right so they wouldn't fall apart or have ragged edges. When we got enough folded, they were sent away and sterilized. The small group I worked with was organized by a woman who had been a doctor. I enjoyed the social afternoons.

My husband was not sent overseas. He was stationed at nearby Treasure Island where he taught radar. This was great for us since he could occasionally come home during the week. We even got to go to a dance at Mills and have a little social life.

Finally, the war ended with V-E Day and then V-J day. We went into San Francisco to see how everyone was celebrating. People (men) were grabbing strangers (women) and kissing and hugging them. Everyone was smiling and laughing. Men were climbing the light poles and anything else climbable. A lot of alcohol was consumed — the bars gave free drinks to service people so some people had overindulged. Some were sick.

Bill kept pulling me away from approaching revelers and we both had to be careful because we were in a large, raucous crowd. After walking up and back down Market Street, we boarded our train and went home. We didn't have enough sense or money to go to the big hotels to see what was happening there.

After the elation of having the war end came the horror of the extermination camps. The revelation of what happened to our forces in both the Pacific and Europe when they were captured came to us with their release. So in a way, the war continued in our minds and lives for a long time. It is a lesson that our generation never forgot.

The war made me more aware of world politics than perhaps I would have been otherwise. It is possible that the Great Depression created a climate of introspection and exclusion of the rest of the world that allowed us in the U.S. to be blind to the dangers to come.

I learned that it is agonizing to say goodbye to someone you love at a train station and know it might be the last time. Our soldiers were getting killed by the thousands. Times were uncertain. People were sent overseas without much notice. Transportation was difficult. However, we had a sense that we were all in this together and needed to do our best.

Fifty years after the Normandy landings, my husband and I went to the beaches and saw how naked they were, lying under the big guns on the cliffs. We marveled that anyone could climb those cliffs carrying guns and packs while being shot at. We went to the US Cemetery, so near those cliffs and beaches where our soldiers gave their lives, and I stood there looking at the huge bright-green field with thousands of pristine white crosses shining in the sunlight. There was a beauty about it, but it was a terrible beauty.

Voices of
Government
Women

Weathering the War

Marge Hopkins

I wasn't familiar with our Bakersfield, California, airport, so I parked behind a long, low, tile-roofed building which appeared to be the only structure aside from a very large hangar and assorted smaller buildings around the perimeter of the field. Walking around to the front, I spotted several doors and then the one I was looking for, with the sign "United States Weather Bureau." I opened the door cautiously and peered around it. There was a small room filled with unfamiliar equipment and at the center a man was seated at a table. He looked up. I summoned my courage and said, "I understand you have job openings?" He replied, "When can you start?"

And so began twelve years of a job I loved. It was the summer of 1942, the country was at war. My brother and many of my friends were scattering around the country and the world. I was twenty-two. Forgoing a senior year of university because of family responsibilities, trained for nothing, I had been working at a minor clerical job for, as I recall, fifty cents an hour. As the men went off to serve, new jobs were opening up for women. A friend's young brother had an after-school job at the airport and had told her that the Weather Bureau was desperate for help. Small wonder, as I was to learn. They were keeping the place open seven days a week, twenty-four hours a day with just three people, and one of those was a young man slated to go into the armed forces in a few weeks. The two others were a young woman who was planning to leave soon and the man at the table, the chief meteorologist, the boss.

My application was soon accepted and I was overwhelmed by the fabulous salary, $1,414 a year! That was, I realized, more than $100 a month, which at that time was considered adequate for a man with a family. Oh, yes, and some overtime pay for extra hours and holiday work was included, plus some wartime perks such as extra gas coupons for "essential occupation."

I started as an observer, learning to read various thermometers and barometers, calculate humidity, estimate the amount of sky covered by cloud layers, know the names and estimated altitudes of these clouds and the extent of the visibility — how far I could see with the unaided eye. I learned to code all of this information into various symbols and numbers and pass it through a window to the communications office next door where it was sent out by teletype and, in yet another code, to pilots flying over. This was done every hour, or more often if the weather was changing rapidly. I took these observations from all over the country and made the information available to pilots who came in person, first ascertaining that they were authorized to receive it under wartime restrictions. The codes were international, so language differences were no barrier, at least in peacetime.

Twice a day, at 2:00 o'clock morning and afternoon, the observer on duty "took a Pibal." This meant going to a small shed across the road, inflating a balloon with helium and climbing with it up a short flight of stairs to a small enclosed platform. The balloon was released and its course followed through a theodolite such as those used by surveyors. For the nighttime balloon run, a tiny battery with attached light bulb was tied to the balloon. Every minute the readings were entered on a clipboard. In the daytime there might be a second person in the office and the balloon observer called in the readings via radio. The readings were plotted on a chart in the office and again, transmitted to the waiting world, showing wind directions and speed at various altitudes.

At night and on cloudy days, the balloon might be out of sight in perhaps twenty or thirty minutes. On a 100 degree plus afternoon it might be visible for an hour. Then, or on a freezing night, was no fun. All of my shoes had a criss-cross pattern on the soles from my standing on the floor furnace in the office to get warm after the balloon run. A kindly Army pilot found a pair of padded flight pants for me, and they helped considerably. Incidentally, all of us women observers wore pants suits throughout the war — no nylons were available anyway!

Gradually enough people were hired to relieve the pressure on the chief. We were mostly women. In time, by means of correspondence courses through the Weather Bureau and Pennsylvania State College, I qualified as a meteorologist, authorized to make local broadcasts. During the war, weather information on the West Coast was closely guarded (although we learned later that the secrets had not always been so well-kept after all). We could give information in person only to pilots having proper clearance. There was a popular story about the radio announcer in the Pacific Northwest who might abruptly announce that the baseball game he was reporting had been called. His listeners had to guess that the cause was rain!

In spite of the hours, working at the airport was fun. A small Army Air Force unit was stationed there, its personnel not unwelcome to almost-all-girl staffs. We civilians were glad to welcome them to our little group of control tower operators, Civil Administration staff, and United Airlines and airport administration people. Although many of these men and women came and went frequently because of wartime conditions, we were close, partied frequently in our free time and came to know their families. Many became my lifetime friends.

After World War II ended, I continued on with the Weather Bureau. Gradually the other women staffers went off to families or other jobs and were replaced by returning veterans. Finally, in 1954 I was "RIF'd"— displaced by "reduction in force," now called "downsizing." I had more years of service than most of the men, but they had "veterans' preference." I didn't consider it unfair. After all, they had done much more for the war effort than I.

It did present a dilemma, though. Meteorology doesn't exactly lead into other jobs! I placed many applications, but with my specialized experience they led to nothing. Finally I obtained a clerical job with the local high school district. A year later, a local television station offered me a job giving the weather forecast for their evening news. I said "no" emphatically. Despite speech training in school, I was a nervous speaker. The station manager was evidently desperate and I finally agreed to try it for a week. The week eventually became nineteen years. For some unknown reason, television weather in those early years was always a woman's job — the only one aside from children's shows and cooking programs.

Much has changed. The Weather Bureau, now the National Weather Service, no longer has a local office. Data is taken electronically and transmitted to a regional office, which issues reports and broadcasts. No doubt much is transmitted by computer — pilot briefings, etc. A network of satellites fulfills our old wish for more data from the Pacific, and maps are transmitted ready-made. Magic! I hope the meteorologists now enjoy their work as much as we did.

Station Attendant
in the Boondocks

Marjorie M. Culpepper

When I was growing up in the Portland, Oregon, public schools, my grade school mid-year class had only 18 students: nine girls and nine boys. By the end of World War II, two of the boys had been killed in France. In 1944, my college roommate's brother was killed in Italy and four more Portland friends died in Germany.

On September 3, 1939, England and France declared war on Germany. I was just entering the ninth grade. There was little concern about the war because the United States was *not* going to get involved in *this* one. We listened to Edward R. Murrow give his reports from England, but that seemed so far away. After all, everything was normal here. At the end of July, 1941, my older brother joined the 41st (Sunset) Division of the Oregon National Guard. By the end of October, "blackouts" had begun every night from 10:00 PM until daylight. By the end of November, the 41st Division had gone to San Francisco and my brother said they would be leaving for the Philippines on December 5.

We later learned that on December 7, the division was about 500 miles out to sea when Japanese planes bombed Pearl Harbor. April 16, 1942, was the last time we saw my brother before the division left for Australia, this time with a naval convoy. So much for non-involvement in the war.

The reality of war became even more shocking when orders were given that all Japanese, even those who were citizens and born in this country, were to be sent to internment camps. My high school had quite a few

Japanese students and I knew several of them. A school party was held for them and then they were gone. I never knew if they received their diplomas.

Many military men came through Portland and numerous times we brought two or three from church to our home for Sunday dinner. My brother was treated the same way in Australia. Their camp was near Melbourne and he became lifelong friends with several families. One of the mothers wrote to our mother and always told where the division was.

My best friend and I enrolled at the University of Oregon in the fall of 1942. When the term ended, I applied for work with an airline. The airline headquarters were in Chicago. After passing the written and physical tests, I was hired with the understanding that when the war ended, so did employment. Before the war, the only women hired were registered nurses who served as stewardesses. Air flight was new, planes were small and bumpy and a lot of air sickness occurred. The theory was that if women weren't afraid to fly, men would lose their fear of flying. It didn't always work that way! That had to change also as nurses were called into the military. They certainly received a much better deal there. The pay with the airline was very low, but our "prestigious" jobs made up for that! This was the way business operated then and I didn't think much about it because "that was the way it was." Girls were supposed to marry and become housewives.

Assignments were given at the end of the six weeks of training and I was to be a station attendant at the Rock Springs, Wyoming, airport. Some of the girls went to large cities to work at the airport counters. (None of the assignments turned out to be very desirable.) I arrived in Rock Springs in mid August and was met by two employees who let me share their rooms while I looked for one. Rooms were scarce but I finally found a furnished apartment. It was one of a row of three adjacent to the owner's home. After I spent three days cleaning it, it was really quite nice.

The airport was ten or so miles east of town on top of a barren plateau. I had never been out of Oregon and western Washington, with its lush forests and green undergrowth, so Wyoming's wide-open ruggedness was quite a shock, especially after learning the field had recently been fenced to keep the wild horses off the runways! People hated to get stuck in Rock Springs!

A station attendant's duties included everything from cleaning the ladies' restroom to operating the radio. We were paid less than the men although we worked the same hours and shifts. The excuse given for less pay was that we did not gas the planes (although I did once or twice). We were also expected to wear the company uniform — gray wool in winter and a light blue suit for summer.

The DC3s looked like big planes in that day. The luggage area was toward the tail and a person standing on the ground could easily open the door and put in or remove anything necessary. The Post Office brought the airmail out to us when a plane was due and we put it in a special mail pouch kept just inside the door of the luggage compartment.

An aerial photographer who worked at the station owned a new 2-door Oldsmobile with the gear shift on the steering column. We were very impressed. He and his pilot went up almost every day to photograph the area. I don't know who he worked for, but he always had plenty of gas for the car and the plane. The people who worked at the airport never had a gasoline problem either. When the men fueled the planes, they always made sure they cut the gas off while the hose was full. Since it was a very long hose, they could supplement what they bought with their gas ration coupons.

In June, I was told there was a vacancy in Fresno, California, and I could have it if I was interested. It didn't take long to decide! On June 28, I left Rock Springs on the 2:00 A.M. train. No seats were available, so I joined others in the same predicament and we sat on our suitcases all the way to Salt Lake City, arriving about 10:00 A.M. My supervisor in Rock Springs had given me the name of a reservation clerk and told me to contact him immediately upon arrival. The clerk gave me a reservation for an upper berth on the July 1st train and told me to board as soon as that train was called and to get into bed immediately.

I followed instructions, even though I thought 9:30 P.M. was too early to go to bed. A short time later, an answer came when I heard a woman tell a porter that mine was supposed to be her berth. The porter told her he would take her to the next car and find a place for her.

On August 14th, we heard the radio announcement of victory over Japan and that August 15th was to be V-J Day. The next day I heard that my brother was in Seattle and would be discharged — home without injury after almost five years of active duty.

True to their word, the airline notified the girls on September 6th that priorities would take effect on October 15th, and those of us who worked at intermediate stations would be replaced by men. I flew into Portland on November 5th, and started the old routine of filling out work applications.

Fifty plus years later, the memories have softened, but occasionally I still think of friends who died during that awful time. So young, so much potential unrealized.

Carolina Moon

Muriel I. Hornaday

It was the end of September 1941. England had been fighting Germany since 1939. I had just received an associate's degree in secretarial science at Northern Montana College in Havre, Montana. Just before graduating, for practice, I took the civil service examination for work in Washington, D. C. to prepare for the later examination given for the Eleventh District in our area. To my surprise, a telegram came from Washington, D. C., the Office of Production Management, requesting me to report on October 15, 1941, to work as a clerk-stenographer for the agency.

I didn't want to leave my family, especially my three little sisters, but I couldn't stay on the farm. My father encouraged me to take the job and co-signed a note for a loan so I could make the move from Montana.

Several of my girl friends from college were already working in Washington. They were living in an old mansion, the Molin Home for Girls, with about 50 girls from all over the United States. I loved to listen to a girl from Mississippi talking to one from Massachusetts. Local accents hadn't yet been affected too much by radio and television, and people had not been moving from state to state as they did after the war. Our house mother, who had been in the AFS in France during World War I, took care of all of us.

Most of the girls were working for some part of the government involved in the war effort. Our house mother had all of our ration books and managed to feed us very well. She made sure we had meals saved for us when we had to work overtime. We went to all the plays and shows that came to town, especially when buying E-bonds would include tickets.

61

The name of my agency was changed to the War Production Board (WPB), and Donald Nelson became the head. Many men from industry came to work as dollar-a-year men, and industry pushed production of war materials on a round-the-clock basis. I was in personnel for a few months and then was transferred to the mica-graphite division as a statistical clerk. I always did prefer accounting, but the statistical work along with the secretarial work was very good experience for me. And soon I was given a permanent appointment. Later new hires received only temporary status.

We were responsible for the allocation of controlled minerals to industry. The war restricted our world-wide sources. A shipload of graphite from Madagascar (the main source of that material) did arrive in the United States just before shipments from there were cut off. The source of the highest grade of mica is India. We tried to develop sources of mica in the United States, mainly in North Carolina. It was not as good quality as that obtained from India, which we continued receiving. We had requests from offices in New York City for allocations of mica for the Manhattan Project. The request was, of course, classified as top priority, and we did not know it was involved with the development of the atomic bomb.

Sunday afternoon, December 7, 1941, my girl friend and I were visiting the Capitol. On the way home, on the street car a paper boy, with an "EXTRA," shouted that Pearl Harbor had been bombed by the Japanese. We knew that President Roosevelt had been meeting with some envoys from Japan, so could hardly believe the news. That evening, employees of the German embassy which was a block from our home, were seen burning boxes of papers in their backyard. That also happened about ten blocks northwest of us at the Japanese embassy. All of the service men were alerted to return to their bases.

Just before the war started, I saw President Roosevelt go by in his convertible with the top down. But that all changed. Spotlights on the buildings were turned off, we had blackout drills often and security was very strict.

We were on our way home from work one afternoon in April 1945 when we heard the announcement of President Roosevelt's death at Warm Springs, Georgia. His body was taken by train to his family home in Hyde Park, New York. But the train did stop in D.C. so the funeral procession could go up Pennsylvania Avenue and the body lie in state at the Capitol.

On V-E Day in May 1945, we joined the celebration in front of the White House, as we lived only six blocks from there. When General Dwight Eisenhower came home from Europe in July we helped to honor him with a parade on Pennsylvania Avenue. Then came the dropping of the atom bombs which resulted in V-J Day in August 1945. Another huge celebration was held all over the country, and we were all in front of the White House again. It was hard to believe it was all over.

I was volunteering at the United Nations Service Center near Union Station on a Friday night in May 1945, checking baggage for servicemen. A young sailor from North Carolina was killing time waiting to take a plane back to the naval air station at Norfolk, Virginia. We had a long conversation about Montana and North Carolina. He was very interesting to talk with, had a sense of humor, was good looking and my age. I told him when I was in high school in Montana that I would ride herd on our cattle and sing to the moon — "Carolina moon, keep shining, shining on the one who waits for me." Many years later, he told my girl friend that he knew that night I was the girl he would marry. It was meant to be.

He talked me into taking a taxi with him to Washington National Airport, promising to send me home. That would not have been approved by the people in charge of the center, but I did it anyway. He sent a special delivery letter that day and called me on the phone on Sunday. During the summer, he came to visit on several weekends. Our housemother approved of him and my girl friends thought he was great. We continued to correspond as I started working for Trans World Airlines, moving into an apartment with three of my friends.

In January 1946, just before he was discharged, he spent a week with me in D.C. After his discharge, he began working for Eastern Air Lines in Cleveland, Ohio, and after many letters and phone calls, we were married on July 2, 1946, in Alexandria, Virginia. My friends had a big party for us, my housemother taking all the credit for our having met. We called his parents in North Carolina and mine in Montana. They were surprised but happy for us.

I was able to obtain work in Cleveland easily as I had civil service status and good experience. So I continued as a career woman and ended up working for General Motors until I retired. I was involved in the development of the procedures for doing accounting with the computer. Fascinating! We did spend our summer vacations in Montana with my family and weekends with Lee's family in North Carolina.

A Government Girl in Washington

Betty Louise Wright

In July, 1941, at the ripe old age of 19 and at the urging of my father, I passed a federal civil service examination for junior clerk-stenographer. I was asked at the time if I would accept an appointment in Washington, D.C., if it were offered. I said that I would, thinking I could always refuse.

Along came Pearl Harbor, which changed everything. On Christmas Day came to our door a boy on a bicycle, not with friendly Christmas greetings, but with a telegram asking me to accept a position in Washington and to be there on January 5. All of my friends were going off to the far corners, so I thought I might as well see the country and have a new experience. I wired my acceptance and began the furious activity of preparation

I left Portland, Oregon, at 9:30 PM on New Year's Eve, knowing only that I had a job. It was a long, lonely trip to Chicago. Our train was late getting into Chicago and I missed my connection. While waiting for a later train, I met two girls from Portland and the father of one of them, who were also bound for D.C. Finding people from home was a comfort to me. We spent the evening in the club car playing hearts as we rode through Indiana, Ohio and Pennsylvania.

I ran into one of the girls the next morning when I finally arrived at the YWCA dormitory in a rather poor neighborhood of downtown D.C. It reminded me of skid row in Portland when I heard the Salvation Army band playing on the corner. The other girl was staying with her father temporarily at the historic Willard Hotel for the scandalous price of $5 a night.

My dormitory room had five beds occupied by girls from all over the country. Some were just starting work the next day. Others had already begun. I became friends with a girl from Minot, North Dakota, and we decided to look for housing together, as our stay in the dorm was limited.

We found a small room with shared bathroom in the home of a couple in a modern row house on the outskirts of the District, a long ride to and from work. Some of our first purchases were an alarm clock and a Kodak camera.

On Monday, January 5, I reported with many others to offices in the Kresge Building. After much processing and standing in line, several of us were sent to the Munitions Building on Constitution Avenue, the home of the War Department. It stood on ground now occupied by the Vietnam Memorial, and had been built as a temporary building during World War I. We were now members of the Secretary of War's pool of typists and clerks.

The rest of the day was spent filling out forms and more forms. The room was full of girls, but finally three of us were ushered into the chief of staff's office where we faced more forms. Then we were directed to the office of the assistant chief of staff G-3, known as operations and training. We also took an oath somewhere along the way and, from then on, our pay began.

The next morning, we had pictures taken for our badges, without which we could not enter the building. A rumor had it that a man had put a picture of Hitler over his own on his badge and it had not been noticed by guards for two weeks.

I was seated in a room with apparently not much activity for me, but I was told to keep my steno pad handy. After a couple of days, a dignified but kindly officer, a lieutenant colonel, asked me to take some dictation, after which one of the girls in the room instructed me in its preparation for draft and then for final form. Evidently I passed the test, as I was assigned to take the places of two girls, at different times, who wished to go on vacation. Their leaves had been canceled on December 7. Not long after that, I was assigned permanently as the secretary to an officer and given my own desk, typewriter and telephone. The work concerned mostly the mobilization and transportation of troops to and from Army installations and staging areas for shipment overseas.

How much there was to learn! First of all, the insignia. How to tell a colonel from a lieutenant or a captain, or someone who was assigned to the Signal Corps from one in the Air Corps or Field Artillery. There were new words such as practicable, materiel, cadre, concurrences, ETA (estimated time of arrival) and TAG (the adjutant general).

There were many new things to learn about Washington. I had never

Betty Wright

seen milk that came in cartons instead of glass bottles, nor streetcars running on a third rail instead of a trolley. Fireflies were new and fascinating. And it seemed we had to stand in line for everything: to cash our checks, to see a movie, and, most of all, to eat. Most restaurants, even the very best, were cafeterias. There were new foods, such as kale, butter brickle ice cream, and all sorts of strange sandwiches.

My roommate and I decided to part company. She was working nights and did not want to be so far from town. As a result, I found myself sharing a room with other girls in a rooming house close to the center of town. In those days, if you rented a room in a *rooming* house, the room was yours, either single or double. A *boarding* house furnished a room, but the number of beds to a room was determined by the management, and usually held as many as space would accommodate. If you found your roommates working different hours from yours, it could be most annoying.

Of course, we had no air-conditioning and fans were not available because of the war. But we managed, even sharing the bathroom with five other women. We had a radio and a small phonograph for entertainment. I learned to put up with insects, bugs, worms, etc. No bedclothes were left near the floor.

There was no lack of outside entertainment. Once we jumped into a cab (we were in the 20 cent zone) and rode to the steps of the District Building where Kay Kaiser and his band were performing for a war bond drive. What fun to see him, Harry Babbitt, Ginny Sims, and Ishkabibble. On another occasion, we were downtown to cash our paychecks and while standing on a street corner saw a parade of Army jeeps going by with movie stars riding in them: Ann Rutherford, Virginia Gilmore, Bing Crosby, Irene Dunne, Hedy Lamar, Kay Kaiser, Edward Arnold, Greer Garson, Jimmy Cagney, Abbott and Costello, Ginny Sims, Walter Abel, and Ralph Bellamy.

We walked back to work with stars in our eyes and didn't get over it for the next three days.

We worked six days a week and even on holidays. Our typewriters were all manual and everything was in ten copies. There being no copy machines, carbon paper was the only way to duplicate information. Accuracy was the name of the game. All final work had to be proof-read with another secretary. Any used scratch paper, used carbon paper, steno pads (even partly used) and unfinished work went into the safe at night. One officer was assigned to lock the safe and the general's executive officer came in later to check again.

At one point I was secretary for an Air Corps officer. He was being sent to the Pacific as executive officer to General Nathan Twining (a Portland native). Late one day, he came to me with a loose-leaf notebook filled with specifications on many types of Army aircraft. He wished copies of this material to take with him, and asked that I stay late to make them, which I gladly agreed to do. His instructions were that I put the original and my copies into the safe which would be left open for me. This material was *top secret*, so if for any reason any of it was left out after the safe was locked, I was to phone him at home and he would return.

We had been warned against intruders, in spite of the great security, especially after working hours. I sat alone at my desk typing and the rooms grew dark until the only light came from the long fluorescent lamp over my typewriter. Suddenly, I began to hear footsteps in the hall. They grew louder, obviously coming close. Then they stepped into the room and I was very afraid! I was in the back of the room where there was no escape.

At last a face appeared. Who was it? The executive officer coming for his nightly checkup to see if the safe was locked. He was one of the most kind and gentle men I had ever known. He apologized profusely for having frightened me. I explained my work and the colonel's instructions and we had a good laugh.

Secrecy was very much a part of our lives. I lunched regularly with a girl from another section. We often discussed incidents which had happened in our sections but seldom anything regarding the work. One day at lunch she told me that she had been chosen as a secretary for a new branch which was being formed. She said the project was *top secret* and that General George Patton had warned them that if any of it leaked out, the whole project would have to be abandoned. We decided to continue our lunch dates, but promised not to discuss anything about work. I asked her if she would tell me when the project was completed and what it was. She said, "Don't worry. You'll know." And that's all that she ever said on the subject.

In the fall, after my 21st birthday, I transferred to another government agency in Portland and had returned home and put this out of my mind.

One evening when I was listening to the radio with my family (possibly in November 1942), the program was interrupted by a special bulletin. The Allies had begun the invasion of North Africa with a successful surprise landing at Casablanca. General Patton was in charge. My friend was so right! I knew immediately. And what a thrill to know that my friend had had a small part in the huge undertaking.

I have many wonderful memories. I am sure my Washington experience was a help to my self-confidence as I matured and it has been fun to recall this period of my life.

Wartime in Washington, D.C.

Evelyn W. Stotler

In the fall of 1943, when I was twenty-three, I took a position teach-ing fifth grade in the Algona, Iowa, public schools. Almost every teacher had a husband, boyfriend or brothers in service. We spent many a night worrying together and commiserating with each other. We went to the movie theater every chance we could because that is where we would see action pictures of the war which, by now, had escalated much more than people had envisioned. We had fighting forces practically all over the world, so it seemed.

Soon, memorial services were springing up in the towns and cities honoring those who had been killed in the service of their country. I played the piano and organ and had to play for some of those services. It was dev-astating emotionally.

About four miles out of the town of Algona a huge prisoner-of-war camp was built. It had been a hush-hush project until it was completed. It was a large complex built on flat ground which had been cornfields. Young women of the town were often invited by some of the officers to have Sun-day dinner at the officers' club at the camp. The waiters were young Ger-man prisoners of war. They were handsome young men and I wondered at the incongruity of us sitting there being waited upon by these boys while our young men were over there killing their brothers and friends, as the German military were doing to ours.

Because of the prison camp, a USO was set up in town where the US soldiers could come for recreation. Algona didn't have a lot of single females, so the single teachers were recruited to serve cookies and to attend the dances. A few of the gals got burned and fell in love with the wrong guys. Two of the men were married, but claimed their wives were divorcing them. I was lucky and met a really nice young soldier and we became friends. However, he turned a bit too amorous for me right then. I was carrying the torch for a certain soldier named Don Stotler who was stationed on an island named Shemya at the tip of the Aleutian Islands. I wasn't sure I would ever see him again, but I hoped I would.

In the summer of 1944, I went to Washington, D.C., to visit my sister Eleanor. She worked in the map making department of the War Department out on MacArthur Boulevard. Army Map Service was built all underground but camouflaged on top by being painted various shades of green and brown. Trees were planted on the building's roof—protection from possible enemy air attack everyone hoped.

While I was visiting, Eleanor was due to take her civil service renewal exam, so I went along with her. The lady at the desk asked if I wanted to take the test, too. I thought it would pass the time so I took a clerk-typist test. The next day, Eleanor told her boss, Mrs. Wellener, that I was visiting and had taken the test. After seeing the results, Mrs. Wellener asked if I would like to work there. I explained that I had signed a contract to teach the next year. She said that was all right, that I could work just for the summer. I jumped at the chance.

The first three weeks, I worked at Army Map Service in the map design department. I didn't know it at the time, but I was making maps for the pilots to use in night flying. The maps showed locations to be bombed, but the locations showed on the maps only when the pilot shone a beam on them with a small flashlight.

Then I was transferred to the payroll department where Eleanor worked. I spent the first week going through all the records hunting an error that no one else had been able to find. I sort of accidentally found it. Well, from then on, I could do no wrong. Each clerk had a payroll to do so when a clerk went on vacation, I moved to her desk and did her payroll. No computers at that time, just adding machines and calculators—but they worked. Every two weeks I moved to a different desk.

I was particularly happy to have the job because my best girlfriend, Lois, worked in an office at the White House and we would have the summer to do things together. Because of Lois I had some rare privileges. The Marines stood guard over the grounds and White House and I guess they must have checked me out because I got to see a movie in the White House theater and weighed myself on F.D.R.'s scale, which was a chair down by the swimming pool. The gardener gave me a big bouquet of roses one day.

And once I was with Lois and met Eleanor Roosevelt and Frances Perkins, Secretary of Labor and the first woman cabinet member.

When Lois first went to Washington, she worked in Senator Russell's office. When Jimmy Byrnes was appointed Secretary of State, she moved to his office in the East Wing of the White House. I have notes in my diary that one night she was working late and I helped her proof a copy of his speech to be given to Congress the following day.

That summer was fun, even if it was war time. Everyone was working hard on various war activities; but also people were craving emotional release, going to plays and band concerts and other entertainment. El and I would meet Lois downtown and go out to dinner early and then stand in line to see movies, plays, etc. On weekends we bicycled over to Arlington, Virginia, to visit the cemetery and Lee's mansion, then all around the Lincoln Memorial, Jefferson Memorial, Washington Monument and Haines Point. We went to Watergate concerts which were held on a barge on the Potomac River. We sat on the back of the Lincoln Memorial and all around the area. Many people came in canoes and small boats to hear the music. Several from our office went roller skating together. We also hiked along the Baltimore and Ohio canal running through Georgetown, which was not far from where we stayed.

The day I left to go back to Algona for my next year of teaching, Lois saw me off on the train. She said she thought she had seen Don Stotler on a streetcar, so she would check when she got back to the White House and find out where he was stationed. She found him and invited him to dinner at Mrs. Donaldson's boarding house where El and I stayed and where Lois took her breakfasts and dinners. He asked for my address and that began nine months of writing letters between us. At the end of May I went back to D.C. to work at Army Map Service.

Don met me at the train and we spent as much time together as we could. The next week I had to report for work. Don asked me if I could meet him in Lafayette Park, across from the White House after work on Monday. I did and he said, "I pulled some money out of the bank and I thought we could go to a jewelry store." That was his proposal. I was willing and we hurried to the nearest jewelry store, on Constitution Avenue, picked up the rings and went to dinner. That was on June 13, 1945. We decided to be married when he could get his next three-day leave, which would be July 13th, 14th and 15th.

The next month was hectic — war time — most of our male friends were in service. There was gas rationing so our folks couldn't drive from Iowa, and it was hard to get train reservations. We decided to be married at the Emory Methodist Church on Georgia Avenue. In back of the church was a fort where, it was said, Lincoln had visited and was shot at during the Civil War, so Don thought that was an appropriate setting — now that he was under matrimonial fire.

So, we were married on Friday, July 13, 1945. About forty people were present. Lois couldn't be there because she was in Potsdam at the Big Three Conference held with Churchill, Truman and Stalin. My sister, Eleanor, was my bridesmaid and one of Don's Army buddies from the Aleutians was his best man. Our friends had helped us stock the cupboards in the upstairs furnished apartment we had been lucky enough to rent. When we arrived after the wedding dinner, we found a coal black cat sleeping peacefully in the middle of the bed — which had been short-sheeted with cornflakes strewn inside the sheets.

Don was in the Army Medical Corps stationed at Walter Reed Hospital. At Walter Reed, they were doing research on a flu vaccine and they used the lab workers as guinea pigs. One week after our wedding Don barely made it home and was so sick with flu shot reaction I thought I was going to be a widow after only one week of marriage. Fortunately, he recovered fairly soon.

In August, Lois called me and said something big and exciting was going to happen, to listen to the radio and come down to Lafayette Park as soon as possible. Don and I hopped on the streetcar and rode downtown to the park. By the time we arrived, the news was out — the Japanese had surrendered. VJ Day! Lois was right, a big news break. She had typed the original Japanese surrender terms.

It was a wild, mad scene. People milling about everywhere — several climbing lamp-posts, yelling, blowing whistles— sailors, Marines, secretaries, young girls, old women — everyone kissing and hugging each other — perfect strangers united in a moment of victory.

During the next few months Washington was an exciting place to be. We all got off work when they had big parades honoring returning war heroes. The one for General Eisenhower was the largest and most spectacular. He was wearing the jacket that was named for him.

By the end of October, Don knew his military discharge was due. He had been in the Army four years. We sent applications to three universities for Don to enter graduate school — the University of Maryland, the University of Chicago and Stanford University. We had agreed to attend whichever university accepted Don first — hoping at least one would. How fortunate for us that Stanford accepted his application.

The first week of December, we were on our way to Iowa, to visit there before going on to California. We had been advised by the university that practically no housing was available and to come at our own risk. Being an adventuresome duo, we decided to take our chances. Stanford, here we come!

Everything Was Segregated

Grace Ridgeley Drew

The second of seven daughters, I was born in Washington, D.C. where my father, Albert Ridgeley, was a physician. I graduated from Dunbar High School in 1927, and was awarded a scholarship to Smith College in Northampton, Massachusetts. In 1931, I graduated from Smith, where I was the only colored member of the class. (In this account, I shall use the words "colored" or "Negro" to refer to persons who are now called black — a term which was not used during World War II.) Soon afterwards, I married Joseph Drew, who also graduated from Dunbar in 1927. He later graduated from Howard University in Washington, D.C.

In the spring of 1942, I was living in Arlington, Virginia, with my husband, our three sons, my husband's mother, and his sister. Arlington County was once part of the District of Columbia. In Washington, everything was segregated — schools, churches, theaters, restaurants— everything except streetcars and buses, the National Zoo, the public library and the Library of Congress. In Arlington, the buses were also segregated, with colored passengers required to sit in the back.

The schools for colored children in Arlington were inferior to those in Washington, so we sent our boys to school in Washington, where my husband was a physical education teacher in one of the colored junior high schools. We used my parents' Washington address and the boys attended the same elementary schools I had attended. It was not unusual for colored parents in the suburbs to send their children to Washington schools,

73

which were superior to most segregated schools in the suburbs. Some suburbs of Washington — including Arlington — did not have colored high schools.

The colored citizens of Washington lived in several widely scattered areas of the city. Some of the areas had distinctive names — Foggy Bottom, near the Lincoln Memorial; Brookland, in the northeast section; Anacostia in the southeast section of the city. The leading colored area in the war years was the northwest part of the city, north of New York Avenue, between North Capitol Street on the east and Sixteenth Street on the west, extending north beyond Florida Avenue, which was once the city's boundary line. That area was the site of the colored high schools, the normal school, Howard University, and colored-owned businesses and theaters. It is now called the Shaw district.

Members of the Drew family had lived for many years in the Foggy Bottom area. In 1920, my husband's parents moved to Arlington and purchased a home. The family then consisted of the parents Richard and Nora Drew, and three children: Charles, Joseph and Nora. A fourth child, Eva, was born later. The oldest son, Charles, a graduate of Dunbar High School (as were the other children), went on to graduate from Amherst College in Massachusetts, and from McGill University Medical School in Montreal, Canada.

When World War II began, Dr. Charles Drew, my brother-in-law, used laboratory experiments and the research of others for mass production of plasma for shipment to Britain. This project was terminated when Hitler failed to invade Britain. But the United States decided there was need for a stockpile of blood reserves if an invasion occurred here. A pilot program was set up through the Red Cross to begin in February, 1941. Dr. Drew was selected to serve as medical supervisor of the project. He resigned in April, 1941, and returned to Howard University Medical School, where he trained many young colored surgeons until his untimely death in an automobile accident in 1950.

During the war we had very little contact with whites unless we left the neighborhood. Business people were usually polite; in most stores we were served courteously; in others, we might be ignored or denied service. There were several prominent department stores — Woodward and Lothrop, Kann's, Lansburgh and Hecht's. Only Hecht's has survived and grown. Scattered all over town were numerous 5 & 10 cent stores. We shopped at the larger department stores and had charge accounts at some of them.

The federal government was the largest employer in Washington, D.C., but it employed very few colored workers in clerical and professional jobs. In the spring of 1942, I took an examination for the job of clerk in federal government. I chose a low-ranking job as a better chance of getting hired.

As the result of the examination, I was offered a job at the National Labor Relations Board as a grade 2 clerk, at a salary of $1,440 per year. This amounted to $60 every half month ($57.50 after deduction for retirement). My mother-in-law agreed to babysit for my youngest son, who was then less than two years old.

The National Labor Relations Board (NLRB) was one of the "New Deal" agencies established in the Roosevelt Administration. It had two responsibilities: (1) to decide which union, if any, had the right to represent a specific group of workers, and (2) to determine whether an employer had committed an unfair labor practice, such as refusal to bargain with a qualified union, or discrimination against employees for union activity. If an employer was found guilty of committing an unfair labor practice, the NLRB could order remedies for employees, such as reinstatement and/or back pay. The office in which I began to work was responsible for determining how much back pay, if any, was required.

Only two female employees worked in my office — one professional and one typist. I was the only colored worker in the section. All the other employees were men, mostly from New York or other northern areas. Some of them were older than I, some were younger. They could not understand why I — a college graduate — would accept a low-paying clerical position. They were all friendly and treated me with respect and admiration. Most of them would have been willing to go to lunch with me, but the local restaurants and food providers would not have served me. It was not until the Supreme Court decision in *Brown vs. Board of Education* in 1954 that Washington restaurants, schools and businesses ended segregation. I often brought my lunch from home, or purchased carryout food from a lunch counter. In mild weather, I could eat lunch on a bench in the park across the street from my office.

As other jobs opened up in the section, I was promoted, first to higher clerical jobs, then to professional jobs, so that by the end of the war my salary was $2,500. But that was also the end of my job. When the permanent workers came back from military service or jobs in wartime agencies, temporary workers were let go.

Some of the men in my office seemed to feel it was their responsibility to find a job for me. They put me in touch with a man who was in the process of setting up a research office for a labor union. I met him and he hired me. I worked for that union for many years.

My life was completely altered when I began to work for the government. I changed from a housewife financially dependent on my husband to a working woman earning as much as my husband earned. But it wasn't always easy. At first, I tried to do most of the household chores in my free time, but it just was not possible. We had plumbing and electricity, but no washing machine. Clothes were washed on a washboard in a tin tub, and hung on a clothesline to dry. After I started working, I tried to do the laundry in the evening or on weekends, but it proved to be more than I could handle, so my husband took over the job until he was able to purchase an electric washing machine. We did not have a car during the war (no cars were being made then), and had to use the bus or depend on neighbors to get to Washington to school and to work.

As I recall, the schools were involved in issuing ration books and coupons. At times, my children would say their teachers would like me to help with issuing ration books and coupons, but I was unable to do so. I was working six days a week, while my husband had Saturdays off. It became his responsibility to do the grocery shopping. He and the older boys would walk several blocks to the grocery store to bring the groceries home. There was a small grocery story near my office, where I could sometimes find items not always available elsewhere.

I had assumed that I would stop working when the war ended. But, by that time, all of my sons were in school, so there was no compelling reason for me to stay at home. When I was offered a job that interested me, I saw no reason to refuse. We had become accustomed to two salaries, and it would have been difficult to manage on only one. My husband wanted me to accept the job offer. I had become a career woman!

Better Than Crossword Puzzles

Adelaide Hawkins

While tensions rose and democracies fell in Europe during the 1930s, President Roosevelt's administration was preparing for war in small ways that would not provoke America's numerous and vocal isolationists. Among the preparations was the enhancement of our intelligence gathering and analysis capabilities. The armed services and the State, Agriculture, Commerce and other federal departments all had some experience in the field, but there was no system for coordinating their work to maximize its effectiveness. So, not only did the various intelligence units expand their activities, but at the persistent request of General William Donovan, Roosevelt created the office of "Coordinator of Information" for him. The growth of the field was the reason my husband was offered a job in Washington, and the centralization of the process was the reason I was offered one.

The unsettled conditions of my war years on the home front were presaged in my life as a young person in the Great Depression. Wheeling, West Virginia, is on the Ohio River, a steel mill town of 65,000 people in the 1920s. My father was a machinist. During my high school years, work was scarce for him so I lived with a sister of my mother to ease the financial strain.

A year after graduating from a Catholic high school, I married Ed Hawkins. He was three years older than I. Ed's father was a Harvard graduate and a successful businessman. Ed's mother was also well educated, including time in the sculpture studio of Augustus St. Gaudens. The differences in their backgrounds was a frequent source of problems between Ed's family and mine.

Within four years of our marriage we had three children: Sheila, Eddie and Don. Ed had neither the training nor the instinct for business so that, when his father died suddenly, we lost most of the benefits of his labor and investments.

Ed joined the Army Signal Corps Reserves and began studying cryptanalysis in their extension program. Col. William Friedman, the premier intellect in American cryptanalysis, was authorized in 1939 to increase the size and capacity of Signal Intelligence Group. He did this through a competitive training and screening process which resulted in Ed's being offered a job in Washington. By February, 1940, we were all living in a little wooden rented house in Silver Spring, Maryland, a suburb of Washington. Later my mother lent us the money for a down payment on a place of our own in Silver Spring.

The crypto community in Washington was still fairly small, so I got to know socially some of the people who were attempting to modernize and professionalize America's work in the field. Colonel Friedman's wife, Elizabeth Smith Friedman, was particularly kind and helpful to me. She was working at that time for the Coast Guard, for whom she broke the rumrunners' codes. I found the work these people were doing intriguing and simultaneously became bored with crossword puzzles, so I began doing cryptanalysis lessons along with Ed. Before long I received permission to send in my duplicate lessons for grading by the Signal Corps.

After about a year and a half in Silver Spring, Ed's mother and newly married sister came to live with us. Our household consisted at this time of four adults, three children and two dogs. Sheila was seven, Eddie was six, Don was four, Kurt was Ed's doberman and Woozy was his sister's cocker spaniel.

Within weeks of my in-laws' arrival, Ed's boss asked him if I might be interested in a job. He knew of my duplicate lessons and thought they might be useful to an organization just being put together. They wanted me to work for the coordinator of information (COI)! This seemed like a timely offer; my mother-in-law was now available to look after the kids while I helped supplement the family income.

I arrived for my first briefing in the old National Institute of Health (NIH) building at 2430 E Street, N.W. in Washington, D.C. The briefing was given by James Roosevelt. Here was a son of the President of the United States telling me, a 27 year old mother of three from West Virginia, that when the U.S. got into the war, this new office would be extremely important. I was most surprised at his saying "when" not "if." Though my husband had been working in the intelligence field for two years, I still did not think war was inevitable. The date of my briefing was December 3, 1941. In my first three days at the office I saw very few military uniforms. The following Monday it seemed that everyone was in uniform. Ed's commission was activated immediately and he was sent to the Pacific in fairly short order.

My assignment was to set up the Message Center for COI. At that time the entire staff of COI consisted of twelve people. Mrs. Friedman was still employed by the Coast Guard, but came under contract to guide me in my totally unfamiliar role. I began interviewing and training employees with the first objective being a competent staff to keep the Message Center operational 24 hours a day and seven days a week. A great cross section of people came to us, many from universities and many from the services. I needed to determine their aptitude for cryptanalysis and related tasks. Many of our successful applicants were good at mathematics and puzzles. Albert Sheinwold, the authority on bridge, became a member of the staff.

The National Institutes of Health had only recently vacated when we moved into the second floor of their building. We were instructed if we saw any stray white rats to disturb them as little as possible and call the guards, who had all been trained in rat-catching. Our working space shifted downward in stages until we settled permanently in the basement. One day some movement attracted my attention and I turned to see one of the no-longer-authorized occupants skittering along a pipe up near the ceiling. I backed out of my office, closed the door firmly and went a considerable distance down the hall before stopping to call a guard to do his duty.

We had a disproportionate number of applicants from Dartmouth College, largely because of another early hire, Bob Lang. Bob had been director of the Dartmouth Glee Club and he let it be known among its members that there was interesting work to be done at the Message Center. One result of this was that, at the frequent parties attended by the staff, there was wonderful group singing. Walter Lord always insisted upon hearing "It Was Sad When the Great Ship Went Down." Bob became a producer for Fred Waring after the war.

General Donovan was known as a person who did not stand on ceremony when it came to getting things done. The creation of the OSS is evidence of his effectiveness in tackling a problem head-on. One Saturday shortly after moving into our basement quarters, the general himself brought a message down to us for transmission instead of sending it down by messenger. He mentioned the all too noticeable stuffiness of the place in spite of the winter cold outside. The windows had been sealed — I suppose to keep the white rats in — and the air conditioning repair men had not yet found time to fix our system. General Donovan sympathized with us in our discomfort and left. A few minutes later we heard the sounds of splintering glass and turned to see a well-shod foot kick a ventilation hole in the window. Our problem had gotten the Donovan treatment.

To run the Message Center, General Donovan chose a New York lawyer with a Wall Street clientele: Captain, later Major, John Delafield. He remained director throughout the War. I was made deputy director and remained until the war was over also. Our duties included the transmission, reception, encryption and decryption of messages, with a huge range of sources and destinations. We handled communications for the OSS, but we also dealt with the departments, the armed services, embassies, the Congress and others. We trained people in communications not just for headquarters work but for the field also. Many of them spent time in enemy territory using the skills we taught them to get information out. It was shocking occasionally to see a former student in the halls, wearing the soiled clothes appropriate to his most recent assignment, on his way to a debriefing. We usually met our students before they had any experience of war. The change was always surprising.

A few months after I began work, my sister-in-law's husband, who was in the merchant marine, transferred to New York. She went with him, having found a position with the Coast Guard there. Within a few more months my mother-in-law found that the stress of caring for three children was too much for her. The solution for her problem was to move to New York and live with her daughter. I suddenly had no one to care for my children while I was at my job.

About this time, my father received a letter asking him to come to work in the torpedo factory in Alexandria, Virginia. Luckily for me, the timing of my parents coming to the Washington area nearly coincided with my mother-in-law's departure. My parents moved in with us in Silver Spring. My father took the hour and a half trolley and bus ride to and from his Alexandria job six days a week. My mother took care of the children and ran the household. Don had begun kindergarten in the spring and Sheila and Eddie were in school in the neighborhood so they did not need care all day long.

Our living situation for the next year and a half remained stable: my parents, my children, me and Ed's doberman Kurt. When he went off to war Ed was concerned for Kurt's welfare, and with good reason: Kurt was not well-liked in the neighborhood. He was troublesome and scary. I suppose Ed thought of him as protection for the family. I saw Ed himself possibly eight or ten times during the war, sometimes for a day, sometimes for a few days. After the Pacific he was assigned to a number of stations in the States and then in Italy. I received a regular portion of his captain's pay for the mortgage on the house.

By the end of 1943, the effort and time my father was expending to get to and from work, added to the overtime, was beginning to wear him down. My parents made the decision to move closer to his work. They found an apartment on the north edge of Alexandria, a mile and a half from the factory.

This time I made a radical decision about the children's welfare. Instead of depending upon family members for their care, we would send them to boarding school, two boarding schools, actually. So Eddie was sent to Longfellow School for Boys in Bethesda, Maryland. Sheila and Don went to Mrs. Walton's School, just a little further down the road in a darkish Victorian mansion on the edge of the countryside. Don was only in the first grade, but Sheila was in the fourth and I thought she could help look out for him.

So the family did not have a home together for a while. I moved into a house on Butterworth Place in the American University Park neighborhood of Washington with two young women from the office. Kurt went off to a series of kennels where he pined for Ed.

Eddie had always been the least healthy of the kids, missing a lot of school in his first few years because of illness. During his second school year, his nervousness became more obvious along with a few other indications of his just not being quite well. Finally, in February of 1945, I realized that he needed to be in a settled home environment and that I was the only one who could give it to him. Major Delafield allowed me to take the time I needed.

I withdrew both boys from school and took them off to Sarasota, Florida, where we rented a tiny house on Lido Beach. We fished, swam, boated and walked. There was really not much else to do. At the beginning of June we packed up and came back to Washington.

When we came back there was a feeling in the air that the war was going to be ending in the foreseeable future. I had already decided to buy another house as soon as possible. I found one in South Arlington that had the one most important characteristic: enough room for three generations to live comfortably for all the mutual support they could give one another.

Mother, Dad, Sheila, Eddie, Don and I moved into our house a few weeks before the surrender of Japan. This house really felt like mine. Mother was home all day to monitor the children and Dad was a kindly male presence, especially for the boys. Ed remained on active duty for some time after the war. He came for short periods to the house, but he didn't ever really come back to the family. We were divorced in 1947.

The OSS was disbanded after the war. Some of its functions were transferred to the Central Intelligence Group, a much smaller organization. I stayed on with CIG but wondered about its permanence. With the creation of the Central Intelligence Agency in 1947, the United States government committed itself to an active role in the intelligence field into the indefinite future. I joined the CIA in 1947 and continued to work there until 1973.

Voices from
the Laboratories

Army in White

Jane N. Aldrich

In 1928, Alexander Fleming observed that colonies of staphylococcus failed to grow in areas where penicillin had accidentally been spilled. Thus the therapeutic value of penicillin mold was recognized. World War II came along and suddenly the need for this wonder drug was desperate. Government funds poured into Cutter Laboratory at Berkeley, California. They were used for new buildings and equipment, including the largest refrigeration system on the West Coast at the time. Speeding up the production of the "miracle" drug was essential. Young women scientists were being recruited from all parts of the United States. As the *Oakland Tribune* of February 26, 1944, stated "the saga of penicillin is being written by a feminine 'army in white.'"

Jane Aldrich with letter from Elmer, Berkeley, '42.

My husband, Elmer, was stationed in Pearl Harbor, serving as a lieutenant JG in the Navy Photo Laboratory there. I was living in Berkeley with a college girl friend whose husband was off with the merchant marine. As a former biology and art teacher, I thought I might be qualified for a position in that "army." I don't remember much about my interview, but I was hired.

About 75 percent of the technical staff working on the penicillin project at Cutter

Jane (right) with two unidentified colleagues at Cutter Labs, '42.

were women. The purpose of this particular lab was to find new sources for different varieties of penicillin. The actual growing of penicillin mold was done in adjacent rooms. Our staff was experimenting with all kinds of bread, trying to discover which kind produced the best, most potent mold. In the area where I was, we used the liquid derivative of penicillin on agar plates that had been inoculated with staph. Measured amounts of liquid penicillin were pipetted onto the plates in a prescribed pattern; then, after incubation, the sterile circles were measured to determine the potency of the fluid used.

The exact output of the drug was a military secret. Practically all Berkeley penicillin went to the Army and Navy. A small amount was claimed by the National Research Council for civilian cases. All treatments were rigidly controlled by authorities so that results could be scientifically computed. The process of penicillin's course from jar to jar, incubator to refrigerator, to the day when the tested, finished product in sealed ampoules was ready for a serviceman's wounds made us feel that we were contributing significantly to the war effort. This was especially important to most of us because we had husbands and sweethearts on active duty.

In my lab the workers were all young women. I don't remember any special personal protection we workers used, except, of course, white lab coats, which were provided — no face masks or hair nets — and very clean surroundings.

We have had a neighbor for the past forty-seven years who was badly wounded in a Navy battle in the Pacific. To this day, he insists that penicillin saved his life. It is a good feeling to think that I might have had a tiny share in his recovery and that of others.

Personal Chemistry

Ellen S. Capps

At seventeen, I had enrolled at Kent State University to major in dietetics, which required a minor in chemistry. During summer break, I got a job in my home town working in a drug store at the soda fountain. It wasn't long after starting to work there that I decided to quit. The new young pharmacist who had just been hired was too cranky to work for. My parents gave me the standard lecture on responsibility and integrity. I had promised the manager of the store that I would be there all summer and there was no other option. The next day, my mother came into the store and invited the cranky pharmacist to dinner. Her point was that he needed home cooking. Her home cooking certainly made working for him easier and we became friends.

The cranky pharmacist joined the Navy as pharmacist mate and was assigned to Great Lakes Naval Station. He got home on weekends occasionally.

I graduated in the spring of 1944. Our neighbor who was in a management position in a company that made porcelain enamel asked me to work for his company doing quantitative analysis of the raw materials that came in. I took the job.

As its part in the war effort, the com-

Ellen Capps, college graduation.

88

pany also made napalm. Mixed with gasoline, a sticky syrup was produced which burned more slowly than raw gasoline and was easier to control in flamethrowers. In World War II, flamethrowers were used against the Japanese in the South Pacific to draw them out of caves and pillboxes. As part of my war effort, on weekends, I went in to test the viscosity of the napalm. The laboratory where we tested the napalm was not very large. We sat at tables and dropped weights down tubes of napalm noting the time that it took for the weights to get to the bottom. In this way we could ensure that the mixture was of the right consistency. We all sensed the importance of the effort, since we felt the napalm would be a help in winning the war. I think that probably it was, but I always cringe when I hear of innocent people being burned by it.

In the fall of 1944, the pharmacist mate and I were married. He was sent to the South Pacific on an airplane parts supply ship. We met in Brookline, Massachusetts, for the wedding in a pastor's home. We had a week together in Newport. He shipped out soon after that. I went back to my chemist job.

The war ended the next spring. Bob came back to a pharmacist's job and I continued as a chemist.

Bob's goal was to get a Ph.D. in pharmacology. So, in the fall of 1945 we went to Madison, Wisconsin. Bob was a student at the University of Wisconsin, taking advantage of the G.I. Bill.

If there hadn't been a war and life had been smoother during those early years, I don't know if we would appreciate now as much. That is not to say that war and the consequences are good. But I am saying that the struggles that we faced made us appreciate now.

Make Mine Manhattan

Kay Watson

"Manhattan Project." What a mundane name for what was probably at the time the most organized, stupendous, extensive, yet secret operation ever undertaken by the United States government. Many thousands of people at all levels of activity were involved. From May of 1944 until my husband's return from military service in the spring of 1946, I lived with my parents in East Bound Brook, New Jersey, and worked six days a week in the Manhattan Project's office at the Bakelite Division of Union Carbide. Comparatively few of us had any concept of what we were working on. Work was done at many places—the University of Chicago (Enrico Fermi was the director there), Los Alamos, Oak Ridge, and our small town in New Jersey were just a few of the sites. My job seemed so insignificant. Yet, when we learned that the first bomb dropped on Hiroshima was tied to *our* war project, those with whom I worked were stunned. When V-J Day was declared about a week later, we really did feel that we had a role in ending the war!

The Bakelite Division was one of the two largest employers in our community and it was one of the pioneers in the making of plastics. We looked upon it as a glamour place to work. Stenographers were often asked to wear "patent-leather" shoes made of plastic, or take home bright-colored molded cups and saucers to get reactions from their neighbors. I think these were only sales gimmicks to show what could be fashioned from the bulk plastics made at our local plant. Some of the early plastic dinnerware was called "Bakelite."

My sister-in-law worked in one of the labs which was co-opted for the Manhattan Project. She recruited me for the office segment of the program and for her car pool. I was primarily a payroll clerk. The production building in which I worked was a small, rather nondescript structure surrounded by several larger buildings—in essence, part of a campus. Several labs in different buildings were developing different kinds of plastic materials—rigid, pliable, etc.

There were about 120 men working on a small production line on the ground floor and in an office suspended on a mezzanine above it. The men were brought up to Bound Brook from the part of the project located at Oak Ridge, Tennessee, and most of them were "colored." The government bought or leased or rented the only hotel in town and housed these Tennesseans there.

I don't know what the pay rate for the men was but I do know they worked round-the-clock shifts and got a five-cent bonus for the swing shift and a ten-cent bonus for the midnight shift. I was paid something like $20 for a 48 hour week.

One duty I had was to mark down the gross and tare weights of barrels of a black powder that arrived from somewhere. There was speculation that it came from overseas, quite possibly the Belgian Congo. The ore, or maybe the purified part of it, was very volatile. Barriers had to be developed to handle it. I suspect one of the barriers they came up with was plastic and that the "powder" that I witnessed was actually pulverized ore to be embedded in the plastic to keep it separated. These powder-impregnated sheets of plastic were then sent on to Oak Ridge. Many years after the war, I came across a book on the Manhattan Project by Stephane Groueff and I fully expected to learn about the part of the project in which I was involved. Alas, I discovered the statement that "the technical details of the process developed are still classified." So, the above conjecture is not to be taken as fact.

Each day when we arrived and left, we had to sign in and sign out. We were told that whatever was below us was extremely incendiary so to be prepared to vacate the premises as quickly as possible in event of fire. One day there was a fire — and they made the firemen sign in before letting them fight the blaze! Fortunately, it was a little fire or I would not be here to recount these memories.

At home, everyone had black-out curtains at the windows, perhaps unnecessary since we were 35 miles inland. But I recall a trip to Asbury Park where the Boardwalk was draped in black-out curtains every evening and a person could be arrested for lighting a cigarette after dark if facing out to sea. The sand was coated with oil and debris from sunken ships, and submarines lurked close off shore.

Kay Braithwaite Bilabran (to become Watson).

I shall never forget one day, while riding the ferry from Jersey City to New York City, I watched the Queen Mary, loaded with khaki-clad young men, pull out into the harbor as we passed by. We solemnly lined our rails, looking up at hundreds lining their rails. There were some waves and some tears, but no cheers.

Mike embarked for the battle front from Goldsboro and it was two months before the first letter came from him. His letters were quite heavily and neatly censored. Most of them came in batches of three or four at a time and with rather long intervals between each batch. Afterwards, I learned that he had sailed through the Panama Canal and across the Pacific to India. From there, his team ascended one of the mountains in Burma and, by radio, guided the planes supplying China with flights "over the hump."

They spent months on their mountain top and they were supplied via parachute drops. That probably explains why the letters came in batches. I don't remember (if I ever knew) how they sent them from their mountain top but I suspect they had local workers who would climb up and down the mountain on foot or by horseback. Once I received a package containing four separate panels of parachute silk — one each of yellow, green, blue and red. I don't know how many panels made up a chute. There was plenty of material in each panel. I had a pair of pajamas made out of one, along with a couch cover and various other items. I think the colors of the chutes indicated the contents of the drop: maybe yellow for medical, green for food, etc. More than one war bride's wedding dress was fashioned from parachute silk.

Another vivid recollection of the war years was going into New York City periodically to socialize with college friends. Two of them worked at the information desk at Pennsylvania Station, sharing a bed and alternating 12-hour shifts at the desk. Servicemen were always traipsing through Penn Station. They soon fell into the habit of checking in with Betty or Peggy, so we had a pretty good grapevine of information available about our friends.

Civilian hospitals and medical personnel were in very short supply. A few months after I got home from Goldsboro, I became quite ill and found myself bedded down in the corridor of a nearby hospital. They removed my appendix and I was released the day after the November 1944 election. New Jersey did not have absentee balloting then. I had hoped to cast the very first vote of my life for FDR and I have always accused my doctor, who was a staunch Republican, of keeping me in the hospital one day longer than necessary.

On April 12, 1945, I returned from work and switched on the radio, catching just the final words of a newscast: "...burial will be at Hyde Park." I was startled but jumped to the conclusion that it must refer to the death of the President's mother or one of his sons. Then, as the family gathered for our usual session to listen to the nightly news, the content of the bulletin was made very clear: it was the President himself who was dead. That, perhaps was one of my lowest moments. I remember blurting out, "What will become of us now?"

In recent days, particularly since the opening of the FDR Memorial in Washington, D.C., there has been considerable discussion and dissension about whether to include a statue of the President in his wheelchair. I was not aware of the President's handicap in those days and I doubt that many of us were. Remember, we had radios, not television, and pictures in news-reels or newspapers usually showed President Roosevelt in motorcades or sitting at his desk in the Oval Office, or delivering one of his famous "fireside chats." The media was much more protective of the privacy of presidents in the days before the Watergate fiasco, as well. The announcement of his death to our generation was much like the shock of President Kennedy's assassination a generation later.

When Mike returned in the spring of 1946 (his was one of the last units demobilized), I barely recognized him. He was almost as yellow as the parachute panel he had sent me. All the months he spent in Burma he had had to take atabrine in an effort to ward off malaria. I don't recall how long it took for the yellow to fade away, but about two months after his return, I woke up to find him shaking uncontrollably. Apparently, the tablets had merely suppressed the disease. It took a long time to control it.

Had it not been for the war, I doubt that Mike and I would ever have married. When we wed in 1943, we were both just twenty-two. Our "courtship" had been mostly through letters and dates during the vacations when I was at home. He was the football and basketball star of the high school and his main interest academically was to qualify for the teams. Faced with civilian life, we discovered that we had very little in common and were divorced in 1951.

Terrible and tragic as the war was, it was also romantic and exciting. There was a sense of camaraderie and solidarity hard to recapture. To be young and connected and able to cope with crowded trains and poor housing and little money produced a strength and a joy for living in many of us that was unique. Initially, I think we all thought we'd survive and this was just an interruption. Of course, we soon learned otherwise. Nonetheless, marriage and the vicissitudes we encountered on the home front gave many of us a sense of purpose and a rock to cling to during the war years themselves.

As I recall these memories, I am struck by the fact that, unwittingly perhaps, I had a very small part in saving the life of my second husband, through my participation, ever so minor, in the Manhattan Project. Don was assigned to a baby flat-top, a small carrier, destined to take part in the invasion of Japan. The invasion was canceled after the dropping of the atomic bombs and he was as assigned to a minesweeper. He did get to Japan but under much safer conditions.

He was called back into service during the Korean War and sent to the East Coast. I met him on one of his visits to Washington in 1952. Meeting and marrying Don was the best thing that has ever happened to me. We have just celebrated our 47th wedding anniversary.

Voices from
Wartime
Opportunities

Doing a Man's Job

Jean Reed Prentiss

My wartime experiences were not as glamorous as Rosie the Riveter's, but somewhat in her field.

Soon after the Pearl Harbor attack, when my husband, John, decided to join the Navy, I had to face a war-winning effort of my own. My sister, Ruth Morgan, wrote from her home in Longview, Washington, that there were jobs to be had in the lumber mills there. I could live with her and her little girl. Her husband, a surgeon, was already being inducted into the Air Force and would soon be off to England. Her offer sounded good to me.

Most mill workers were considered to be doing valuable work where they were, with wartime contracts being awarded in several departments. Women had always found jobs in the mills, and there were some openings where men had enlisted and been called up.

John received notice to leave for a training camp in Virginia in December 1942. He was to be a Navy Seabee, which he preferred to join, being in his thirties and with some skills working with tools and with small boats. His high school experience with ROTC had left him uninterested in Army attitudes. We stored our possessions and put the car up on blocks in a friend's garage, and off we went to Longview.

I was hired by the Weyerhauser Mill. I went first to the planer mill in the enormous plant. It was a revelation—constant noise from the machines, and the people working fast around me, shouting instructions. We worked at machine speed, sorting boards as they passed the grader, pulling and stacking them behind us. My muscles were sore at the end of the day, and my ears rang all night. But I soon got used to that.

I learned that there were women aged 30, like me, who had been employed there since high school, in the same mill, doing the same work, year in and year out. Of course, the pay was pretty good compared to working in shops. I started at 85 cents an hour, and a year later got a raise to $1.05! Most of the women used their money to buy nice clothes, and then spent almost every evening at their favorite bar. This seemed to be their entertainment of choice, except for an occasional dinner out and a movie.

In a few months, I was sent to another big shed to work with three other women on a Navy project. Enormous planks were hoisted in, about 12 to 15 feet long and three feet wide (called dimension lumber), moved into place in front of us in layers, each layer being sprinkled by us with urea salts. When the right number was salted, the stack was swung away by the hoists and another stack begun. It was explained to us that the urea salts affected the wood in a certain way, hardening it — a sort of curing process — and then the layers were laminated. This lumber was to be used in making very fast, small boats, possibly the PT boats such as Jack Kennedy served on!

When that project was completed, I was sent to an open shed to learn to use a drill bit. The mill had a contract to prefabricate roof trusses for an airplane hangar up in the Maritime Provinces. (I can't recall the name of the place.) This was interesting work. There was a large crew working on the machines, and the foreman was good at employee relations. I remember when the project had all its parts, a whole truss was assembled on the shed floor for us to see what a truss was — I could see the bolts fitting into the holes I had so carefully drilled.

My next assignment was to spend the summer months outdoors, "counting" stacks of lumber on the dock, and Longview in summer is *hot!* But it was interesting watching the ships come in and tie up and then load their cargo. Generally the ships were described as filthy, and the Russian ships were the worst. I never did find out what the counting of the piles of lumber was for. I guessed it was to be sure each ship got its correct load. I got a beautiful tan, though.

In the fall, I had a new assignment, using a cut-off saw in an unheated shed in another part of the plant. Boards were shoved on rollers to reach my station, and with my saw I beveled the corners of the 4x6s, flipping them to complete the process. When a proper load was made, these were sent on to be assembled into pallet boards, which were used to load cargo into the holds of Liberty and Victory ships. Interestingly, out on Guadalcanal John saw some pallets with our Longview mill numbers on them, he told me later.

This was cold, monotonous work, with its constant reaching and lifting, and Longview was into its usual chilly winter. I developed a bad back

and had to take a month off for treatment. There was nothing like the therapy of today, and not even an osteopath in town. The doctor gave me heat
treatments, but the problem remained until he put me into an old-fashioned corset (like the ones the Gibson Girls wore around their tiny waists)
and that worked. I was back to work in a week.

During that year, 1943, there was a War Bond sale, and I took part in
that. We volunteers did so well that we got the mill an Army and Navy E
Award (E for excellence).

In the spring and summer of 1943, I was sent to work in the loading
shed in another vast building with railroad tracks running right through
it. I was the first woman to ever work in that mill's loading shed, and I had
never really understood the method of figuring the number of board feet
in a certain car-load, etc. It was a mystery to me, really. But the men who
worked with me loading the cars saved the day. They also saved my neck
and got the right load into the right railcar every time.

In the fall of that year, I learned that John was coming home for a six-
month leave and for retraining. I told my sister that this was it, I had
decided to give up my job as soon as I had a final word on John's arrival.

I had learned a lot, had some money in the bank, and I hoped I had
really done something good while I was doing a "man's job" for a couple
of years. In a few months we were expecting our first child, and I had a
joyful reason to go back to "woman's work."

Grinding the Groove

Grace H. Kaiser

With the end of World War II in Europe, America directed its undivided attention westward to Japan. Factories continued to hurl smoke and grind out parts around the clock for the machines of war. We still complained about rationed butter, sugar and gasoline. Sacrifice and work in a defense plant were patriotic. Work was also college tuition money for me.

I was twenty in 1944. While my sophomore college classmates rolled bandages, entertained service men at one of Philadelphia's hospitality centers or bragged about rare dates, I learned that the SKF Ball Bearing Company near Hatboro, Pennsylvania, was hiring women for full and part-time work. SKF was a Swedish company known in the USA as SKF Plain Bearings USA Inc., manufacturers of steel-on-steel metric spherical plain bearings and rod ends.

Previous employment had taken me behind the food counter at an amusement park and I had sold everything from shoes to underwear in Goldman's Variety Store, but entering a factory gave me shudders of apprehension. I signed for Saturday and Sunday work, full time during vacations, trying to ignore the nervous jitters as my pen completed the application forms. I did not know one person inside the big factory.

The men in the plant—foremen, office managers, setup men — were older than draft age, deferred from service or rejected for physical reasons. My job was explained to me by a setup man. It was his duty to keep the women-operated rows of machines running in our department, realign

100

machines when they were out of sync and change adjustment when the race size we polished changed. He showed me how to push a spindle called an arbor through the central hole in the disk containing the race, pull a handle to insert the arbor into the rocking arm of the machine and advance it against a grinding wheel with its washing flow of honey-colored water. Each machine had two arbors. While one groove was grinding, I checked the last one with a micrometer, and dropped it into a bin of completed races before reloading the arbor from a pile of work on the table to my right. By the time a wheel finished grinding and backed away from the spinning grindstone, I had to be ready to reload the machine.

Each machine and size of work piece had its quota, depending upon the size of the bearing we ground. If the bearing was tiny, I had to twist a nut onto the end of the arbor. Awed at first by the speeding hands of women working around me, within days I was meeting my quota.

The best example of my job is the wheel of a roller skate where balls spin between outer and inner grooves—the outer and inner races. I had become an inner-race groove grinder in SKF's fight against friction.

Long rows of whirring, head-high machines stood around me in monotonous columns, like grotesque soldiers frozen at attention. It seemed a mile to the far end of the factory. Concerned with making my quota, I never walked the length of the gigantic building to see the many other operations concerned with plant production. Some shifts I ran a lapper machine that polished the sides of bearings several feet in diameter. I wondered about the use of all the bearings, so many sizes. Did they swing great guns during the heat of battle? Did they move tanks through conquered cities? Were they used in airplanes?

As we worked, night became day in a windowless brick building where florescent lights hung from an open ceiling fifteen feet overhead. When the great rolling doors at the loading docks slid open, winter air swept across the room guzzling our heat. The rasp of polishing wheels in my department answered the clatter of metal on metal in surrounding departments. Lubricant flowed over polishing wheels in a never-ending watery stream, turning fingers into bleached prunes and splashing oily blotches onto blue jumpsuits. We were issued two pairs of navy blue gabardine coveralls. The blotches washed out but the pungent odor of solvent lingered forever.

SSSSSzzzzz! Trouble. The flow of coolant running over the grinding wheel washed away sparks and smoke, but the acrid odor of hot metal burned my nose. I grabbed the handle, released the arbor from the rocker arm, wanting to use language I'd heard from women machine operators around me. An arbor fit into the machine like a toilet tissue roll into its slot. If inserted by mistake at an angle, the grinder burned metal. I tossed the burned piece into the reject pile with those not meeting micrometer specifications and I paid with *down time.* "Setup man," I shouted above the din, stepping from the wooden pallet cushioning my feet from the concrete floor. Three machines away, a man girdled with tools acknowledged my call with a wave of his wrench. Every piece polished had to be micrometer perfect. Burning one knocked the grinding wheel out of kilter. Burns happened to every operator sometime.

Our 12 hours over, we punched out at the time clock. In my first days I thought I had to wait until my shift started to punch in. The tide of workers punching out from the shift before mine nearly trampled me until I learned I could punch in before my shift started. Women exited the plant via our rest room. Before leaving the building, we washed oil and lubricant from our hands at huge circular troughs with knee-operated hot water controls.

Outside, late afternoon summer sunshine reminded me I had worked the day shift. Soon it would be the alternate two weeks at night. I boarded a public bus for the ride home to Ambler. My thoughts dwelled on that day's lessons of life, conversations of co-workers at lunch, awesome and shocking revelations of how other women my age lived.

Judy had said, "My old man came home drunk again. See my black eye? Bad heart gets him outa the damned Army. Don't keep him from running around and drinkin'."

Betsy snickered. "Yeah. Know what ya mean. The kids and I been sleeping on the floor. Ain't made a furniture payment in months. They come and hauled it away. Hafta get some on time another place."

"Yep." Sue leaned closer. "Iffin my mom ain't looking after my four kids we'd be outa rent and living on rice and macaroni. The Army pay I get outa Bill ain't worth dirt."

I had listened, amazed, thankful that piece work at SKF was only weekend and summer work. Thanks to college, I could look forward to a better life. I would not stand in an assembly line forever.

D-Day was behind us. How long would it take to defeat Japan?

I will never forget lunch break, midshift at SKF, August 6, 1945, standing in the serpentine cafeteria line as it lazed toward the food counter. "Attention!" The loudspeaker interrupted Frank Sinatra singing "The House I Live In." "The United States dropped an atomic bomb on Hiroshima, Japan…" The rest of the announcement blurred, blown away by the shock and the significance.

My college major was chemistry. Repeatedly, professors had emphasized that if anyone ever found a way to split the atom the world would change forever. A second bomb fell on Nagasaki August 9th, and Japan opened negotiations for peace. Factories soon became as silent as the war's acres of white crosses.

The next day we were called in, one by one, from our machines to speak with Mr. Shock, our department foreman. Seated at his desk behind our lines of machines, the slight, pale man ruffled papers, tugged his long tan lab coat, and smiled as he informed me that the plant would close. Only several weeks until fall semester began, it meant freedom to relax. I turned in my jumpsuits. As I left, I wondered what would happen to Betts, Judy and Sue? What impact would come from the awesome atomic bomb that erased cities as easily as the grease washed out of my jumpsuits? What would it mean to me and to future generations?

From Job to Job

Trudy Rulofson

We were living in Arkansas when Pearl Harbor was hit on December 7, 1941. My husband had already signed up in Tennessee for the draft, which was required of males of a certain age in the months before Pearl Harbor. After Pearl Harbor, he decided to move back to Tennessee and joined the Tennessee Volunteers in April of 1942. He was sent to Santa Anita, California, along with the rest of the Tennessee Volunteers. Their base camp was the Santa Anita race track!

About two or three months later, I took a train from Memphis to Los Angeles to join my husband. The housing around the base was practically nonexistent. For the first few days after my arrival, I shared a motel room with another soldier, his wife and small child. Privacy was hard to come by. Each couple took many walks to accommodate the other, all in good humor.

I had to find a job immediately as the small stipend the government gave for spouses didn't go very far. Finding a job was no problem. I went to work in Pasadena for a mining company owned by one of President Hoover's sons. There was a single lady working there who had a small apartment and she rented me a room. I was a very young and naive secretary and the employees liked to tease me. I remember one incident in particular: one of the engineers asked me to order a can of white lamp black! I picked up the phone to order the paint and couldn't understand why the clerk at the store was laughing so hard until I turned around and saw all the men laughing.

About two or three months later when I was all settled in my new job and room, my husband finished basic training and was transferred to the Cow Palace in San Francisco. About one month later, I quit my job in Pasadena and headed for San Francisco. As soon as I stepped off the train, I fell in love with San Francisco and my love has never changed.

Again, housing was a problem. After three days in the Palace Hotel (which I could ill afford), I found a room over a dry cleaning shop and shared a kitchen with three other G.I. wives. The situation was not pleasant. Their attitude bothered me. Their husbands had the rank of staff sergeant but mine was just a corporal and they gave me the treatment.

In San Francisco, I had to remember at night to close the blackout curtains tight. We had block wardens patrolling the streets to make sure no light was showing. Everyone was so afraid of San Francisco and environs being bombed because of our proximity to the Pacific Ocean.

Again, I had to find a job quickly. It was no problem as so many were joining the service. This time I worked for an auto and truck rental agency. And again it was office work, keeping track of the gas stamps that we had to give our customers who rented the cars and trucks, writing down what they were used for and reporting to some government agency, the name of which I have long since forgotten.

Our social life consisted of going to the movies and visiting the USOs where there was always food and entertainment. The Hollywood contingents were wonderful in entertaining the G.I.s. The two performers I remember best were Bob Hope and Dorothy Lamour. My husband was a huge fan of Dorothy and went to see her when she was on stage.

After working at the car rental agency, I decided I wanted to work at something which was more related to the war effort. So many men had joined the service that there was a great demand for women in ship building. I found a job at Western Pipe and Steel Company where two female friends of mine worked. Many of the women were doing the work of men there. However, my job was in the office. My boss was a good looking male who was sixteen years older than I. I liked him, and we worked well together.

A few months later, when our husbands were transferred to the East Coast and shortly thereafter overseas, my friends invited me to move in with them and share one bedroom, two small beds, a closet and one dresser, for which we each paid seven dollars a month. We had a lot of fun living together. We always had someone to go to the USOs with or the movies. There was only one drawback — the two small twin beds. Two of us had to sleep together in one twin and one got to sleep alone. How we treasured the night (every third night) we got to sleep alone. I stayed friends with the two roommates I lived with in 1942 and they remained in San Francisco after the war, as I did. Losing them in death about five years ago was very hard.

Trudy Rulofson, 1942.

Several months after I had gone to work for Western Pipe and Steel, I had a call from the owner of the car and truck company, telling me his son had joined the merchant marine and would I consider coming back as assistant manager of the company. He made me an offer I could not refuse. So again I changed jobs and abode.

With my finances greatly improved, I moved into a room with a private bath in the Sea Cliff home of a lady in San Francisco. It was on the trolley line, so commuting to work was easy. Sometimes if I worked late, I took one of the rental cars home.

The longer I lived in San Francisco, the more I loved it. From my new room I could hear the fog horns and loved their sound. To this day I have a fondness for the fog and fog horns.

The war changed our lives in so many ways. My older brother was in the Navy and his ship was torpedoed outside Cape May, New Jersey. He was the first casualty of the war in our small town in Tennessee. My younger brother joined the Marines as a tail gunner and was shot down several times but came home safely.

I had moved several times, changed jobs several times, and I knew my feelings for my husband had changed. We were very young when we married and, during the war, we had very little time together. We were almost strangers. We agreed to a divorce, and shortly thereafter, I married the handsome man I had met at Western Pipe and Steel. We had three lovely daughters together and settled in Palo Alto, California, where I still live. My husband died twenty-five years ago and I still miss him. I wish he could see his grandchildren and I wish they could have known him.

We Called Them Business Machines

Helen Putnam Rudd

I graduated from Salem High School in 1938; college was not an option for me, so I searched for a job. I found one as a receptionist/typist for a real estate and insurance office. I earned $1 a day. This was a one-man office and I soon learned that the job required avoiding my boss's sexual advances. When my boss turned out the light at about 4 o'clock I knew it was time to put on my running shoes. He would come behind the counter and put his arm around me. I quickly evaded him and left the office. There were no laws against such behavior at that time.

It didn't take me long to search for another job. The State of Oregon hired me to work on the annual renewal of driver's licenses, a part-time job. December, I believe, was the month for renewals. My earnings were tripled to $3 a day. When the license renewal job was finished, I was without work.

My brother-in-law, Bill, knew a man named J. W. Carter, who was the manager for the International Business Machines office in Portland. Bill felt that the keypunch school offered by the IBM would be great for me. When he told me that a keypunch operator was nothing more than a typist with no brains he convinced me that I qualified.

The keypunch machine was used to punch cards with data to be submitted to the accounting machines. It was important that all information be accurate so it was necessary to repeat the keypunch process in a verifying machine. These machines had a keyboard much like a ten-key adding machine. As the keys were depressed, they would put a hole in the card to be read by the EAM machines (electric accounting machines). The cards were fed into the big, bulky machine automatically. Everything was checked carefully to see that the numbers balanced. It was not an exciting job, but one that was necessary in the accounting field at that time.

While I attended the school, I was also trained to operate the EAMs being used in the IBM service bureau. We provided payroll support as well as data for many services needing statistics for their business. It was fascinating to be working in a field that was becoming a standard for future technology. IBM was considered a very high class company. I remember seeing scientific magazines in the waiting rooms.

Ted VanVeen was the manager of the service bureau and was soon inducted into the military. I was put in charge of the service bureau. The war had just started so women were in demand in many fields which men formerly dominated. It was a bit terrifying, but I was assured support from the salesmen who were soliciting the jobs for the service bureau as well as selling equipment to businesses. This experience would not have been available if the war had not started. Women just weren't being hired for such jobs.

At that time there were two wage scales…one for men and one for women doing the same work. IBM did not allow married women to work for them. Fortunately, the salesmen and other men I worked with were very kind and helpful.

The Putnam women: Mom Put, Barbara, Helen, Polly — about 1942. Barbara became Barbara J. Sloan (see "Small Town Girl" in this book); Helen became Helen Putnam Rudd (see "We Called Them Business Machines"); and Polly is Pauline E. Parker (the editor of this volume and the author of its story "Coast to Coast and Back Again").

Clients who came to IBM began offering me jobs with much better wages, so it wasn't long until I accepted work at Swan Island Ship Yards in Portland. I worked with the supervisor of the EAM room setting up jobs, wiring machine boards, testing, and training the operators to use the program. My boss was able to get raises for me based on my initials (rather than using my first name). Illegal, I'm sure. It just didn't seem right that the men I was training to run the machines were making more money than I was. This has been changed since the "women's libbers" fought for equality in job pay.

At that time I was engaged to a boy I had known in Salem. He was stationed in San Diego and wanted me to come to Los Angeles and get married before he was to go overseas. I quit my job and off I went. After arriving, I had uneasy feelings about getting married and postponed the date. Friends offered me a place to stay, so I accepted their kindness and found a job at Gladden McBean's (the pottery company) working on EAM equipment there. Eventually I broke the engagement and went back to Albany, Oregon.

My sister Barbara and I worked for the Selective Service Board processing men into the service. Our supervisor was out of the office a great deal — especially when an officer came to oversee our work — so Barbara and I were alone much of the time in the office. It was an interesting job

Helen Putnam at work, 2nd from left. The other three women are unidentified.

but sad, too. While there, several calls from my ex-boss at Gladden McBean asking me to please return to my old job started me thinking about it. Barbara and I discussed the possibility and decided to spread our wings and head to Los Angeles. Barbara also got a job with Gladden-McBean in Glendale where she painted the well-known Franciscan dinnerware.

During the war, our lives were not in jeopardy when we went out at night. We enjoyed many a night at the Palladium in Hollywood where name bands played and we met many wonderful service men.

My two brothers, Jim and Bill, were in the thick of the war. One was in Alaska and later Iwo Jima while the other was in the Pacific war zone. It was devastating to me to receive letters from them and know that they were in harm's way. My brother-in-law, Bill, was also in the Pacific war zone. We were very fortunate to have all three of them return from the war with no physical injuries. However, my older brother, Jim, suffered nightmares from his experiences.

Mother was very active in the war effort. She spent much time at the USO helping to cheer the soldiers. She and Dad also opened up their home to wives of the soldiers who needed a place to stay while visiting their loved ones. It was a good experience for the whole family. We became acquainted with some wonderful people.

Mother even involved my sister and me to help entertain the soldiers.

One of the business machines Helen Putnam worked on.

May 7, 1944 — Jim Putnam and Borge Hanson's wedding. Jim, Borge, Polly, Helen, Barbara and Bill Putnam.

At one time she asked us to go to a dance at Camp Adair, which was near our home in Albany, Oregon. Having dated a few of the second lieutenants (known as shave-tails) we weren't eager to attend. Some of the aforementioned lieutenants were quite conceited and aggressive. Mother assured us that it would be for enlisted men and that there was a shortage of girls who could go. Barbara and I agreed to help out. As we entered the dance hall there were two lieutenants overseeing the party. Lo and behold, they flipped a coin to see which one would get my sister, the redhead, or me, the brunette. Little did we know the impact they would have on our lives! My sister became engaged to Buck and I later married Jack. Life holds many surprises!

When Jack returned to Southern California after being discharged from the service, we dated for a time and then married. We lived in a one-room place where meals were offered in a central house. Housing was very scarce so everyone did what was necessary to carry on with his or her life. It was not a very pleasant arrangement but sufficed until something better came along. That was in the form of a rented room in a private home in Eagle Rock. We ate all of our meals out which soon became old. Later, a family friend in Glendale knew of a neighbor who had a guest house on the back of their lot, which they would rent to us. We were so happy to have a place to live, do our own cooking, and start a family. We are eternally grateful to those people.

During those war years, people were more than willing to assist anyone they could. After, it was a great time of receiving our soldiers home from a victorious war and starting to heal the wounds that wars bring. I wonder if war happened again if we would be so supportive. The Vietnam soldiers weren't so fortunate. Hopefully, we will not be tested for this again.

The experiences that led me to further my capabilities in the machine accounting field during the war gave me great career opportunities. While I was married and living in Glendale, a service bureau offered me a job preparing EAM reports, which I could work whenever I had time. This was great for a new mother. Jack would arrive home from his job at the Broadway department store and I would go off to my job. The boys were fed and bathed early and Jack would put them to bed. It worked fine for us until we moved to the San Fernando Valley. I gave up my job in Glendale and was hired to work for Lockheed in their EAM office. I worked nights so we again split the childcare. I vowed to work just one year to help pay for the new home we had purchased.

We stayed in the valley for several years, then decided to relocate in Sacramento. Again, the experiences which began during the war helped me find work with the California State Controller's office. My brother-in-law, Bill, came to my rescue again and helped me obtain the job there. Bill has had a great influence on my life, as you can see. I am eternally grateful to him.

The war opened up this whole new area for women, although there were few at my level. We proved ourselves during the war.

At the controller's office, we were confronted with the task of converting EAM work to a computer in 1959. I was supervisor of the 1401 programming section. The 1401 was an IBM printer; the 7070 was the IBM mainframe that took up most of one floor of our building. It was huge! We did the payroll for all of the state employees in California, including teachers and railroad employees.

We programmed the machines to handle the state payroll. The 7070 was only a 10K, 10-digit word machine. One 1401 was an 8K machine; the other 1401 was a 4K machine. We had to write many programs to accommodate all of the necessary information to create the payroll and reports necessary to submit to the accounting department. These were written in Basic; FORTRAN and COBOL were not yet available. All programs had to be tested and ready simultaneously or the payroll would not go through correctly. (As I recall, the governor of California once got a paycheck for $9,999.99!) We never missed a payroll but we worked many long hours to do so.

After my career with the early business machines, it is mind-boggling to me to see what the modern computer can do and in such a small container! However, when I struggle with my PC, I sometimes wish I could do a "core dump," as we used to do to follow the program and find the bugs.

Voices from the Services and Military Hospitals

Life in the WAVES: 1943 to 1946

Mildred Joyce Shafer Hulse
(LTJG Mildred Joyce Shafer)

On the day of Pearl Harbor, I was living in South Dakota and was teaching in a junior high school. I had just finished a degree in education and enjoyed what I was doing. Within the next year, we began to hear about limitations on many things...no butter, less gasoline, limits on shoes. By the summer of 1942, we saw people on trains who had been drafted and were traveling to military camps. I saw changes more clearly when I visited relatives in Portland, Oregon, where the shipyards were in full swing. A trip to the beach meant driving the last part of the way in the dark if it were in the evening. The houses had to have dark curtains at the windows facing the beach.

In September, I was back in South Dakota and changed to the high school as the teacher had gone away to do war work. I supervised a group of high school girls as they sold war bonds on the streets on Saturdays. Posters of all kinds advertised for people to join in the work to help with the war. Among these we saw articles about the Army and Navy wanting women to join and do their part. Several of the teachers with whom I worked began to think this sounded interesting. Just after Christmas, one of my coworkers applied and was tested because of her interest in the Navy. When she came back from Minneapolis, we heard her story. A friend and I began to be interested too. Why not see what it was all about?

After we filled out some papers it was not long until we received notices to travel to Minneapolis for interviews, physicals and tests. We went home expecting that if they wanted us it would probably be in the summer after school was out. This was only February.

Surprise! In March I received orders to report to Smith College in Northampton, Massachusetts, to begin training in the WAVES. The school where I worked had said I would be allowed to go if called. In the next three weeks I had to store my things and get clothes in order. I was to report to training on April 10, 1943. I had to first report to the headquarters in Chicago and join a group of women from surrounding states. We boarded sleeping cars in late afternoon and traveled overnight and part of the next day on the train. We were met at the station, lined up alphabetically and marched to the dormitories or hotel we were assigned to. You can imagine how well we marched because the officer finally said, "Just walk!"

From this day until June 1, almost everything we did was done by command from an officer in charge. Each morning we heard the call to get up and what clothes we were to wear. We marched to breakfast and stood in line to pick it up. Then we marched again up and down to classes, to gym or out to the drill field to learn to keep in step in our platoon. Short girls had to run around the corners. In classes we learned to recognize ranks in the military and how to salute properly. We identified ships and aircraft. We took shots—lots of them, had our clothes fitted, had fire drills and probably had a thirty-minute breather before study at night. We slept well! After one month as seaman, we were all promoted to midshipman. During the second month, we were interviewed about a possible job. We didn't feel we had a great deal of choice.

Graduation Day—June 1, 1943—A parade in white uniforms before the admiral, a ceremony and rain. The graduates waited in their whites while others were sent back for their raincoats. The orders were there and mine said, "Report to Washington, D.C. to the Commander in Chief, U.S. Fleet for active duty in Headquarters, Navy Department."

With this assignment I spent my days until November 30, 1945, working in the Navy Headquarters in Washington, D.C., located on Constitution Avenue. The building was a long, box-like structure built during World War I with very plain offices. At first I was in the reception room where we greeted people who came to see Admiral Ernest Joseph King and his staff. Vice Admiral Edwards was chief of staff and Lt. Tennant Bryan was his aide. I worked directly for Admiral Edwards.

As a new officer I was eager to please. Admiral Edwards needed some papers from the mail room across the hall and I went quickly to get them. As I started to cross the hall I collided with a man much taller than I. As I raised my eyes, I saw a navy blue uniform with much gold braid. The man smiled down at me. This was my first introduction to Admiral King.

WAVES had been taught how to meet and salute high-ranking officers, but no one had prepared me for the very highest of all. I can't remember that either of us said much. I did learn to look before entering hallways in our area.

There were few women in our immediate set of officers, but we were treated with respect. I soon discovered that these people had work to do and worked hard at it. I worked a nine to five day and, at first, for six days a week.

The headquarters was made up of people with the experience and expertise to determine ways for the Navy to do its part in the war. They wrote pages of "how to" plans. They did it with pens and pencils, by dictating to yeomen, passing the material around to a number of others who changed it, discussing it and finally issuing plans to carry it all out. Junior officers such as I had to keep track of much of it, file it for immediate retrieval, see that it was secure at all times. Typewriters were manual. Everything was made with a specific number of carbon copies and one had to know where they all were. We were librarians, bookkeepers or whatever.

The first month I stayed in WAVE quarters quite a distance from the building. After that, I had to find my own housing. I teamed up with some women who had trained with me and we were, at first, in a sort of dormitory which had been built to solve the housing shortage. Then we found an apartment to sublet. We enjoyed that apartment because we could cook our own meals. Eating out was boring at times. Our one-bedroom apartment served three of us. We have kept in touch over the years and have visited each other. Only two of us are left, as one of my friends died a number of years ago.

Perhaps the idea of a job in headquarters seems to have a bit of glamour. There are certainly things I will never forget. People whose names I had only seen in the newspaper or in *U.S. News and World Report* or *Time Magazine* were often visitors in our offices. Some took time to chat with members of the staff. *U.S. News and World Report* published an official report of the Navy at war in 1944 -1945. By that time Admiral King had become a five-star admiral. Fleet Admiral Nimitz and Admiral William F. Halsey and their staffs were visitors to our offices when these operations were in the planning stages. Many people were working on phases of this planning. We learned to know them and admit them to see our superior officers. David Lawrence, the editor of the magazine, was a visitor when he was preparing the publication. When Admiral King received his additional star, Admiral Edwards, with whom I worked, received four stars and became deputy commander-in-chief.

Lieut. Commander C. C. Kirkpatrick was the commander of the submarine the USS *Triton*. This submarine was credited with many attacks on

Japanese ships. The commander was the first submarine officer honored with three Navy Crosses. After these experiences, he came to be the flag lieutenant for Admiral King. We worked with him as he carried on his duties. Everyone admired him a great deal. He was a very friendly and personable fellow.

On my first Christmas in Washington, as a junior officer, I had to work all day. It promised to be a dull day. Then we were told that we would be entertained for dinner on Admiral King's flag ship, which was a rather large yacht moored in the Potomac River. We were transported down to the ship and served a beautiful dinner in wonderful style. We were seated at a long table covered with a white linen cloth and set with china, crystal and silver. I believe there were about 20 guests who were served by the stewards who usually did the serving on board. I think one is a bit overwhelmed by a situation like this, so I can't remember that anyone took notes! We were all junior officers who did not work in the same office, so we could just get acquainted. The meal was the entertainment and then we were transported to our respective residences. My roommates were properly impressed when I told them about the dinner.

I lived life in two parts. At work, I was in the commander-in-chief's headquarters, but at five o'clock I returned to life much as a civilian in Washington. I shared an apartment with two other officers. We worked in entirely different situations, and knew very little about each other's jobs. We worked in highly classified places and left them behind when we were home. We had our own friends and did the usual things people do for entertainment. We rode trains— usually very crowded trains— to New York City and Ocean City. Because we were in Washington, we had other service people from our hometowns stop to visit as they traveled to new assignments. We always took them to see the sights. We soon learned to choose different ones so we would see something we had not seen. We learned how hot it could be there in the summer. Air-conditioning wasn't available except in a few public places. Even so, just living in Washington for those years was a treat.

I believe it was in July 1944, that we celebrated the WAVES' birthday by assembling many WAVES, marching down Constitution Avenue and sitting on the grass close to the Washington Monument to hear a program. The news reported 10,000 of us, but I wasn't counting! I know we marched better when we were in training more than a year before

And then, it was all over. My last day of work was November 30, 1945. I was ordered to report to Great Lakes Training Center near Chicago where I was released to inactive duty. I returned to Portland, joined my family and began a teaching career in the Portland schools. I returned to Washington to join a number of the women to celebrate the birthday of the WAVES in 1992. Time had taken its toll on the number present.

I like to think that the work I did was important in those days during World War II. I shall never regret that I chose to join the WAVES even though I still startle some people when I say I was in the Navy.

Life on the Midwestern Front

Margaret M. Freer

Although World War II started formally for the United States on December 7, 1941, many events before that led to it. For me, personally, the first thing that comes to mind happened when I was in fourth grade in Detroit in 1932. For two weeks, we had a little English girl in our class. She was with her parents on the way home to England from China. They had been missionaries and had to leave China because Japan had invaded where they were. That was my first realization that "current events reports" involved real people that I might know. Thus, in 1937, when I was in high school and read about the rape of Nanking, China, by the Japanese Army, it really rang a bell in my mind.

In 1938, we listened to the Orson Welles' radio broadcast of H. G. Wells' *The War of the Worlds*. Although we knew that it was fiction, I remember going out on the front porch to see if there was "panic in the streets" but, at least where we lived, all was silent. We read about Nazi aggression in Europe and war came there in 1939, but it was far away. They were real people, but they weren't us.

In 1940, I enrolled at Wayne University. I remember two classmates being only part-time students since they expected to go into the service shortly. As 1940 and 1941 wore on, more and more went off to serve. In the summer of 1941, I worked as a waitress at Sanders, an ice cream and lunch chain in Detroit — it was a 48 hour week at 30 cents an hour. One time a woman offered me a ten-cent tip, but I declined, since we were not allowed to accept tips.

120

On the morning of December 7, after listening to the news of Pearl Harbor, I remember going out on the porch to see if the world was stirring, but all was silent. It reminded me of when we listened to *The War of the Worlds*, but this time it was broad daylight and it wasn't fiction.

Detroit was a major part of "the Arsenal of Democracy." The war plants were working 24 hours a day with three shifts. The work week all over became 48 hours. The Wayne University student body did become smaller but there were still a lot of people around. Men were home on leave after basic training or before going overseas. Others were stationed in and around Detroit. The city was very busy with civilians, both men and women, doing their jobs. The streets, the shops and restaurants (also the bars), public street cars and buses— all were crowded. Smaller towns may have had fewer people but not Detroit.

In 1943, I graduated from Wayne. Ever since high school, I had wanted to study abroad. I had a cousin who had spent two years in Europe, from 1936 to 1938. It sounded exotic, plus it wasn't the Middle West. Because of the war one couldn't study abroad, but the Red Cross sent women overseas. However, there was a slight problem. At that time, one had to be 25 years old and I was still 20. The only service that did send women abroad was the WAC [Women's Army Corps]. This corps had evolved in 1943 from the WAAC [Women's Auxiliary Army Corps] created in 1942.

A parent's signature was required for anyone under 21 to sign up. My mother, who had led the very traditional life of a woman born in 1890, had the view that girls born in the 1920's were born into a whole new world. She thought my enlisting would be an interesting and rewarding experience. On the other hand, my father, who had the traditional views of woman's role of a man of his generation, took a very dim view of my enlisting. My girl friends all seemed to think it would be a strange thing for me to do, and all the young men thought it was a terrible idea.

Considerable prejudice against women in the service existed, more against those in the WAC than in the Navy WAVES, Coast Guard SPARS or women Marines. It may be that the prejudice stemmed in part from the outstandingly unattractive WAC uniforms. I think the WAVE uniforms were couturier-designed, but clearly no designer was responsible for the WAC uniforms! By the time I enlisted, the WACs no longer had to wear the upside-down cooking-pot hats with a visor. To be a soldier was man's work, even in a non-combatant job. Some men would probably (and understandably) not have cared to have women release them for combat. But there was also, contrary to propaganda, prejudice against women who took what had been men's jobs in factories. I had one college friend who went to work in a factory in Detroit and was subjected to considerable hostility from her male co-workers.

Margaret Freer

Since I was not certain about the Army, I decided on a civilian job with Detroit Army Ordnance, which was expanding its auditing operations, partly because of more contracts for war materiel. Many of these were cost-plus contracts, an opportunity for "creative accounting."

I was hired along with 29 other women from all over the country. I think a degree, regardless of major, was the main qualification. I went back to Wayne University. We studied accounting I and II, plus cost accounting and auditing 48 hours a week for six weeks and then alternated with one week of class and one of on-site experience for another six weeks. During this summer (1943) race riots occurred in Detroit. One of the class was black ("colored" was the word then) and she did not come to class for several days.

It was on one of my on-site weeks that I was the object of sexual harassment, although I didn't realize it at the time! For my first of three on-site training weeks, I was sent to a town in southern Michigan to work for a man who lived there. For my second week, he and I were sent to another southern Michigan town. On that Friday when I was ready to leave for Detroit, this man suggested that we both stay until Saturday. I thought this was just a strange idea and said I had to get back home. It wasn't until I was at home that I realized what he had in mind. I had hardly noticed the man except for work — he might have been anywhere from 50 to 70. (In the '40's, the gap between generations was much wider — people over 30 seemed settled and old and those over 40 quite middle-aged.) The whole incident struck me as merely funny — that he fancied himself as some kind of Don Juan, whereas I had thought of him as Methuselah. However, for my third week I was not assigned to him, which was fine with me, but I concluded that my assumptions about him were probably correct.

As for sexual harassment in the Army, the only thing I remember is one time standing with a group of other WACs in a long line waiting for the base bus. Suddenly on the other side of the line a young soldier made an obscene gesture at us. I don't think that was a friendly gesture.

When we finished our six months at classes and training with the Army Ordnance, we were given permanent assignments. Two others and I went to an eight-person office in Chrysler's Dodge main plant in Hamtramck, a city within the city of Detroit. However, Army Ordnance was renegotiating the contract with the company. We had nothing to do but try to look busy. Looking busy was for the benefit (and, we hoped, happiness) of the much larger and very busy Navy office which had a contract and was separated from us by a glass partition. After nine months of this inactivity, I decided to resign from the Detroit Army Ordnance and join the WAC.

Before I could join, I had to wait three months. During this time, I learned something about photography. I assisted, ineptly, I am sure, a professional photographer on a couple of wedding shoots. I also got photo lab instruction from a little old lady (probably about 60 at the time). On the basis of this experience, I managed to get classified by the WAC as a photolab technician.

I went to Ft. Des Moines, Iowa, for basic training. Alas, after three days, someone said "Fall out" and I did and broke my ankle — not my intention! After a couple of weeks in the base hospital, the staff decided I needed surgery and I was transferred to Lincoln AAF (Army Air Field). At that time the Air Corps was a part of the Army. Lincoln had a surgical ward. Along with me went Jane and her broken arm.

Jane had been a buyer for a major department store and joined the WAC when she was just short of the upper age limit. She was the oldest enlisted woman I knew, although I think a number of officers were about the same age. The officers, at least those I encountered, seemed to be largely ex-school teachers, whereas the enlisted women were far more varied in their backgrounds. Of course, they were all volunteers (no women were drafted), quite a cross section of Americans from all over the country.

At Lincoln I had surgery, physical therapy and infectious mononucleosis. Major G., the surgeon in charge of the ward, said that after repairing us he didn't intend for Jane and me to be marching around Des Moines in the dead of winter, so we didn't start our basic training until March. The doctors seemed to be doctors first and Army types second. Most of the armed forces were ex-civilians and planned on being civilians again as soon as possible.

In March, Jane and I went back to Des Moines. We learned, more or less, the Army way. When I think of the Army, "the sheltered life" is what comes to mind from my personal experiences. When to get up, when to go to bed, what to wear and when and where to wear it, how to do one's hair (off of the collar), what to eat and when and where, etc. We learned how to salute and whom, to tie a tie, to do KP (the pots and kettles were almost as big as we were) and we did a certain amount of marching to and fro. In April, when President Roosevelt died, we had a parade. And we took tests to classify us for assignment.

Because there was no likelihood that we would ever be in combat, there seemed to be a slight air of unreality about the uniforms, the marching, the saluting — a feeling that we were "playing soldier." But we kept on marching and saluting, like good soldiers.

While in basic training, I still hoped to go overseas and wrote to anyone I knew who I thought might help me. This included the cousin who had studied in Europe before the war. I had only seen him twice — when I was very much younger — but I thought he might do what he could out of family feeling. At that point, he was with the OSS in the Middle East. He eventually replied that he couldn't do anything for me and, if he could, he wouldn't. The other answers were similar, although more diplomatically phrased. I suppose it reflected the rather negative attitude toward women in war.

I met this cousin several years after the war and his attitude seemed to have improved a lot — so much so that I married him. It must have been a permanent improvement, since we are still married more than 50 years later.

Instead of Europe, I went to Texas and the P-47 fighter base at Abilene. On the way to Texas, the train stopped in St. Louis, Missouri. I was shocked to see a "Whites Only" sign at a drinking fountain. Although there was a great deal of *de facto* segregation in Detroit in the 1940s, I had never before seen it so blatantly displayed.

While at Abilene I had home leave and my first flight ever — in a B-25 bomber. The transportation office arranged a ride for me as far as Lincoln, Nebraska, where I took the train to Detroit. V-E Day was celebrated not long after I returned from leave and the base started closing. The WAC company was dispersed to various other 2nd Air Force installations. I was sent to Clovis, New Mexico, a B-29 "SuperFort" bomber base. Everything was pretty much in flux there. At first, a lot of men from the 8th Air Force were being redeployed to the Pacific from Europe, but that changed after V-J Day.

There was little in the way of work. As at Abilene, the photo lab at Clovis really had nothing to do. I went to Albuquerque to see a WAC friend and had a ride on a B-29. I remember crawling through the tunnel in the fuselage from the cockpit to the tail gunner's turret, and the pilot let me take the controls for a few minutes and even turn the plane back toward base. In December of 1945, I went back to Des Moines to be discharged.

After the war I worked as a very junior statistician at General Motors' headquarters. After a year and a half at GM, I decided that the two times I had actually worked were as a waitress and as a student. At that point, the G.I. Bill was available and I decided to use it for graduate school.

The war was over, but not its effects. One very positive effect was the G.I. Bill, particularly for education. A number of years ago, while traveling in South America with a group of 22 people about our age, we discussed this. Of the 12 men, only my husband (who had an advanced degree before the war) did not use the bill. One of the group was a judge, one a dentist, one an engineer, one a college professor, the others I don't recall specifically, but all agreed that they would never have done what they did in life had it not been for this bill.

One of our daughters has commented that, from watching old movies, she always thought that practically every house had lost someone in the war. A Canadian friend who had graduated from a university in one of the western provinces said that by the end of 1943 almost all of the men who had been in her class were dead. But, at least among the people I knew in the Midwest, it was different. Of all the people I knew from childhood on, only three were lost: one in an Army tank on D-Day, one a Marine on Iwo Jima, and one in the Coast Guard somewhere in the Pacific. My nine male cousins were all in various branches of the service and all survived. But I am not forgetting that this was not true for all.

Most people supported the war, did what they had to do, tried to lead as normal a life as possible and to pursue their own goals as best they could — and so did I. The war had a major influence, both directly and indirectly, on the rest of my life. My husband's work in intelligence continued after the war. As a consequence, I spent 11 years in Europe and I saw a good many other parts of the world — but that's another story.

Woman Marine

Betty Cooper Thompson

When the bombs were dropped on Pearl Harbor I was a supervisor in the long distance office of Ohio Bell Telephone Company in Akron, Ohio. Soon the West Coast offices were recruiting experienced operators because of the huge increase in calls in that area. I took advantage of this opportunity to transfer to Pacific Tel in Santa Monica, California. While working there, I was loaned out to the Los Angeles office part of the time and commuted from Santa Monica. They allowed two hours a day for the commute which meant I was working six hours a day instead of eight. A Woman Marine was often on the same bus. I talked to her one day about the service and it sounded interesting. After giving it a lot of thought, I visited the Marine Corps recruiting office in Los Angeles. They gave me the big pitch and finally I took the tests and was accepted in September, 1943. It was a month before I was called to active duty.

We departed from Los Angeles on a troop train in October to go to boot camp in North Carolina. Our car was on the end of the train and MPs were stationed in the car ahead to keep the men from entering our car. They also kept us from going forward. I think we were put on a siding for every train we met all the way. At least, we seemed to spend a lot of time on sidings waiting for trains to go by. The only time we were on our own was four hours in New Orleans. About a dozen of us went to the French Quarter for lunch. That trip took us six days to travel from Los Angeles to Camp Lejune on the East Coast.

Boot camp was difficult but I survived the six weeks there. The secret was to remain as invisible as possible. Do what you were told and never question. We learned to handle a rifle but were not allowed to shoot it. One day we had to go into an enclosure and put on gas masks because they were going to spray what they said was poison gas. None of us removed our mask to find out. And then there were the calisthenics at six in the morning. After the first week, I put my trench coat on over my PJs for that. I just couldn't get dressed in time for it. It was pitch dark and we exercised outside so I got away with it.

But there was the plus side. I loved the marching drills. Our platoon was soon adept at marching, and with the drill instructor calling cadence, we marched to classes, to the mess hall and, sometimes, just marched. The biggest thrill was on Saturday mornings when the whole base, accompanied by the Marine Band, marched in a show of troops.

After finishing boot camp, a group of us were shipped to Cherry Point, North Carolina. They had told us to pack a few clothes in an overnight bag in case the rest of our things didn't arrive for a couple of days. We arrived in the afternoon. I was interviewed and took a battery of tests; then, after dinner, more interviews. When I joined the service, I just assumed I would spend my time on a switchboard, but they were trying to fill a couple of classes in Link trainer (flight simulator) and operation tower. I was one of the lucky ones, so the next morning I was on my way to Atlanta, Georgia, to Link trainer school — again on one of those slow trains. My clothes caught up with me two weeks later.

I arrived just a few days before Christmas. It seemed most women had made plans for the holiday, so I was one of very few in the barracks. To add to that, Atlanta had an ice storm that stopped all public transportation on Christmas Day. It was my first Christmas away from friends or family and a lonely time because no letters or cards caught up with me until two or three weeks later.

Learning to operate a Link trainer was so far removed from anything I had ever done that I found it fascinating. We had continuous drills on compass headings. Our classes in Morse code required us to receive at least 12 words a minute. We learned how to read flight instruments, how to operate as well as to fly the Link (flight simulator) and learned maintenance and repair of one.

I was there for three months and during that time made friends and learned my way around the Atlanta area. One thing I never got used to was Friday breakfast. During breakfast, someone read for about 10 minutes from a section of the *Book of Navy Regulations*. I suppose if one stayed on that base long enough, she would have heard the whole book. Also, they served baked beans for breakfast every Friday. It was a tradition of some kind, but hard to face so early in the morning.

I wanted to go back to California, but there was just one opening so

I didn't think I'd have a chance. However, two of us tied for top grades and we flipped a coin. I'm not very lucky in any game of chance but this time I won the toss. I was sent to El Toro Marine Air Base, where I spent the remainder of my military time.

I was lucky in more ways than one. In all three years that I served, I was never assigned to "mess duty." I escaped after boot camp when most new Marines spent two weeks on mess duty before being assigned elsewhere. Because of my qualifications they immediately sent me to Cherry Point for reassignment. Because they needed to fill a class quota at Atlanta, they couldn't keep me in Cherry Point. On the bus from the train to the naval air station in Atlanta they said anyone who had not yet been on mess duty somewhere else should volunteer for it. I did, but they wanted me to start in a Link class the following day so I escaped the duty again. At El Toro, we were needed as instructors so were exempt. By the time they finally sent some Link operators to mess duty, I had a staff sergeant rating and no longer was required to serve.

When I arrived at El Toro Marine Air Station there was one women's barracks, which we shared with the Navy nurses assigned to sick bay. I enjoyed life on the Marine base. We put in our work day and pretty much had the rest of the time to ourselves. There were housekeeping chores assigned each week, some less desirable than others. And one weekend a month we were required to stay on base. The center of the barracks was the lounge area, the utility room with washers, ironing boards, irons and lines strung along one side for hanging our clothes to dry. I declared that when I got out of the service I would never iron another shirt as long as I lived. It all came back to haunt me when I had a husband plus three sons whose shirts had to be ironed.

The bathrooms and showers were also in this area, as well as some semiprivate rooms for the non-coms. The double story wings on each side accommodated about 50 women in each wing. We had double bunks, a dresser and a locker in which to hang our clothes. The bunks were set up so there were four women to a cell, with the dressers and lockers giving us a little privacy.

I was with three women who soon became my very close friends. We all worked as instrument flying instructors on the Link. The four of us became family during the two and a half years we worked and lived together. Probably the testing we went through to qualify for the jobs we had brought together persons with the same likes and abilities. The four of us all had teaching in our background and we enjoyed many of the same things.

El Toro was a great base to be on. We were close enough to Hollywood that we were often entertained by the celebrities. There were craft

Betty Thompson and an unidentified colleague at El Toro Marine Air Station in August 1944.

classes. Golf lessons were offered free; and, eventually we had a riding stable and a swimming pool. The theater on base changed movies every other night and at least once a week there was a dance at the NCO Club which we could attend. Once a week, a private home in Santa Ana opened their door to service people and played classical records. Usually 15 or 20 people took advantage of this.

We went off-base a couple of times a week to eat at a restaurant at either Santa Ana or Laguna Beach. Since I was not far from Santa Monica, I spent many weekends there with friends. Officers and enlisted persons were not permitted to fraternize. Even the movie theater had its officers' section. Since all pilots were officers, they were the people we knew and worked with. It was only natural that some of us managed to get together offbase.

Several months after I arrived, they began building new barracks for women. Eventually there were about 2,000 women on the base. They worked at all kinds of jobs: airplane mechanics, parachute packers, drivers and a host of other jobs. Eventually we had our own mess hall and they served foods that we had been requesting, such as salads for lunch.

Transportation on the base was by "cattle cars." These were semis pulling long partially enclosed trailers. Wooden benches lined the sides. They had tops and wide spaced boards on the sides. They ran a regular route and if we needed a ride, we flagged the driver. There were no regular stops. These semis were driven by women.

Raising the flag at sunrise and lowering it at sunset was quite a ceremony. It was accompanied by a bugler and as soon as it began, everyone came to attention and saluted. If we were on a part of the base where we couldn't see or hear it, we came to attention as soon as we saw someone nearer do so. Even if we were going in the opposite direction, as soon as we saw someone salute, we turned in the direction of the flag and saluted. We held the salute until the one we had been watching dropped his arm. I would love to have had a bird's eye view of the base completely shutting down for those few moments.

After I had been at El Toro a few months the "higher ups" decided that Link operators should get some flight time in the SNJs, which were the planes used for teaching instrument flying "under the hood." This way we could practice in the air what we were teaching on the ground. These planes had a double cockpit. The instructor sat in front and the student sat behind. We didn't learn to take off and land, but we did handle the plane once it was in the air. I logged 28 hours of instrument time before we were grounded.

One of my students was Don (Tommy) Thompson. He later became a flight instructor in the SNJs. We struck up a friendship and became an "item" when I was flying with him as my instructor. Once on the way back to the base, he called me on the intercom and asked me to "cage" my instruments. To me that meant only one thing, he was going to do some acrobatics which I knew would make me sick and which pilots had been instructed not to do with us in the plane. I grabbed the mike and yelled, "No, Tommy, please don't !"

What I didn't realize was that he had tuned his radio to the control tower for landing instructions. So, not only did the tower hear me, but so did every other plane in the air that was on that frequency. By the time we got on the ground we were being teased. What was going on? How did he manage to get in the back seat? We never lived that one down. But we ended up getting married after we were both out of the service and celebrated our 50th wedding anniversary in 1996.

There were two Link rooms, one on each side of the field. During my last year I was the NCO in charge of one of them. I still did a lot of the training, but also had the office duties to take care of. My biggest bugaboo was the weekly and monthly reports that had to be made out in triplicate, *without error.*

We did not train new pilots. El Toro was an advanced base and a lot of the men had already seen duty overseas. But they were required to take a number of hours of instrument time in the air and on the ground. Not even the generals were exempt. Most of the pilots hated the Link because it didn't feel like a plane. A general who needed some night flying time asked the four of us instructors if we would like to go along. He was flying to San Francisco to visit with his parents that evening. Never ones to turn down a golden opportunity, we said yes. After work, we climbed aboard the DC3 he was flying and we flew to the navy base in Oakland. He told us to be back at 10:00 P.M. We went into Oakland to a restaurant for dinner, met him back at the base at 10:00 and flew home. A nice evening out.

After peace was declared with Japan, the military started discharging the Women Marines at El Toro. By August, our barracks was the only one left and even it was thinning out. A few days before the last of us were to be discharged, we had a big party at one of the nightclubs in Los Angeles. We had a great time, but later during the night we all started getting sick. When sick bay had no more beds, they turned one of the wings in the barracks into service. All the Navy nurses turned out to care for us. Eight of the sickest were sent to Long Beach Naval Hospital in ambulances. I was one of these.

It was a hot, uncomfortable ride in the metal gurneys used for transporting wounded soldiers. When we arrived at the hospital and the medics came out to unload us, their first words were, "You didn't tell us they were women." We stayed in the ambulances for another half hour while they made room for us in the maternity ward.

We were all together in what looked like a visitors area. We were there for four days. When we were discharged, we had a hilarious time trying to get into uniform. They had moved us to sick bay at night and we did not have our clothes with us so we had asked our "buddies" to pack a bag for us. I did pretty well. Only my necktie was missing. One girl had no underwear. One had only her dungarees—which we never wore off base. I had the most stripes, so I was put in charge of this motley crew and we were left to our own devices to get back to our base from Long Beach. We had to pool our money to buy bus fare because some didn't have their purses. When we arrived back at El Toro, all our comrades had received their discharge papers and were gone. Our papers were awaiting us too.

After three years and the end of the war in the Pacific, I was discharged with a rating of technical sergeant. Our "family" went our separate ways, but even after 50 years, I still keep in contact with one of them.

I read of the trouble some service women now have with harassment. I do not recall ever having that experience, but in the '40's we had not been introduced to "women's lib." While the war was a terrible thing, my experiences in the service were mostly positive and I have fond memories of the time served.

First in Town

Rhoda I. Mills, LCDR, USNR (Ret.)

In August 1942, the WAVES (Women Appointed for Volunteer Emergency Services) was established. At the time, I was working in Pendleton, Oregon, as secretary to the city schools superintendent. An article in *Mademoiselle* magazine described the WAVES and gave an address to which to apply for membership. I had been writing letters of recommendation for the men teachers who were applying for service, so I decided to apply also. My uncle had been in the Navy during World War I so it appealed to me as a branch of the military service.

Very shortly I received a letter telling me to report to the Navy Recruiting Office in Seattle to take a written exam and a physical on October 26. My mother and I went up by train. I passed the written exam with high marks and the physical the next day. I was sworn into the Navy on Navy Day, October 27, 1942. I was the only officer candidate on that day. My mother was there to witness the ceremony and to meet some of the recruiting staff. Then I went home to await orders to the Officers' Candidate School at Smith College, Northampton, MA.

I was in the second class of WAVE officers and reported on January 4, 1943. It was a very cold winter that year. One day, in fact, it was 20° below zero, which was the record for the day. As a result, we had our drills in the armory. We had to march back and forth to classes and also to meals at Wiggins Tavern. Since we were the shortest in my platoon, my partner and I had flashlights and would run ahead to stop the traffic while the platoon marched through, then fall in at the end until there was another crosswalk. It actually worked to our advantage because the running kept us warmer!

While I was there, the First Lady, Eleanor Roosevelt, visited us and told us how important our work would be. We were quite surprised at what a pleasant personality she had. She was better looking than her pictures.

On April 4, 1943, we were commissioned as ensigns and received our orders. Mine were for Willamette Iron and Steel Corporation, Portland, Oregon. At that time there were 125 men officers, engineering duty only, at Willamette Iron and Steel. At the end of the war there were 12 women officers and 12 enlisted girls. I was the first to report in and was quite a strange sight to them, since I was probably the first military woman in Portland. No one was sure just what I was. People were curious but friendly. Two more WAVE officers reported in two months later, one a woman architect, so I didn't feel so strange.

Since I had joined the Navy to see the world, I was disappointed to be sent so close to my home in Forest Grove, Oregon, but I discovered there were quite a few advantages. Our commanding officer was a Navy captain, a graduate of the Naval Academy and also a graduate of M.I.T. in engineering. His title was Supervisor of Shipbuilding, USN, Portland, Oregon. He was challenged to see that we women officers received the best of care, and, whenever a new ship type went on its trial run down the river, two of us escorted by a male officer, were assigned

Rhoda Mills as a lieutenant junior grade, c. 1944.

to go aboard. This gave us a lot of first-hand knowledge of the ships that were being built.

We were building ships at a very fast rate. There were three ship-building yards in Portland, one in Astoria, and one in Coos Bay. Our yards even built some aircraft carrier escorts for the British Navy. The men had to spend a lot of time inspecting the ships so we WAVES had to see that the office was running properly. We were invited to the commissioning ceremonies when the ships were turned over to the Navy. We went to the British commissionings also.

Another plus for us was that, after they ran out of wives, daughters, and celebrities to launch the ships, the WAVE officers were invited to christen the ships. Since I was the first arrival, I went first. I broke the bottle of champagne across the bow of the USS LCI (L) 46 (Landing Craft Infantry [Large]) as it went down into the water. All the shipyard workers and Naval personnel were on hand, as well as my sister and mother and father. I was afraid I wouldn't hit the bottle hard enough, but I needn't have worried! Everyone around got christened as well as the ship.

At the end of the war, I was promoted to lieutenant. We had to deal with the closing of the command and then went on inactive duty. A year later they gave the WAVE officers the privilege of joining the active reserve. I drilled in uniform one evening a week and spent two weeks each year on active duty for training. When the Korean conflict occurred I was asked to return to active duty in Seattle. While on duty there, I made lieutenant commander. I stayed in the reserve altogether 34 years and retired in 1976, receiving my reserve pension at the age of 60. I have never regretted my decision to become a Navy officer.

The Day That Changed Our Lives

Eloise S. Irwin

I remember vividly my own placement on earth at that time of sudden change. On December 7, 1941, I was twenty-five years old, had taught four years in small elementary schools, and was then at Willamette University in Salem, Oregon, working for a baccalaureate degree. In the fall term I was living at the women's dormitory, Lausanne Hall.

The university football team, along with Oregon's Governor Douglas McKay, his daughter and many civic and school leaders, had traveled to Honolulu to share in the game against the University of Hawaii. Our dormitory housemother, Miss Jack, was among the boosters who accompanied the team.

On Sunday morning, as I came from church up the steps of the dorm, wearing the red coat I loved, some girls ran out to tell us that Pearl Harbor had been bombed by the Japanese and much of the U.S. fleet had been sunk or destroyed. Because the event was too big and horrible to comprehend, we thought only of the Willamette team and the local people we knew whose lives might be endangered there.

We waited for news of them and finally heard the terrible extent of the disaster. Our acquaintances were safe. The young men had been put to work patrolling the beaches; the women were assisting in hospitals. There was no transportation to bring them home. Six weeks later the Salem people returned on hospital ships, which were still transporting the wounded.

Miss Jack called an evening house meeting immediately. She told us

135

first of their trip home—how the smell of burned flesh had pervaded the ship, for many of the injured sailors aboard had jumped into the flaming sea as their ship went down. She further told us how the people from Oregon had all been celebrating the football victory and enjoying their island vacation, when on Sunday morning they had seen a hysterical woman in the hotel lobby, saying she had taken her husband to work at Hickam Field and had seen U.S. planes being strafed.

As they returned to their rooms with troubled minds, island visitors saw Navy and Army officers rushing to the elevators, dressing as they went. The Willamette group went back to the lobby and heard the radio announcer saying, "Be calm, but the island of Oahu is under enemy attack, and the sign of the rising sun has been seen on the wings of the planes." It was some time before they knew the full meaning of those words. The next six weeks they observed many human tragedies as they tried to help.

On Pearl Harbor Day, we had no idea of the changes that were coming to our society or to ourselves. Within a year, Willamette University adjusted to a drop in enrollment, shortages of fuel and commodities, and soaring prices. After negotiations with the military, it began a naval officers' training program.

I received my B.A. while I lived and worked at the State Blind School, taught one more year in the country now changed, and then made a career shift. The government needed occupational therapists to work with nerve and muscle rehabilitation in the new barracks-type Army hospitals across the country. I joined a war emergency course at Mills College in Oakland, California. In the mornings, we were taught medical subjects by doctors in uniform. In the afternoons, we were taught by master craftsmen in hand crafts like weaving, ceramics, carpentry, leather and metal work, and macramé.

After four months, I served an internship at Hammond Army Hospital in Modesto, California. It treated only the nerve injuries of men flown in from the beaches of Anzio and North Africa and the Pacific islands. I was roughly initiated into a ward where all the men had spinal injuries which had left their lower bodies paralyzed. Their injuries had come from mines, from parachuting into transmission lines, from trying to shield a friend.

What was I doing there? In that ward, occupational therapy was a way to make the difficult hours pass. Because most could use their hands, we helped them learn to weave on hand looms, make knotted belts, or tool leather. I was learning how human beings can support each other. Sometimes we were required to accompany the doctors on their rounds as they evaluated the ambulatory patients, who might have a hand twisted into a claw, or a leg drawn and bent, due to nerve injuries. Such patients were summarily ordered to amputation hospitals, and for that, they were glad. Part of the time we worked in locked wards where the men had been mentally broken by the war. The happiest place was the big shop, where convalescing men worked with all kinds of tools to create beautiful things.

I worked in three Army hospitals, and in the Veterans' Hospital in the aftermath of the war. It remains the most vivid and poignant period of my life, as I daily lived with what had happened to the young men of my generation.

During the fifty-year celebration after Pearl Harbor, I wish we could have honored our service people without "celebration." To "celebrate" seems to ignore the costs.

It Was the Patriotic Thing to Do: From Montana to Iwo Jima

Mary Elizabeth Dahl Jorgensen

Everyone on the home front did something for the war effort, my family included. Dad ran the family business, Dahl Funeral Chapel in Bozeman, Montana, almost by himself. Mom was an active member of the Nurses' Reserve Corps, chairwoman of the cancer dressing committee. For the Red Cross, she helped with emergencies at Bozeman Deaconess Hospital, taught home nursing, knit afghans, rolled bandages. Once a week, she did airplane spotting from the roof of the Baxter Hotel. When the Air Cadets were encamped at Montana State College, she was in charge of 57 cadet patients in Hamilton Hall.

My oldest brother, Eldon, a B-17 pilot, was missing in action over Italy. My brother Raymond was a staff sergeant and B-24 bombardier in Europe. Our youngest brother, Bernard, just out of high school, was in the "V-12" program being educated by the Navy to become an officer. We knew he, too, would eventually be in the war.

My older sister, Vera, was married and lived in Tacoma, Washington. Her husband, Lars Jensen, was a civilian employee for the Navy at Todd Shipyard. Vera was a nurse at Pierce County Hospital. Some of her patients were Japanese "internees," American citizens of Japanese descent who were being held at the Puyallup Fairgrounds before being moved to internment camps.

After graduating in 1943 from Montana State College among the top ten in a class of 2,500, I had gone to Stanford University Hospital in California to complete my one-year internship in dietetics. It was then located in San Francisco at Clay and Webster streets. It was 1944, the war was on and I had to make some choices as to my future career.

I visited my sister in Tacoma, and one day we went shopping. We passed an Army recruiting office...no, I didn't pass it. I "just stepped in to inquire," I thought. I could learn about possible career opportunities, where I would go, what my duties might be. The recruiting officer had a hook out for me: he told me one of my college classmates, Dorothy Brewer, would be in basic training at the same time as I would. When I came out, I was signed up to become a second lieutenant in the Army Medical Corps.

I felt I had made an important decision. Excited, surprised, but I hadn't planned it. It was the patriotic thing to do. Vera, her baby, and I took the train to Bozeman to see our parents. At the station, Dad greeted us with the bad news: Raymond was missing in action over Germany. How could I tell them my news? Not then. It was much later in that visit, when things were calm, that I told my parents that I, too, would be in the war. It must have been very hard for them.

I was sworn into the Army Medical Corps in Bozeman, Montana. I had a few weeks to spend with my parents before reporting for duty on July 21, 1944. During that time, we learned that Raymond had been killed on May 29, 1944, in a mission over Germany. It takes a long time for the death to really set in on you...you just keep thinking they're "away somewhere in the war."

I was assigned to Camp White, Medford, Oregon, for one month. We wore green Army fatigues to march, bivouac and pass tests. The exercise put us in pretty good shape. I was sent then to Barnes General Hospital in Vancouver, Washington, where I stayed for approximately two months. From there, I was ordered to McCloskey General Hospital in Temple, Texas. I knew no one on the troop train going to Texas; however, a note was tossed into my upper bunk asking: "Are you interested?" No, I was not! Otherwise, it was a calm ride.

At McCloskey General, I was one of several who supervised food preparations for patients. Stateside, the food was more than adequate, it was good. The officers' mess! They were served the best food. I learned about things like serving nasturtiums on the salad.

While I was in Texas, my mother, "in recognition of the meritorious services of her sons and daughters and herself," was appointed by the Bozeman City Commission to christen the SS *Bozeman* Victory ship at the port of Portland, Oregon. Mom was now a gold star mother. These were mothers who had lost children in the military to the war. Each mother was

Mary Dahl, 1944.

presented with a small blue banner decorated with a gold star for each person lost. Some banners carried as many as four stars. The banner was often hung in the front window of the home, so that people seeing it were reminded of the high cost of the war.

My next orders were to the port of Seattle. I didn't know where or when I would be shipped out. It was "hush hush." I had time to visit my sister again. Before I departed, we learned my brother Eldon was *alive*! He had bailed out of his stricken plane over Italy. After months in a prison camp, he escaped and finally made his way to Allied lines near Monte Casino. He had endured terrible hardships and harrowing escapes along the way. He provided the military with valuable information and taught survival and escape skills to others.

This was it! Finally! Ninety women medical personnel were loaded onto the USS *Ernst*. We were below deck, in hammocks, fairly crowded, allowed on deck only at specified times. All civilians going for jobs in Hawaii were on upper deck. Everything was regulated for everybody: showers, meals, contact with other military personnel. One nurse was seasick the whole trip. She lost 15 pounds en route to Hawaii. The food — not officers' mess — was not good.

We disembarked at Oahu and were quartered at Scofield Barracks, a delightful place. During our stay we enjoyed some tours around Oahu. The pink Royal Hawaiian Hotel was the largest hotel on the beach. Sometimes there were groups of male officers to take us to parties, dancing, drinking. I sent my parents a photo of me on the lovely beach...that's how they learned I was smoking. There was a pack of cigarettes next to me in the photo!

After a holding period of one month, we boarded a ship in a convoy headed for the South Pacific. I do not remember its name but it was better than the last one! Twenty-two days on board! We were housed on the upper deck as officers, and ate in the officers' mess! What food! My first Indian curry, with all the condiments. And we were waited upon. We could go on deck to watch the waves and leaping fish. For someone who grew up in North Dakota and Montana, what an experience.

But I remember the ash cans rumbling at night to keep enemy submarines away. "Ash can" was the slang term for barrels full of explosives propelled from each side of a ship and exploding when they hit the water. I don't know if any of the ships of our company was hit.

We did not know of our final destination — a few rumors — but we disembarked at Guam and were assigned to 203 General Hospital for approximately three months. It seemed a peaceful island: beautiful beaches, clear water to enjoy after duty, the village of Agnew where the natives made baskets and dolls to sell. However, at night the mess hall garbage cans were raided by hungry Japanese military still hiding on the island.

Our ship finally stopped at Iwo Jima, a bleak-looking volcanic island. It is five miles long and two and three quarter miles across at the widest part. We loaded onto liberty boats to go ashore. We saw abandoned ships on the beach, pill boxes scattered high on the banks (enemy machine gun positions), only scrub vegetation and black sand everywhere. Nighttime temperatures were in the high 70's and water came out of the ground at 130 degrees.

We arrived about six months after Iwo Jima had been secured in a terrible battle. Seventy-five thousand soldiers, sailors and airmen participated. There were 25,852 casualties, 6,821 killed in action. One Marine in three was killed or wounded. In the entire course of World War II, only 353 Congressional Medals of Honor, the nation's highest award for heroism, were given. In just over one month, 27 went to the warriors of Iwo Jima.

We were there to set up a hospital for the planned invasion of Japan. Tokyo was only 750 miles away. We had 30 Medical Corps, six Dental Corps, nine Medical Administrative Corps, three chaplains, two Sanitary Corps, 78 Nursing Corps, two physiotherapists, three Red Cross workers and three dieticians. Since I had enlisted a few days before Margaret "Beth" Heap, who was in her 40's and experienced, I was slated to be head dietician. I was much relieved to have her take the job. She was a good friend for years after.

The narrowest part of the island is dominated by Mt. Suribachi, 546 feet tall. The airstrips took up the middle part: Motoya Field, home to fighter planes, bombers and B-29's. Our living quarters were on the widest end of the island, Quonset huts perched before a sharp drop to the beach. Two of us were assigned to a room, just big enough for two single beds. For a while we had only our helmets to wash in, until showers were set up. At night, rats would tickle our feet.

The kitchens were in Quonset huts, too. The dieticians' job was to plan the menus and inspect the food preparation and serving. We did not actually do the cooking and cleaning. Food was served cafeteria style, portions served on trays, but second helpings were O.K. We three dieticians would rotate duty for hospital or regular enlisted men's mess.

Even under wartime conditions so far away from home, we planned full meals, with something hot and something cold, even though there was no refrigeration or air conditioning or iced beverages. The hospital was supplied with "B" rations which consisted mostly of canned foods: gallon cans of fruits, vegetables and meats, cheese, peanut butter and butter. We also had gallon cans of powdered items: juice (called "battery acid"), cocoa, milk and powdered eggs. On rare occasions, something fresh from Hawaii would be flown in. One special day we had fried chicken. I was observing the enlisted men's mess when the air raid siren split the air. It was a mad dash to the nearest shelter...every hand clutching a piece of fried chicken!

Most of the air raids were directed at the air field. One night, it was for all of us. About 90 of us slipped and stumbled through deep black sand to the shelter located by the bank below us. Betty Kribbs and I got there first! The shelter, probably 20 X 30 feet, soon had standing room only. It was dark and silent, smelling of earth. We were all in our nightclothes. The lone, older male among us did some groping, to no avail. We jostled away from him. We waited, hearing distant booms, probably an hour before "all clear" sounded. We never saw combat, and rarely felt a sense of immediate danger, except for those air raids. They were our lowest morale point; we were really scared.

Our duty uniforms were a wrap-around dress, or slacks and pants, hat like a nurse, all made from pin-stripe brown and white cotton seersucker. Dress uniform was olive green rayon, belted shirtwaist dress, or Army "pink" dress, beige with maroon piping, same style. But if there was a festive occasion, we wore civilian clothes. I had a short blue bed-jacket with daisies, from my mother, which I turned into a blouse. Someone gave me a piece of white silk (used parachute) from which I hand-sewed a skirt. I thought it a pretty outfit. But we had little time for beauty. We didn't fuss much with hair or makeup. One date told me I'd look better if I fixed my hair up. I didn't see him again. We could buy bathing suits flown in from Hawaii. They were two-piece, a bra and a short skirt with panties, all in the same fruit print, in red or blue. I chose red. So there we were, a dozen or more all decked out in the same suit, red or blue! I heard that some guys nicknamed me "the Varga Girl." Seems the enlisted men had a poster of a Varga Girl in their mess hall. I was openly called "Dolly" after my name, Dahl.

We were far outnumbered by the men and there was much fraternizing on our free time. Like me, most of the women had someone special back home, and I suppose the men did too. But we needed to have a good time when we could; everyone needed relief from the presence of war.

We had an open air theater with benches so we could see an occasional movie — even in the rain. Daily Mass was conducted at 4:00 P.M. lasting all of 12 minutes. We were invited to officers' clubs for parties, dancing, drinking. One club even had a latrine just for women. We could have a whiskey ration — a fifth — and cigarettes. Mostly I traded mine to enlisted men for paperweights of metal molded in the shape of Iwo Jima (made from exploded shells), sea shell jewelry, watchbands. We could explore the island's caves and go to the black sand beaches to swim in the ocean, although we were wary of sharks.

Letters and food packages came from home. Our mail was censored before being posted. Enlisted men would ferment dried fruit and make alcoholic beverages. Once medical alcohol was stolen and mixed with the other brew. Those who drank it ended up in the hospital going blind. Another tragedy of war: one nurse was suspected of having flushed her aborted fetus into the latrine.

But there were happy stories too. My friend Ruth met Harry when he came to her in physiother-

Mary Dahl (left) and Betty Kribbs, dieticians on Iwo Jima, 1945.

apy to complain about his flat feet. First he brought her a fresh apple, then some shoestrings which she needed but couldn't get. But the gift that won her heart was the *cold* Coca Cola he brought her. In steamy Iwo, this was only possible if a pilot took a bottle of coke up with him into frigid altitudes. She decided he might be worth marrying, so she did.

I visited one of the two huge cemeteries—all the little white crosses, row upon row. I found one with the name Ed Angemeir on it. He had been president of the Newman Club when I was in college. Someone I knew was here. I felt I should write to his parents, but I couldn't. It made it all so real, so sad. A small section of the cemetery was just for the dogs that died in the invasion.

We went to see General Kamimoto's cave. The Japanese troops on the island had lived in these labyrinths. We thought the invasion had cleared them out. Only years later did we learn that Japanese soldiers were still hiding in the maze of the caves! I don't know why all the places on the island were still named after the Japanese we defeated there.

One day, I was called to the desk where we checked in and out. To my complete surprise, there stood my brother Bernard. He was following orders to report to a minesweeper in Tokyo harbor and had maneuvered a stop to see me. He was so handsome I had a hard time convincing others that he was really my brother. He procured a jeep and we toured the island. We went to Mt. Suribachi and pretended we raised the flag again. It was so good to spend a couple of days with him before he went on to the mine fields.

On August 6, 1945, we were told that two planes, the *Enola Gay* and *Bock's Car*, had stopped on Iwo Jima the night before for refueling before a bombing run on Japan. A new kind of bomb had been dropped on Hiroshima. Only much later we learned the devastating nature of the first atomic bomb. On August 15, 1945, President Truman announced Japan had accepted unconditional surrender terms. It was OVER! The invasion we had been preparing for would never happen. We rejoiced. Tracer bullets, like fireworks, blazed over the sky in celebration. In September, General MacArthur entered Tokyo.

In November, 1945, I was promoted to rank of first lieutenant. As we prepared to leave the island, equipment was being buried, rather than being left. Even the waffle irons—what a waste, what a shame. How hard it was to say goodbye to comrades, most of whom we would never see again.

I was demobilized December 6, 1945. We were transported to Saipan, to be flown to the States on an Army transport plane. The plane had bucket seats on the side and I was the only woman on board. Some questioned the safety of the plane. I was *ready!* It was an uneventful flight, actually beautiful, flying above the clouds. We put down at Hamilton Field, California. There I was given the option of finishing the two year tour of duty at Camp

Beal, California, or being discharged at 18 months. I was discharged. My cousin, officer John Dahl, facilitated the discharge. I had been in the Army for eight months, eight days stateside and ten months, 27 days in "foreign service." I was awarded the World War II Victory Medal, Meritorious Service Unit Plaque, and Asiatic Pacific Theater ribbon with bronze service star.

Once again, I took the train to visit my sister Vera in Tacoma. Arriving too early to go to her house, I went to early Mass. Because I was still in uniform, complete strangers invited me to breakfast. But I went on to Vera's even though it was still early. I let myself into the unlocked household, crept in and fell asleep on the couch, feeling at home at last. What a surprise when they found me there!

So, what did we do? We went shopping again, this time to Seattle. I replaced my Army uniform with a pale blue, tailored two-piece suit, a cherry-red wool coat and a jersey bathrobe. A complete civilian wardrobe.

I went on to Bozeman to spend six weeks with my parents. And now I had come full circle, back to the questions I had before I stepped into that recruiting office. Where would I make my home? After a year in the tropics, Montana was too cold. I returned to California, the Bay Area, and took a job at Peralta Hospital in Oakland. Vera's husband, Lars, had a brother in Oakland named Albert. Albert's wife, Lena had a sister, Esther, who was married to Oscar. Oscar had a brother, Frank Jorgensen. This grapevine arranged a blind date between Frank and me. With his bright red hair and yellow skin he was so handsome! He was recovering from a malaria fever he got serving in the Army in New Guinea. We dated for a few months. I was considering a job offer in South America, the tropics again! Frank bet me a bottle of whiskey I wouldn't go. I said I would come back in a year or so. He said, "Well, we could get married..." And I said "When?" He got a bottle of Jack Daniels, and we were married November 2, 1946. He told me later that on our first date, when he saw me coming down the stairs in my red coat, he thought, "*Wow!*"

My husband and I never spoke about our war experiences to our children. This is the first time I have tried to record these memories.

Two Years in the Red Cross

Eleanor Soule Crosby

In June of 1942, I graduated from the University of North Carolina with a lovely B.A. in English literature and no skills at all. So, when I returned home to Tacoma, Washington, I went to secretarial school for a few months to learn shorthand. I purchased a book on medical shorthand, went to Madigan General Hospital at Fort Lewis and asked, if I learned medical shorthand, could I have a job there. The answer was to come right away and they would help me learn on the job. After working as a secretary on the obstetrical ward and in the surgical service for two years, I applied for a job in the Red Cross.

I was soon accepted and was sent a ticket to travel to Washington, D.C., for indoctrination and assignment. There, a whole group of us were billeted in the Colonial Hotel at, I think, 11th and M streets, N.W. We caught a passing bus each morning for the American University where we had lectures on the history of the Red Cross and current functions. I should have liked to ask for an overseas assignment, but I was under 25, and so too young. However, I got what I feel was a prize assignment — Letterman General Hospital in the Presidio military area in San Francisco. When I reported there, I was assigned to their Dante Annex.

Dante Annex was a very attractive, friendly little hospital about a mile towards town from Letterman. The staff was small: a secretary, two or three social workers and two recreation workers. I was to be the second recreation worker. My first assignment was to find a place to live. People came

146

to me with suggestions and numbers to call. One cheerful corpsman came to me with the number of a place he said was not too far away and had vacant rooms. I happily called the number and almost dropped the phone when a deep voice answered "Alcatraz." [Alcatraz was the highest security prison in the United States in its time.] However, I did soon find a room in the basement of an old Victorian house just four blocks from the hospital.

The hospital itself was a three story affair with a sunny recreation room and open deck on the top floor. Much of my work was up there, especially evenings. There we had entertainments for the patients, most of whom were ambulatory. Often groups of volunteers came in and put on evening shows or other entertainment, and there I learned — after some great glitches — to thread the 16 mm Victor machine and show movies. I could also take the movies during the afternoons to patients who could not — or would not — leave their rooms. The pictures shown on pale green walls left something to be desired but did help to entertain. What we could have done with the VCR!

Most of the patients stayed a fair length of time. They were often undergoing treatment before being sent back to duty or on to other hospitals. They had complicated broken limbs, amputations and were awaiting prostheses or, sometimes, grafts for such things as new noses or ears. These latter patients did look very strange, with big rolls of flesh connecting their ears or noses to their chests, rather elephant-like. They were the ones who absolutely refused to appear anywhere. I could certainly understand their embarrassment, but theirs was to be a happy ending.

The amputees, on the other hand, should have been sadder it seemed to me and, basically, they were. But they hopped around the hospital on crutches, or rolled around in wheelchairs while waiting for their wounds to heal so they could be fitted with artificial limbs. Then, the depression was apt to be worse, for their new limbs were often hard to adjust to. Most of those I happened to meet were tank battle victims and their legs were often lost with no stubs at all, so they had to have legs fitted to their torsos. These men seemed to have a very hard time adjusting to both the weight and feel of their new legs.

Most of my meals were eaten in the officers' mess, which was small and very friendly. There, I became good friends with a dietitian named Kit. As she had recently lost her roommate, I was able to leave my first room and share her apartment on Divisidero Street. Imagine the shock I had a few years ago when I saw that very block of buildings absolutely flattened in an earthquake.

Our landlady was a sad creature — an alcoholic — who could be very shrill and unpleasant when Kit and I invited dates up to our apartment. It was here that I met my husband. Kit had a framed photo of a very hand-some Navy officer on her bureau. One evening, I came home from work and there he sat in our living room, just returned from Okinawa. It took me about 10 minutes to realize that he was the man of my dreams. I got to know him quite well in the next few weeks, but what was I to do? He belonged to Kit. One day, when I came home, she excitedly showed me a very nice engagement ring. The bottom dropped from under me, until she showed me a photograph of someone she had never mentioned, but for whom she had been waiting.

In the spring of 1945, some weeks after V-E Day, I was transferred to the main Letterman Hospital, where the patient load was increasing rapidly with soldiers from the South Pacific, complete with atabrine glow and jungle rot. Soon thereafter came the great deluge of soldiers freed from Japanese prison camps. They were frighteningly thin, often very nervous and haunted in appearance, but so full of joy and eager to get on the hospital trains which would take them closer to home. I even saw among them the husband of a friend of mine, though at first he had to shout greetings to me as I had not recognized him.

After V-J Day the need for hospital trains increased dramatically, and I was delighted to accept the assignment of Red Cross worker on the trains. On this job I worked all alone. The trains left San Francisco with numerous cars, each heading for a specific military hospital. The longest train I ever rode had thirteen cars for patients, plus one for the personnel traveling with the patients, and a kitchen car. I had a compartment to myself where I could store supplies and which had a toilet and a washbowl. Across the hall were two showers— a great addition to train travel.

Each car was a hospital ward. Some patients were bed patients, but a larger percentage were ambulatory, only there was no place to go as they had to stay in one car. They were often in groups playing bridge; or, I suspect, poker, but that wasn't supposed to show.

At some long stops, ambulatory patients were allowed to get out to stretch their legs and to enjoy the goodies at the canteens arranged by volunteers from the local towns. The very best of these was at North Platte, Nebraska. The wonderful ladies from North Platte arranged the most astonishing selection of good things—cakes, pies, cookies, sandwiches and drinks — that I have ever seen. Everyone on the trains including the staff, looked forward to that stop. However, I never had time to indulge because my job at this point was to hurry to the nearest phone and call an ice cream company from which I would buy a huge container of ice cream for the bed patients. The company never failed me, but I was always on needles and pins, as they invariably arrived at the last possible moment before the train pulled out.

I went through each car twice a day, getting requests for toilet articles, games and cigarettes, which were so freely handed out in those days. When I brought the patients the things they had requested, I picked up mail to be posted at the next stop. Of course, there was much stopping for small talk.

During that year, I crossed the United States twelve times and before I finished I had been in every state in the Union. As we progressed, the trains got shorter so there was more time to spend talking to individual patients. They were always a very polite and grateful lot. When all of the hospital cars were detached, we "dead-headed" back to San Franciso.

In the early summer of 1946, things were beginning to wind down, so I decided it was time to move on. This decision was tinged with regret, however, as it had been an exciting and rewarding time for me in the Red Cross. I had come to know and appreciate the rich diversity among Americans, had seen many of them in great pain and anguish, and had admired their courage and determination. It was an education and a growing experience I have never forgotten — excellent preparation for my subsequent life in the American Foreign Service.

Voices from Military Dependents

Coast to Coast and Back Again

Pauline E. Parker

I stood alone in an eddy of people milling about between the Boston railroad station and an entrance to the nearby subway. It was a day in October, 1942. For weeks I had been doing everything as correctly as my inexperience would allow. I had quit my job; rented the little white house in Phoenix with the proper lease; packed and stored all of our newly acquired possessions. I had driven the 1450 miles from Phoenix to Oregon, alone and within the new 40 miles per hour speed limit; I had sold our beautiful gray Plymouth coupe in Salem; I had said goodbye to all the family not scattered over the Pacific war zone; and I had endured the train trip from Portland, Oregon, to Boston, Mass. But it wasn't enough.

It was bad that the railroad company had lost my huge suitcase, and told me, as I filled out the claim form, that they had no idea when it would surface. But far worse, I realized as I stood in that crowd, Bill had neglected to tell me where to meet him. He had volunteered for the Navy and been assigned to the US Naval Communication School at Harvard, leaving me behind to tidy up the shambles that war had made of our newlywed life before joining him far across the country.

I was lucky to have gotten this far. Travel space was at a premium. The military were on the move, as were wives, children, parents and lovers, all struggling across the continent to reach each other for a few precious hours, days or weeks before being separated — perhaps forever. So long as our loved ones were still in the States, we camp followers lived on the edge of time and endeavored to be near our men until the bitter moment of farewell.

Where should I go? What should I do now? Bill was blithely confident of my abilities, but I was a young woman of small Western towns, alone in a big city in the unknown East. Panic was closing in at a gallop when a little redheaded urchin came to my rescue.

"Wharya wanna go, lady?"

"Harvard," I said.

The boy grabbed my small case and headed down the cold, clammy stone steps. I followed, fumbling for coins to tip him, too relieved by his decisiveness to worry about his motives. He waited impatiently until the right train came along, handed me my case, took his money and disappeared, off to rescue another bewildered wayfarer and earn another coin. I envied him his savoir faire.

I arrived at the Cambridge station about lunchtime. I was weary and hungry and still lost. Fortunately the Harvard gate was close by. I entered and found the famous Yard absolutely deserted. Wandering forlornly with my traveling case, I finally located Hollis Hall. A brass plaque on the stoop informed me that "George Washington quartered his troops here." I stepped inside the hall and saw no one. I fluctuated between anxiety and indecision and finally returned to the stoop, wondering what to do next. Just then, with a "hup, two, three, four" a wave of long blue overcoats and white hats came swaying across the Yard. At the foot of the stoop, the impressive formation broke apart and one piece became distinguishable as Bill Parker. The intimidating officer metamorphosed into my handsome husband, and my world was secure again.

Bill had rented a room for me on the third floor of a quiet, dignified, old home not many blocks from Harvard Yard. Gradually I became acquainted with other Navy wives. We would go to lunch and shop or explore Boston and Cambridge, then hasten back to Philip Brooks House at Harvard to await the one precious hour with our husbands before their call to dinner. The weary men poured in at 1705 hours (I was learning military time), collected their women and struggled to find tiny spaces of privacy where couples could talk about their day. At 1755 hours, the men filed back to the barracks and the wives went off to dinner in small groups before facing another night alone. At noon on Saturday, the officers were released until 2100 hours Sunday evening. We wives endured the long, idle weekdays for these few hours with our men.

In December, Bill completed his first session of communication school. We were delighted when he was chosen to remain for the air communication session. That meant that he and his colleagues were now allowed to live away from the Yard — with their wives at last.

Bill and I joined with another member of Bill's company, Stan Arthur, and his wife Gale, and rented one unit of a four-plex in Arlington, just north of Cambridge. We soon learned that our landlady had failed to have the furnace converted from oil to coal, as strongly recommended soon after Pearl Harbor. The men were the fortunate ones. They stayed in warm classrooms during one of the coldest winters in Boston history.

Gale and I found that even with the thermostat set at 65 degrees, the fuel tank was empty several days before the allotted oil delivery arrived. We piled on clothes and lived in the kitchen with the doors closed and the gas oven on. It is a wonder we were not asphyxiated.

Polly and Bill Parker May 1945. Oregon State, Corvallis, OR.

At night, when the temperature was well below zero, going upstairs to our unheated bedroom and ice-cold bed demanded all the courage Bill and I could muster. "Closeness" took on a new meaning! If electric blankets had been available, I'd have stayed bedridden until spring.

The second session of school drew to completion in February. Tension had risen since Christmas—we all knew active duty orders awaited everyone. The men quietly dreaded duty in the North Sea, where the weather was horrible and where many ships had been sunk. PT boats were flamboyant but chancy. Destroyers pitched and rolled. Cruisers and battleships were considered good duty, and aircraft carriers were the best possible sea duty, just like floating hotels. The wives were in dread of any kind of sea duty for their men.

Bill and I were relieved when he opened his orders to see: Commissioning duties on USS *Yorktown*, CV-l0 — an aircraft carrier! Commissioning duties meant that he would take part in fitting out the vessel, which was being built in Newport News, Virginia. We would have a few more weeks together. We hoped fervently that this carrier would fare better than the one carrying its name which had gone down in the Pacific on June 7, 1942.

Through the ever-present Travelers' Aid, savior to many during the war years, we found a room without kitchen privileges in the home of an elderly retired couple in Newport News. The following morning, Bill reported for duty at the Newport News Shipbuilding and Drydock Company, and I went searching for a restaurant.

Sitting alone at a table, I watched cockroaches as big as mice racing about on the ledges of the windows. I was puzzled to see a member of the Shore Patrol stationed at the entry. All was made clear when Bill returned that evening. The eating places in Newport News could not pass the armed forces sanitary inspection and were off-limits to military personnel. Of necessity, officers and men assigned to the *Yorktown* and their accompanying dependents were eating at a special general mess established for the ship's company. So, daily, we trekked over to the yard for meals and enjoyed the social interchange with other *Yorktown* people.

Bill believed that idleness and isolation would not be good for me. He saw no reason why I should not apply for employment at the huge shipyard, which was hiring on a vast scale. After two or three evenings of being greeted by "Did you apply today?" I found my courage, put aside my books and presented myself at the employment office of the Newport News Shipbuilding and Drydock Company.

The shipyards were tremendous, the massive buildings exploding with sounds of riveting, hammering and the shouts of men and women. Several Navy ships lay in various stages of construction. Towering above them all was the *Yorktown*.

The lineup at the employment office was long; but eventually I filled out a form and was hired. Next came a physical examination modeled after an assembly line. After that ordeal, I found myself in a large room filled with desks, typewriters, and women. I joined other wives and sweethearts, typing deferment forms for shipyard employees who were eligible for the draft.

When I sat at my typewriter and raised my eyes to the windows, I could see the skeletal form of the *Yorktown* looming above the buildings. Daily, the form became less a skeleton and more a ship. Each day was one nearer to the next shift in our lives.

Bill was busy helping organize the communications department of the ship but he frequently took me aboard. Work never stopped; the deafening racket of welding, jackhammering, and shouting went on around the clock.

Too soon, the day came to move her out of drydock and over to Portsmouth. Now the commissioning crew and officers had to live aboard ship. The day after the ship left the Newport News Yard, I looked out the windows from my desk and saw only sky. I knew that our time together was running out.

At each visit aboard the *Yorktown*, after an arduous trip by bus and ferry from Newport News, I was very aware of how much more finished and military it appeared. Fewer and quieter civilian workmen were about. More and more officers and crew were settling into their new life. I became accustomed to Bill's "Permission to come aboard," the replying salute, and his hand at my elbow directing me down the ladders and through the hatches to the wardroom where dinner was served — our only time together.

We had become acquainted with a veteran petty officer, Chief Steward Dordas, when he was supervisor of the general mess at Newport News. He was now supervisor of the mess aboard ship. His crew had come aboard with him.

Here, preparing and serving meals was quite different from the cafeteria system at the general mess. Despite chaotic conditions while the ship was readied, the officers' meals were served true to Navy tradition — individually from silver trays and dishes at linen-covered tables with great formality. Among many other things, the steward mates were learning to hold a heavy serving tray in one hand and, with the other, to manage the large silver serving fork and spoon somewhat in the manner of chopsticks to place food upon each dinner plate. Those first meals were fraught with uncertainty for all involved!

Dordas approached Bill each weekend to tell him to be sure to bring his little wife (he was all of five feet six himself) to dinner. "Sunday, we gonna have chickun" — or steak or whatever. So, in the first days aboard ship, Dordas used the few women guests as the focus for part of his men's training. Eleanor Roosevelt, the ship's patron, would have been impressed at the intensity of the service we received.

Far too soon, it was time to officially turn the ship over to her first captain, Joseph J. Clark. He came aboard a few days before the commissioning and was already known to be tough and gruff, his disposition conditioned by a longstanding ulcer. But he knew his stuff and, over time, his became a taut ship, known as "The Fighting Lady" for its record in battle.

The officers' wives received formal invitations to attend the commissioning ceremony. I fussed over the proper things to wear for so momentous an occasion. Aboard the ferry, I faced up to the fact that "This is it.

U.S.S. Yorktown

After today, the Navy will be Bill's world completely and I will be on my own for a long time." I felt a kinship with the *Yorktown*. As her framework had emerged into a fighting ship and she had developed her own identity, my dependent life was disappearing and I was slowly gaining confidence in my own ability. We both had to face the future with fortitude. I felt both proud and apprehensive.

Polly (Pauline E.) Parker, Lake Oswego, Ore., Sept. 1996.

April 15, 1943, was a clear, bright day. Flags and pennants were flying and the ship sparkled in the sun when I arrived at the dock. Bill barely had time to usher me aboard and take me to the guest area on the flight deck. Soon the dignitaries arrived and the officers and men, all in dress uniform, lined up on deck. It was a glorious, tear-inspiring sight. The bugle sounded "Attention!" and the chaplain gave the invocation. Rear Admiral M. H. Simons, Commandant, Fifth Naval District, introduced the Assistant Secretary of the Navy for Air, whose address to the officers, crew and guests has escaped my memory long since. Newport News Ship Building and Dry Dock Company officially turned the USS *Yorktown* over to the US Navy.

The commandant ordered "Sound colors" and the Marine guard presented arms while the band played the national anthem. We all stood while pennants snapped smartly in the sea breeze. The proper colors were hoisted and the commandant turned the ship over to Captain Clark, who read his orders and accepted the ship. The watch was set and the captain ordered "Pipe down."

Officers and crew were dismissed. Official guests and the few wives present joined the officers for an impressive reception in the wardroom put on beautifully by Chief Dordas and his steward mates. The USS *Yorktown* (CV-10) was ready to join the fleet. And ready or not, I had to wend my way back to the West Coast to wait out the war.

The Unpredictable Life of a G.I. Wife

Roberta Jamieson Locher

They also serve who sit and wait.

During the fall of 1940, all single men of the Selective Service age bracket watched anxiously as the draft numbers were drawn. My fiancé, Calvin Locher, found his number far enough down the list that we calculated his call-up date would probably be in the summer of 1941. We planned to be married on Saturday, February 22 of that year. That meant I could pass up a teaching contract for 1941-42 since Calvin would not have to go into service. At that time, only single men were drafted. But we had miscalculated badly.

As Calvin and I prepared for our wedding, several things happened to challenge us. First of all, an arsonist set fire to my dad's church in Colusa, California, where we planned to get married. Fortunately, the big parsonage next door to the church did not burn. The second problem was the weather. It rained every day in January and February until the day before the wedding. The last straw was Calvin's letter from the President which arrived just a few days before the wedding. It contained his call-up for the draft officially set for February 24, two days after our wedding date! After the small, but beautiful, wedding, and an overnight honeymoon tempered with the knowledge of our pending separation, he left to report for duty.

This was the beginning of our becoming a part of the armed forces. We were rapidly learning that the Army was not always to be counted on to do what was expected. Calvin thought he was going to Ft. Ord, California, the induction center near Monterey. He went there overnight and was sent on to Ft. Lewis, in Washington State, to become part of the 162nd Infantry of the 41st Division. This set of events began my own G.I. training—"Learn to be patient while you wait." I began a new routine, writing a letter every night.

Our first chance to see each other was at Easter in April, just before Calvin's initial six weeks training time would be over. I met him at an Olympia hotel. We made the most of our short time together and too soon, we were getting me ready to catch a Sunday bus back to Sacramento. We knew we would not see each other again until school closed in June. From the bus window, I observed the Easter Sunday flowers all the way home. This was the first Easter Sunday I had missed church.

It was back to the tasks at San Juan High School near Sacramento where I was experiencing my second year of teaching. My personal project for the next few weeks was to get my driver's license so I could drive to wherever Calvin was to be located for the summer.

As the time neared for vacation, I learned that Calvin's Army unit was to be at Hunter Ligget Military Reservation to take part in extensive maneuvers. Hunter Ligget was near King City, California, south of Monterey. Things worked out well. I rented a motel room in King City, near the base, and Calvin came in as often as he could. Each time, after I drove him back to camp, I would drive the twenty or so miles over a twisty, dusty road back "home" by myself. I felt very much alone and inexperienced, as I drove our big black Nash, the only civilian car in the midst of constant Army convoys. I always felt safe, but I usually felt blind. The high-bodied trucks in front and behind me had glaring lights. All I could see was the shadow of my car in front of me. I just followed red tail lights.

Soon our days there met with a pleasant surprise. The California troops were given passes of several days to report for duty at Ft. Lewis individually. We packed and drove north together to Tacoma, Washington, where we located an apartment before Calvin had to be back at Ft. Lewis. We were happy to "set up housekeeping" using some of our wedding gifts. Once settled at Ft. Lewis, Calvin found out his commanding officer allowed no soldiers, not even officers, to live with families on-base or off-. The men were given passes from late Wednesday afternoons until ten P.M. and half days Saturday and Sunday. No one was happy with the CO.

Our summer grew short and Calvin's outfit was to leave for a second set of maneuvers. Training was to be in the rain forest of the Olympic Peninsula—a real contrast with the California maneuvers. This time Calvin and I knew it would be Christmas before we could see each other again. Soon I welcomed in my third class of freshmen.

Calvin and Roberta Locher, February 22, 1941.

National plans were being made to alternate the current draftees in the service with a new crop and to muster out the early ones after their year of service. This talk was heartwarming to us and I began to plan for Calvin's return to civilian life. Then came Pearl Harbor.

On the Monday after, we turned radios on at school to hear what was going on. The news was sobering to teachers and students alike. During that week we began to notice an increase in the fly-overs of pilots training at nearby Mather Field. Sometimes the planes would dive over a girls P.E. class on the outdoor fields. Once in awhile on a weekend, they would "bomb" the school parking lot with bags of flour. There was an increase of truck traffic on our main road, Greenback Lane, as they transported gravel to the air bases.

At school we participated in the community war work. As the result of being assigned the drama activities, Phebe and I were asked to produce programs to take to the Army hospital in nearby Auburn. The local Red Cross chapter hired a bus to take us there once a month. Our students were faithful in working on our performances. Sometimes they would present part of a play we were producing for school. Other times, we'd develop a variety show. Often portions of these were taken into wards after the main show was over.

The performances in "locked wards" were different. Here, special numbers, usually musical, were done for young men suffering nervous shock from battle experiences. The nurses hoped the music and the young people would touch the faraway minds and bring them home.

A ward episode not to be forgotten was the Can-Can line dance in the paraplegic ward one evening. The nurses had a glint in their eyes when they took those girls into that ward. The girls made their line down the middle of the big ward and did their dance. Part way through, the dancer on the end slipped on the slick floor and the whole line went down! The girls were mortified, but as the nurses had hoped, the patients all howled. The nurses wanted these crippled men to see pretty girls fall down, too. The event was helpful to some very despondent young men.

We often had scrap metal collections which were subsequently used in making items for which supplies were short. One interesting collection we had was used postage stamps. As the war went on, some dyes for our stamps were in short supply. They had come from Germany. We turned in our stamps in large quantities so the dyes could be extracted and reused.

While we were becoming accustomed to a wartime tempo, Calvin was working with his company as they, too, took on a wartime complexion. As Christmas drew near, Calvin put my name on the list at the new guest accommodations at Fort Lewis which were to be ready for occupancy during the holidays. Right up to the day before vacation we had not gotten word that the guest accommodations were open for occupancy.

A teacher from Salem, Oregon, was driving home and offered me a ride that far. Calvin met me in a borrowed car, and settled me into the new guest quarters. I ate at the troop mess and met the fellows with whom

Calvin worked, some of whom I had met on previous occasions. Later we went to our quarters and I took out Christmas decorations I had made.

That evening, the officers received sealed orders to leave for another assignment. This brought a lot of confusion to Company K of the 162nd Infantry. The menfolk had expected to be sent to Missoula, Montana, to guard a railroad point. In true Army style, the orders did not fit expectations. The move was to guard the local airport at Olympia, just a few miles down the road. The whole unit left the established living quarters and set up a tent bivouac under tall evergreens across the road from the airport.

Two young officers' wives and I changed our plans from driving to Montana to apartment hunting in Olympia. We found a very nice one a couple blocks away from the state capitol building. We made a trip to the commissary at the fort to shop for food and supplies. The Military Police showed no hesitancy in letting us in, and we had no trouble purchasing supplies. When it came time to leave, the guards balked at letting us out. After a time, the MPs came, told us how to get the proper ID for exiting the base and let us go. I was glad to be with officers' wives.

The men were now in uniform all the time. They carried their gas masks, rifles, and side arms. The atmosphere became very much like the movies we saw of World War I. The civilian folks from Olympia came out on sightseeing jaunts to experience the feel of being in the Army. I remember one man asking Calvin if the pack over his shoulder was his lunch. Calvin explained it was his gas mask. The civilian's eyes grew large.

The airport had three places to visit — our husbands' tents, if it was O.K. with his tent-mates; the office/waiting room of the small airport; and the diner across the road from the airport. The troops tended to seek refuge inside the diner. They enjoyed the nickelodeon which they played constantly while they nursed their sodas or beers or ate food. One of the tunes played over and over was "San Antonio Rose."

We dependents were to have Christmas dinner with the troops. This, like all of the meals, was to be held outdoors like a huge picnic. The ladies in Olympia had roasted turkeys for the whole unit. The Army cooks were operating from a field kitchen. The drawback was the sub-freezing temperature all day. A large washtub had been set up with a fire built under it. The idea was, as you passed through the food line, to dip your aluminum mess kit into the hot water to warm it just before being served. The idea was not too successful because the water froze before the food was all on the kit. We ate with one hand until it was too cold, then we swapped hands and put the cold hand in a deep, warm pocket and ate with the other hand for a while. We continued this swapping through a tasty meal of usual holiday fare.

The beginning of 1942 found all of us digging in, doing our jobs to the best of our ability. For those on the Pacific Coast, the slowness of our comeback in the conflict depressed us.

Events of those early months of the war included the internment of Japanese Americans on the Pacific Coast. We had only a few Japanese students at San Juan, but we were deeply saddened to see these second generation, loyal, hard-working children and their families be locked up at Camp Kholar with its barbed-wire fences until they were moved to permanent camps at Tule Lake, California, or to other camps on our high deserts.

At school, we had more and more young men being drafted or volunteering. Many of them would write back to their English class or just to me. I wrote my "book" over those years, one letter at a time—Calvin got his letter first, then the students.

One thing hard to realize is that for all the first year I lived without easy access to a telephone. The Bogarts, where I lived during the school year, had no phone. We borrowed a neighbor's in a pinch. So when Calvin was supposed to telephone me at the high school on the Sunday of our anniversary, I was there waiting. When no call came, I hurried to the telephone office and placed a person-to-person call to him. The response on the other end of the line was "The 42nd Division has left—destination unknown!" Another unexpected Army action—a gift for my first anniversary.

In the mail a day or two later, I received a long letter. Calvin had worked around the clock helping to prepare his unit for shipping out and could not stand in line for hours to use the phone. He wrote while on a troop train headed for New York.

Then I got a letter from Fort Dix, port of debarkation. After that, there was nothing but silence until Easter week. One of my neighbors across the street came running over to say the Western Union Office in Roseville had a cable for me. That was scary! The message they read me over the neighbor's phone was from Calvin who was in Australia! This was the first war-area cable the Western Union office had received and they wanted to get the word out promptly. They had checked with the phone company to find the telephone nearest to my address. Their action certainly impressed me and gave me relief. His 80-plus-year-old grandfather, who had raised him, had a stroke from worry a week before I got my message and was dead when it arrived.

Calvin's outfit spent the entire war in the South Pacific. They trained in Australia, and moved north for combat engagements through New Guinea and an assortment of islands. He was with the company headquarters most of the time and had hair-raising experiences and attacks of tropical fevers. His "points," accumulated from time on active duty and factored into the decision as to when a military man would return home, were high.

In the early summer of 1945, while U.S. troops were taking back the Philippine Islands, Calvin began his trip home. He came back on a ship that kept breaking down all the way across the Pacific. The war was still on and enemy submarines still did some roaming. A stalled ship was highly vulnerable. When the ship got to Hawaii, the passengers headed for the Pacific Coast were put on a different ship, much to their relief.

On August 6, the ship Calvin was on received word that the A-bomb had been dropped on Hiroshima! Calvin arrived in Bremerton on August 9. He was transported to Camp Beale near Marysville, California, to be discharged. Since he had been quite sick on the way home, he had a round in the base hospital for a checkup.

On August 15, the Japanese surrender was announced. Everything, everywhere broke loose. The powers-that-be decided everyone in the hospital able to walk would have a pass. Calvin came with me to his uncle's house in Yuba City nearby. After that weekend he had to go back to the hospital. He finally had his records completed and was ready to get his discharge papers after slightly more than four and a half years in the service.

After the war was over and Calvin was home, I received a bag of his "effects" from the Effects Quartermaster Office. In the box were some interesting battle area trinkets, other personal things and only the large frame from a picture of me he had carried with him. Throughout the war, the Effects Quartermaster Office personnel selected out anything in a soldier's effects that might possibly be construed as indicating indiscreet conduct, to protect the dependents as well as the soldier. They were not sure the picture in the frame was of Calvin's wife, so they did not send it home.

The one thing I want to leave this account with is a recognition of the pervading feeling of loneliness and sense of something missing that filled the whole time until Calvin came home to stay. This was a time when I prayed without ceasing, with soul-felt prayer for the well-being of Calvin and his counterparts underlying everything I did. God did give comfort, but the empty spot was always there. Our joy was full when he got home. We had waited so long for these hours that we found it easy to solve problems which came up. Serious family health problems found us strong enough to work together to take care of them. We were ready to begin a new phase of life: our long awaited family. We gave our thanks to God and launched our new life expectantly.

Missing Myles

Roberta I. Ludwig

My husband, Myles Gordon Ludwig, and I were married at a Presbyterian Church in Vancouver, Washington, on November 10, 1940. We were only 19 years old. My father, Paul Dawson, was a disabled World War I veteran. He died shortly after we were married. We were so glad that he got to see us married.

We had our first home in Albany, Oregon. Myles worked in a meat market six days a week, from 7:00 AM to 7:00 PM, for $16.75 a week. I baby-sat for ten cents an hour and for twenty cents an hour I did heavy house cleaning.

Myles was drafted when he turned 21 and joined the Navy on August 27, 1942. After boot camp in San Diego, he was sent to cooks' school in San Diego. There he learned to cook and bake bread, pies and cakes in big quantities the Navy way. When he left Albany, his boss at the meat market hired me to wash pans, grind meat for hamburger and keep the showcases clean.

We had wanted a child but decided we would wait until Myles came back. So, a week after he left, I got up to go to work, ate my breakfast and lost it. Here was our baby coming! I moved out of our apartment and in with my mother, now a widow. Our baby was due April 28th. On the 27th, Myles sent me a telegram telling me that he was going by train to Norfolk, Virginia. When he got there, he sent his new address and said, "What do we have?" So I sent back that I was still waiting. On May 5, 1943, Jane Mylene Ludwig was born. I paid the doctor $35 for delivering Jane and had a private room for $6 a day. I stayed ten days flat on my back and was very weak when they said, "Get up and go home."

I received $50 a month that came out of his pay and $30 more from the military after our baby was born. Congress passed a bill in June of 1943 that the maternity expenses of servicemen's children would be paid for. I sent them all of the information on Jane Mylene Ludwig and got a nice letter back saying that she was six weeks old when they passed the bill so they would not pay her expenses.

Myles and his shipmates were sent from Norfolk to Orange, Texas, where their ship was being built. It was a small ship with about 250 men, a destroyer escort that was to accompany troop ships and supply ships over to the Italian side. It was named the USS *Farquhar* DE139. He and his shipmates were all "plank owners" of the USS *Farquhar* because they were the first crew to man this ship. He was on board until the war ended. In the summer of 1944, they were in the Atlantic taking a convoy to Italy when a German sub surfaced ahead of them. They left the convoy to chase the sub when another German sub came from behind the convoy and sank the USS *Fiske* DE 143. The *Farquhar* stopped to pick up survivors but 33 men were lost. The *Farquhar* put into Boston with the wounded.

A side note: In September of 1984, my husband and I flew to Charleston, S.C., to the National Destroyer Escort Convention and I saw a man wearing a hat that said, "USS *Fiske* DE 143." I said to him, "Were you on the *Fiske* when it sank?" and he said, "Lady, I was." I told him that my husband was on the *Farquhar* that picked them up and he said he had waited all of these years to thank them. The last weekend in April, the shipmates of the *Farquhar* have a reunion on the east coast. In 1984, they invited the shipmates of the *Fiske* to join them and they have every year since.

In the spring of 1944, Myles wrote me a letter from Casablanca asking me to meet him in New York. I was to go to a certain hotel to wait for him. The letters were censored and words were cut out, but I knew he would be in New York about May 15th. When I got that information, I didn't think about clothes, the train ride from Oregon or anything. I only thought about getting to see him. My mother stayed home from work to take care of Jane and I went by train five nights and four days, sitting up, to meet him.

I got off the train with my luggage because if you checked it, it might not be there when you got off. I took a taxi to the hotel and waited for several days. The manager was very nice and told me some sights to see that didn't cost much money while I waited. I didn't go out at night. Myles didn't show up and I didn't have money to stay any longer, so I went home. About the middle of June, he called one night and said, "I'm in New York." I said, "Well, I'm not." The ship had left Casablanca and sailed up off the coast of France, chasing German subs on D Day, and, like he said, "There are no mail boxes in the Atlantic."

In the spring of 1945, he once again got word to me to meet him in New York at a certain hotel. That time, I took two-year old Jane with me. She was very good on the long train ride. We got to the hotel and that night she was asleep and the phone rang. I answered it and I could hear my husband's voice talking to the desk clerk and the clerk saying that there was no Mrs. Ludwig registered there. I was yelling into the phone, but nobody heard me. I heard him say, "Well, when she does get there have her come to Boston." The clerk said, "What's wrong with our hotel?" and he said, "Probably nothing, but my ship put into Boston and she should go to the Minerva Hotel." I picked up my daughter and went downstairs to see the clerk and give him a piece of my mind. He had me down as Mrs. Myles.

The next morning, Jane and I got on another train and went to Boston. We got off the train and I tried to get a taxi, but every driver said, "Get the next one." Finally I asked a man selling newspapers why they wouldn't take me and he said that they only wanted to go between North and South train stations because they were sure of a fare each way. He said, "Just get in the cab and then tell them." Another Army wife was trying to get a taxi to go to a hotel to see her husband, so I told her we would share the taxi and we got in. The driver said "Where to?" We told him and he swore all the way there about how we had tricked him. I paid him the fare but no tip because of his language.

My husband got to come every other night to stay all night and Jane wasn't a bit afraid of him. She had seen lots of pictures of her dad in his uniform and I talked about him a lot to her. The ship was in Boston for 18 days for repairs before they went through the Panama Canal to the South Pacific. Our being together was worth all the struggle.

The war ended and Myles had enough points to get out. He got so many for the length of time he had served, for being married and for having a child. His ship was going on to Japan, but he and a shipmate were taken off and they sat on a small island in the South Pacific waiting to come home. I didn't hear from him or know what was going on. Finally they got on an old Dutch freighter that broke down and had to be towed to San Pedro, California. There he was put on a train and sent to Bremerton, Washington, going right through our home town but he couldn't let me know. He was discharged in Bremerton and came to Portland on a bus, but didn't have enough money for fare to Albany, so he called and my brother, daughter and I picked him up at the bus depot. It was a happy reunion.

My mother had said we were welcome to stay with her as she had a three bedroom house, but my younger brother was home from the Navy and she told me, "If you are smart, you will get a place so you can adjust and he can get to know Jane."

We rented a three-room apartment in the upper part of an old house for $20 a month and got furniture at an auction house. Jane's crib was in the kitchen. We had an old refrigerator in the bedroom with a hot plate on it so Myles could eat breakfast and get to work by 7:00 and we wouldn't wake Jane.

We were so happy to be together again. Susan Kay was born ten months after Myles got home and Sally Jo twenty-two months later and little Mary Lou seven years after Sally. He loved all of his daughters and spent time with them. Myles passed away May 11, 2000, on a golf course in Placerville, California, while golfing with our oldest daughter.

We would have been married 60 years on November 10, 2000.

A Different View of the War

Luree Hughes

We read lots of stories about service and combat experiences during World War II. They are exciting, horrifying, tragic, and dramatic. Then we hear about those who were on the homefront — Rosie the Riveter — those who worked 12 hour shifts in the defense plants, and those who helped develop products for prosecuting the war more efficiently.

Then there are those who did not fit into any of these categories. I was one of them. My husband, Ken, was called to active duty in September of 1942, after waiting two years for admittance to Air Force Officers' Training. When he left, we were living in Berkeley, California, where he had found a job in August, 1942, as a food inspector for the Army procurement service while waiting for active duty.

I had worked part-time at the Berkeley Public Library during those months; but, faced with an unknown time of supporting myself, I sought a full-time job. Jobs were not hard to find, and almost immediately I went to work in a biological experimental laboratory at the University of California, Berkeley, raising experimental animals (rats).

Apparently the management deduced that I was capable of something more, so I was transferred shortly to the place where the experiments were performed. There I met Mig, another service wife, whose Navy husband, Rudy, had just left for duty in the Pacific. We immediately were attracted to each other and made plans to share an apartment, if one could be found. I was living in a rented room and she with an elderly distant cousin. By great good fortune, we did find an apartment just five blocks from the campus. It was the lower floor of an old house, and rented for $65 a month. Since our salaries were $125 a month, we could easily split the cost.

So Mig and I settled in. First we had to pool our ration coupons and agree on how to spend them. We decided on margarine instead of butter. But we had to agree to take turns mixing the little packet of color with the margarine, a fairly unpleasant task! In those days it was illegal for the manufacturers of margarine to pre-color the butter substitute. We vowed to drink coffee sans cream or sugar, which freed more rationed goodies. We also agreed to be free at any time to veer from our intended path to wait in lines for such scarcities as steak, cigarettes, or certain cosmetic products. If we couldn't use all the cigarettes, they were a good bargaining agent.

And what did we do for amusement? Well, there were always movies. Since this was before television, we had to go out to a theater, which was more of a social experience. Often we'd see someone we knew, and that meant a trip to a local confectioner for whatever they had in stock to drink. This choice might be quite limited. "There's a war on, you know!" We rode crowded streetcars, carrying home groceries in two bags, one in each arm, standing in a mob that kept us upright when the car started and stopped. Or we walked.

If there was any hint of difficulty we found someone in uniform and didn't hesitate to ask for assistance. Once another friend, Marian, and I were going to Modesto to visit her in-laws. Her husband had just shipped out to Europe with a field artillery unit. She was driving a Model A Ford coupe, and had saved ration coupons to be able to buy gas for the trip. Rain was coming down in sheets, and suddenly the windshield wiper fell off. We stopped and searched in the pouring rain but couldn't retrieve it. There was nothing for it but to go on, which she did by leaning out the window to see the road. Shortly we came by a sailor hitchhiking in our direction. Without giving it a thought, we stopped and picked him up, reasoning that under the circumstances, it would be good for us to have a man along. It never occurred to us to be cautious. We showed the sailor what the problem was, but he didn't mind going along with us. Needless to say, the traffic in central California was quite different at that time. We laughed, joked and sang all the rest of the way to Modesto. He didn't ask questions about us, nor did we question him.

Sometimes we could find a small ethnic restaurant, which were not nearly so numerous then as now, but there were Italian places offering pizza, baked in the old-fashioned stone ovens. It was the original Italian lunch, a delicious dough with tomato sauce and cheese, a great novelty in our diet. Or we would transfer from the Key System train to a streetcar and spend the day in Golden Gate Park. It was a lovely, green, restful place, a retreat from noise and reminders of the war. It was also a favorite place for servicemen on leave to spend time with their girls.

Having an "in" with the Navy, Mig often knew of the pending arrival of a naval vessel in San Francisco Bay. Sometimes they came in for repairs at one of the shipyards. One of our favorite activities was to take the train to San Francisco, then a streetcar to near the south end of the Golden Gate Bridge. From there we could walk out on the pedestrian way on the bridge and watch as the Navy vessels came in through the Golden Gate and under the bridge. They often came in during daytime, with all hands in dress whites standing in formation on the deck. What a thrill to watch it! We located a piece of flag-like bunting and waved it enthusiastically from the bridge, shouting and whooping.

The day Rudy's ship came in through the Golden Gate we both played hooky from work to be on the bridge. We did inform our usually stern and rigid boss of what we intended to do and she responded with reluctant permission, but there was a twinkle in her eye.

And then, in the spring of 1945, the United Nations Conference on International Organization was held in San Francisco. What an opportunity! We came home from work, grabbed a quick bite, and hopped a train for San Francisco. We stationed ourselves outside one of the major hotels where the delegates stayed, and watched as the limousines pulled up and the passengers descended. We could occasionally recognize a famous face, such as Anthony Eden, British Foreign Secretary; Jan Christian Smuts, Prime Minister of South Africa; or Commissar M. Molotov of the U.S.S.R. Edward R. Stettinius of the U.S. was often visible. If we did not recognize the person, then we could play a guessing game about who it might be, recalling all the famous names of which we had read. And then might come a series of limos, discharging tall, impressive Arabs in their flowing desert dress.

And, finally, came the drama in the Greek Theatre in Berkeley, at which the principals of the conference were awarded honorary degrees by the university. Of course, the general public did not have access to the theater, but there is a lot of hill rising up behind the constructed seating. Believe me, the bare hill was well populated during the ceremony. The lucky ones had binoculars, but the rest of us just enjoyed the drama of the ceremony and watching the famous people on stage. What a different world it was then! No one worried too much about snipers on the hill.

And then there were the long evenings spent reading and writing letters. I was very blessed, as Ken was stationed in a non-combat zone in Alaska. But Rudy was "somewhere in the Pacific," and fortunately Mig did not know the whole story. After he arrived home we learned that he was on a destroyer escort with the Fifth Fleet, which spearheaded the whole island-hopping drive in the Pacific. His ship had even taken two kamikaze attacks.

The end of the war was a stunning event. When we heard of the dropping of the atom bomb on Hiroshima, Mig and I held each other and cried. But then came V-J Day! Once again we took off for San Francisco to whoop it up with the deliriously happy crowds there. I'm glad to have experienced it, for never again could one feel joyously safe in a milling, celebrating crowd of thousands of total strangers, cheering, singing, and hugging each other.

We service wives spent many lonely hours, and for some, like Mig, there was always the question: "Will he come back?" But at the same time, we experienced a society unknown to the next generation — one of uniformity of purpose, overwhelming honesty, and caring for each other.

Three War Wives and a Rooster

Lunette Mulkey

I had just dozed off when that rooster crowed. His cock-a-doodle-do reverberated in and out of my semi-consciousness.

Now, I've never held any resentment toward a rooster. In fact, I've always had a high degree of respect for the fowl. God must have had a good reason to endow him with the ability to see over the horizon in order to tell us that another day of life is on the way — long before most of us are ready to wake up and face that day.

So I really feel a guilt complex developing when I think of what happened to that certain rooster that January day in Overland Park, Kansas, back in 1945. Of course, the rooster didn't know that we three war wives living in that house had not heard from our husbands for over three weeks. And further, that sleep was a commodity so elusive we dared not utter the word.

That rooster didn't know that Leah's husband had closed his plumbing shop, joined the Seabees and was somewhere in the south Pacific — a long way from Kansas. He didn't know that Kay's husband had turned the keys to his appliance store over to an assistant and was now running trains across Germany, carrying wounded men and supplies to and from the front lines. And, of course, that rooster had no way of knowing (although I had probably told him) that my dear M C and I had closed our upholstery shop, that M C was no longer building new custom upholstered furniture and tufting antique loveseats.

That rooster couldn't have known that M C was over in Belgium where the Battle of the Bulge was raging all around him. He couldn't have known that Montgomery's army was on the north and that Bradley's was on the south, while Von Rundstedts' army was pushing from the east, showering German buzz bombs on the Allies' ordnance companies caught in the middle.

At that time, we war wives were not privy to all this information either. We were to hear the details some weeks later. So, on this particular morning, anxiety and exhaustion reigned supreme. We knew that something of grave consequence had to be taking place. Something sufficiently important to prevent, for three weeks, the arrival of letters from our loved ones.

We three sisters had decided to keep ourselves busy, pool our resources, and add to our war-time incomes by making slip covers and drapery. We were all living in Leah's home. A drapery work shop was set up in the basement, but we carried our portable Singer and all our tools and equipment needed for slip-cover making into our customers' homes. We alternated, two of us working in the customers' homes, and the third remaining at home to care for the two children — my toddling son and Leah's five-year old daughter, Patty.

The previous day, Leah and I had worked long hours finishing a slip cover for Mrs. Potter's large wing-backed chair. The Potters lived well into Kansas City and we were living at the outskirts of greater Kansas City. We could not afford to make a second trip. Every gallon of gas must bear fruit. The "boys" had left us a '39 Chevy, boasting three slick tires and one good spare.

For me to be away from my young son for 14 hours was something he had not previously experienced. Leah and I arrived home long after sundown that evening. When Y.B. (Young Bill) saw me, he came bundling toward me — his torso ahead of his inexperienced feet. As I knelt down, he stumbled into my arms and the expression on his face is something that is etched in my memory forever. I was his whole world, naturally. He had never seen his father. His life had consisted of one long kaleidoscope of unfamiliar scenery and persons. In order to assure him that I would not disappear and to get him to sleep, I tucked him into bed with me. So the night gave both of us only a fitful rest. It seemed the deepest portion of my slumber was just before that rooster crowed.

Now I have heard a rooster crow when the cock-a-doodle-do was as soothing as the music of the carillon wafting over from the church belfry across the town. But on this particular morning, my tolerance held no compassion for that singing fowl. He surely was right under our bedroom window. I jumped out of bed, pulled on some heavy shoes, threw on an old coat and started toward the outside door.

"Where are you going?" Leah asked. She couldn't sleep either.
"I'm going to catch that rooster,"
"Well, I'm going to help you."
We agreed that I would go to the northeast corner of the house and wait for Leah to circle in the other direction and shoo the bird toward me so I could lunge out and catch him. I lunged, the rooster eluded me, flapped his wings and took off toward a patch of weeds at the back of the yard. Leah was not far behind him. I gathered myself up and joined her. The weeds were mostly frozen stubble and the rooster was using his wings more than his feet to keep from being submerged in it. All the while he was uttering raspy, deep-throated sounds as though he were scolding us.

We continued to lunge — always missing. Leah made one long thrust and fell so hard I felt sure she was hurt. I went to where she had landed in the stubble and helped her to a sitting position. The rooster, who had found a perch on a stump, stood with his head cocked to one side, still uttering his scolding. (It could have been cursing.)

The ridiculous situation finally touched our sense of humor. We sat in the weeds, our arms around each other, both crying and laughing hysterically. The tensions of the past weeks broke loose and we relaxed for the first time in days.

"Aunt Kay said that breakfast is ready, and for you not to bring that rooster in the house." Little Patty stood at the edge of the weeds in her robe and slippers. The expression on her face caused us to break into further wild laughter. The rooster, still on his perch, had stopped his horrid screeching and I was sure he was about to come out with a victorious cock-a-doodle-do. We put our arms around Patty and rushed to the house and breakfast.

That evening we had a knock at the kitchen door. A neighbor handed us a package. "We thought the performance in the weed patch this morning deserved a chicken dinner." We thanked him, of course, but our faces blanched.

"Oh, your package doesn't contain the rooster," he added. "He was a pet so we gave him — alive — to my nephew."

We had another good laugh. The chickens had been raised to be killed and put in their freezer, and our little episode gave the neighbors a good excuse to get the job done. Needless to say, that rooster never crowed under our bedroom window again. And, in due time, all three of our husbands returned home from the battle grounds.

I'd Rather Have Joined the WAC

Virginia Raymond Ott

I would rather have joined the WAC (Women's Army Corps) but, with three children under fourteen, I was not eligible.

As the wife of a colonel of the U.S. Army Corps of Engineers and a person who grew up in an Army family, I was used to the exigencies of the service. To me, the home front in World War II was like having the men off on maneuvers, only, of course, we knew they were in deadly danger. I admired so much the civilian wives to whom this was all new, strange and frightening.

At the time of Pearl Harbor, the children and I were at Vancouver Barracks, Washington, while my husband was on temporary duty at Ft. Lewis. Afterward he was issued permanent orders to Ft. Lewis. I packed up our belongings and, with a bit of trepidation, set off in the car, before dawn on New Year's Eve, into the dark with snow falling. We made the trip safely and were lucky enough to be given quarters on the post instead of having to find housing in one of the nearby towns.

After six months, my husband was ordered to a new division, the 104th (Timberwolves) at Camp Adair, Oregon. The nearest we could find a place for the family to live was in Salem, and there our third child, Elizabeth, was born. When she was six months old, my husband was ordered overseas, destination unknown. It turned out to be England.

My parents lived in a small town in upstate New York and I decided to go there. We packed and headed east by train. My husband had to report first in Washington, D.C., so we parted company at Chicago. The children and I went on to Erie, Pennsylvania, to visit his parents. While we were there, I accompanied my mother-in-law to the Red Cross to make bandages and dressings.

Our car had been driven across country by a couple of young officers. I drove it the rest of the way to my parents' home. Their house had plenty of room but my eldest sister and an aunt were already living there and I thought that adding four of us would be too much of a burden for my mother. I kept looking for a house of our own. Eventually, one turned up just down the street and I moved in on New Year's Day 1944. A few weeks later, my father died. That was the week our troops landed at Anzio. One of my brothers was there.

The night before my father's funeral, the telephone rang. My husband, Chester, was calling from New York. Could someone come pick him up if he could get on a train to Albany? I nearly collapsed! While I thought he was in England and had sent word to him there about my father's death, he was actually on the north Atlantic on a secret mission to Washington. He sailed on the Queen Elizabeth, which at the beginning of the war had been converted to a troop ship and was so fast that she dared to sail those U-boat-infested waters without an escort. He had a few days of leave before reporting in Washington. As the officer in charge of all engineering supplies for the European Theater, he had come to speed up delivery of materiel needed for D-Day.

He spent several weeks in the U.S., and after a few days of lonely living in a hotel, called and begged me to join him. It took a bit of doing to persuade me to leave my recently widowed mother with the three children, but she had good help and Chester's wooing was hard to resist; we had some precious time together.

During that winter of 1943–44, I spent a great deal of time hauling stuff between my mother's house and ours. My kitchen had no source of heat and was built over a cistern so the floor was always cold. I was able to buy a gas stove for cooking, which required a propane tank. One tank lasted three weeks. This became pretty expensive, so I used the oven as little as possible. My mother had a big old coal stove. Every day she put a potato in the oven to bake for my baby, who was by then on solid food. I would collect the hot potato and go home with it in my coat pocket.

My house was heated by a coal furnace and part of my daily activity was shoveling coal into it. The previous occupant had left a large pile of ashes in the cellar and the pile kept getting bigger and bigger. I was able to find a local man who agreed to remove the ashes if he could find a helper. Since most of the men were off to the war and the boys were in school, he couldn't find anyone. So I volunteered. We spent the better part of a day shoveling ashes out of the cellar and, when I finished, I had a head of beautiful gray hair.

During the summer we lived with my parents, we worked very hard, "doing our bit." My parents had a large vegetable garden and we were always shelling peas or snapping beans, most of which my mother canned. We were allowed to pick up wind-fall apples on the grounds of the local hospital or in a cousin's orchard, which Mother made into applesauce and canned. With such an extended family, we had plenty of ration stamps so we ate well. Six family members had back-to-back birthdays and we celebrated them with one cake, thus saving sugar. The only problem was shoe stamps. You could buy sandals or non-leather shoes without a stamp; but, when the baby was ready for her first pair of real shoes, none were available in the stores so she inherited a pair from one of her small cousins. Elastic was unavailable, too, and her training panties were held up with tape drawstrings. She was a real war-time baby!

That summer, my ten-year-old and I were recruited to act as official airplane spotters. We spent many hours in the tower of the J. B. Rice Seed Company, scanning the skies for enemy planes. It seems far-fetched now, but we never knew what the enemy might do and our town was on the direct flight path to the General Electric plant in Schenectady.

After I had been in my house for three months, I got word that my husband was ill with tuberculosis and soon to be returned to the United States, or Zone of the Interior, as it was called. His job in England had been planning and preparing for the invasion of France. On D-Day, he was already back in the U.S. in Halloran Hospital on Staten Island, New York, and the children and I were still up in the country.

On D-Day, early in the morning, we heard on the radio that the invasion had begun with landings in Normandy. I unfurled a large map of Europe I had been saving and taped it to a wall, and — still in my nightgown, bathrobe and slippers — hurried up Main Street to my mother's house to tell her the news. All the church bells in town began to toll. Later, my family and I joined others in our parish church to receive the Eucharist and pray for the safety of our men. Our own family had 20 in uniform.

I was back at my mother's when the Japanese surrendered on V-J Day and the war was over at last. When we heard the news, I remember saying about my two-year old daughter, "This is the first night she has lived in peacetime."

Chamber Pots and Steel Findings

Margaret Bader Crawford

News of the attack on Pearl Harbor caught me dusting my apartment in Silverton, Colorado. I felt stunned. Such shocking news. I was particularly fearful because the young man I was dating was the right age to be called up for military duty. Despite Pearl Harbor, Robert ("Bud") Crawford and I became engaged at Christmas in 1941.

My fear for Bud became a reality in May, 1942, when he volunteered and was accepted into the Army. He was sent to Camp Stoneman in Pittsburg, California. We decided I would visit him during Christmas vacation. I had two weeks off from the school where I was teaching. In the give and take over the phone, the issue in my mind kept being skirted, so I finally suggested we get married while I was visiting. Bud agreed, to my delight. I would then return to Silverton and finish my school year. Bud's mother and my mother quickly volunteered to accompany me to Pittsburg.

December 23, 1942, the day Corporal Robert A. Crawford and Miss Ruth Margaret Bader were to tie the knot, arrived on a blustery breeze, bringing both rain and fog to the nuptials. Chaplain Major McClain led us down an aisle to the front of the Camp Stoneman chapel, which was decorated with pots of red poinsettias. There we were met by our mothers, a couple we had befriended and who agreed to stand up for us, and Bud's best buddy, Sergeant Tenkhoff. Our mothers treated us to a wedding brunch at a local restaurant, and then we took the bus to San Francisco to spend the three days of Bud's leave seeing Golden Gate Park, riding the cable cars and finding any attraction we could enjoy for free. Whoopee! That was the sum of our honeymoon.

After we returned from our San Francisco sojourn, I had to begin thinking about returning to Silverton and my teaching job. The more I thought about it, the less I wanted to leave my new husband. So, I wrote to the president of the school board and resigned. Looking back, I have to concede that it was a scurvy trick, especially with a war on and a substitute hard to find in the middle of the year. I don't think I was ever forgiven for it either.

We had to find a place for me to stay. Bud was fortunate that he had some good buddies at Camp Stoneman who tipped him off to a room available over the garage of a house in the vicinity. We rushed to contact the landlady, Mrs. Boomer, and soon we were moved in.

Bud had been transferred from headquarters to the new school to train officers for transportation procedures. In true Army fashion, the school was given call letters: PCTCOTS, which stood for Pacific Coast Transportation Corps Officers Training School. And further in keeping with Army tradition, the call letters were made into a nickname — Petticoats. Bud was a file clerk when we married, but was soon upped to school photographer and then to sergeant.

Since Bud was now a non-commissioned officer, he could live off the base, so my room at Mrs. Boomer's became our first home as man and wife. Mrs. Boomer came with a suspicious personality and a collie dog named Lady. There was something about Lady neither Bud nor I could stand. I think we decided she was just like Mrs. Boomer and we never could warm up to that woman either. She had quite an obvious German accent and wore flowered aprons — always. She worked in the kitchen at the camp hospital, so she was gone all day except Sundays. We were fortunate, however, even to have found sleeping space during wartime.

Oh, the trials and tribulations of our one-room apartment! It was a little gray room with no running water or bathroom facilities. A key to Mrs. Boomer's house gave us bathroom privileges — peachy keen! We carried water from the hose in her yard up to our room for spit baths, but once a week we could use her bath tub. We had a key to her house but had to go all the way downstairs from above the garage, down the driveway and in through the front door. There we were always met by suspicious Lady, who sniffed us with her long nose.

Keeping our clothes clean was a major chore. We rinsed things out when we took baths and hung them in the room. Laundromats were not around then. Bud and I resolved that we would use Mrs. Boomer's washing machine while she was at work. We figured if we asked her, she would turn us down. She took great pride in that washer.

The day of the Great Washing Caper came. We hauled loads of dirty stuff down to her laundry room, washed carefully and cleaned up even more carefully, making sure everything was left the way we found it. That evening, we were called onto the proverbial carpet. Mrs. Boomer knew we had used her washer and she was very unhappy about it. We were not to use the machine again. Bud and I surmised that Lady had sniffed out the truth for Mrs. Boomer. Consequently our regard for Lady soured even more.

Bud and I also suspected there were spies in the neighborhood and our suspicions were confirmed after another sneaky episode. We were magnanimously allowed a chamber pot in our room. This we were supposed to carry, slopping and dripping, down the stairs of our room over the garage, down the driveway, around through the front yard to the front door, putting pot down on porch while fishing front door key out of pocket, inserting key into lock, unlocking door, opening door, holding door open with one foot while retrieving pot with both hands, and trying to keep Lady from getting out. We would probably have been evicted on the spot if Lady had got her freedom.

That routine wore thin fast. I told Bud that I would be damned if I was going to go through that embarrassing situation in daylight one more time. So I began surreptitiously emptying the chamber pot onto Mrs. Boomer's cactus. It was at the back of the garage, away from the house's view. Our secret dumpings went on for quite awhile. The cactus seemed to be thriving and I figured all was, indeed, well. So much for figuring.

We were again called over to stand on the carpet. Mrs. Boomer reported her neighbor across her back yard fence had seen Bud or me emptying our chamber pot on Mrs. Boomer's cactus. We were properly contrite, with heads hanging in shame, promising eternal abstention from yard polluting. From then on, I was very careful to empty the pot in a more secluded spot — after dark.

I knew that the two of us could not live on Bud's Army pay, so I tramped the streets for several days; and, finally, got a job at Pittsburgh Steel in the lab. At personnel, they figured I knew all about chemicals and chemical reactions since I had been teaching chemistry in school. I bluffed my way in, having no idea what chemical reactions I would be expected to know. As it turned out, I didn't need to worry. As low gal on the steel pole, I was put to grinding heats, steel ingots — a hard, hot, mindless job. For an eight-hour shift, I ground steel findings to be tested for various reagents in the chemical lab. At least it helped keep Bud and me in groceries and a roof over our heads.

To complicate our lives at a time I already found complicated enough, I discovered that I was pregnant. I became increasingly dissatisfied with my job at Pittsburgh Steel; but, due to the war effort, workers were locked into their jobs by government regulation. Luckily, the regulations changed. I was one of the first people in my working area to get a release from my job of grinding heats. I wanted less physically demanding work, so I got on at Army personnel at Camp Stoneman, working as a clerk/typist copying lists of troops being sent to the South Pacific. It was an eight-hour day job in contrast to the three different shifts I worked at Pittsburgh Steel.

Bud and I knew we would need more space than our room above Mrs. Boomer's garage. A new apartment complex was rapidly being constructed for steel plant employees and married military personnel. As soon as the apartment rental office was open and taking reservations, we signed up for a one-bedroom apartment. Early in the summer of 1943, we transferred our meager belongings from our bedroom over Mrs. Boomer's garage to a brand new apartment. We said an ecstatic farewell to Mrs. Boomer and Lady.

Our apartment was furnished with two single beds, a couch, dining table, four chairs, range, refrigerator, sink and cupboard. Of special delight was the bathroom complete with shower and hot and cold running water. I gloried in washing clothes and hanging them outside without interference from Mrs. Boomer and Lady.

I worked at camp personnel until I was six months along in my pregnancy. By then I was becoming quite rotund, nothing fit anymore and it was time to request a release from my clerk/typist position. I soon settled into practicing the home economics skills I had studied in college. I'm not certain I was the all-American housewife, but I don't recall complaints from Bud.

Finally, the future arrival was clamoring for admission. Jerry Mark Crawford was born at 10:30 P.M., January 19, 1944, at the camp hospital. He was a beautiful child with lots of black hair. I had to remain in the hospital in bed for thirteen days, due to the afterbirth not being expelled — quite a difference from today's fast turnover.

Bud got a furlough in May, 1944, so we made quick plans to go home to show off the first grandchild and nephew. Traveling with Jerry was a challenge. I'd had to wean him, so additional baggage of bottles and formula were in tow. He was then six months old and weighed close to twenty pounds. We stayed overnight in Salt Lake City, found a quiet room and put our little boy to bed in a dresser drawer. The next day, we were met in Grand Junction by a good neighbor of Bud's mother who had enough gas coupons to get us to Silverton and back. Both families received their first grandchild with open arms and a firm belief that Jerry was a most worthwhile addition to the family.

Back in our little apartment in Pittsburg, California, on a fall morning in 1944, we were breakfasting when a terrific explosion shook the whole apartment. Bud shouted to me to put Jerry under one of the beds, and for me to get under the other. I slid Jerry under one bed, but there was no way I could force my body under the other one. I gave up and joined Bud at our west window where we could see a regular Fourth of July fireworks display at Port Chicago, ten miles away. Dishes rattled, furniture swayed and we wondered if our walls would hold.

Soon, rumors reached us that the Japanese were bombing the Bay Area. Military personnel and families gathered outside apartments, fearfully theorizing as to the cause of the explosions. It was not until evening when Bud returned from Camp Stoneman that I learned that a munitions ship at Port Chicago had blown up while unloading. I never learned more about the explosion. War was hush, hush.

Bud was promoted to tech sergeant at Petticoats and then to staff sergeant. Colonel Kardis, Petticoats' commanding officer, felt Bud was officer material and urged him to go to officer candidate school for training. But Bud was stubborn about it. He did not want to be a "ninety day wonder"—a popular term for the officers the Army was rapidly producing to ensure enough staff to serve overseas. As a result, the colonel told Bud he would be sent overseas in the infantry. Bud would not budge from his decision to refuse O.C.S. Colonel Kardis issued orders and Bud was soon transferred to Camp Plauchet near New Orleans, where he was to begin his overseas infantry training. The Army allowed Bud travel time to accompany Jerry and me back to Colorado before reporting in at Camp Plauchet, but as a result of his transfer he missed his son's first Christmas and birthday.

Bud spent three months at Camp Plauchet and was then transferred to a camp outside of Gainesville, Texas, for final training. His next stop would be overseas. My husband prevailed upon his mother and me to visit him before his departure. I wanted so much to see him again, yet I did not feel Jerry was old enough to do so much traveling. Reluctantly, I left him with my mother and father in Durango, Colorado. Bud's mother, Helene, and I began our journey. It was February, 1945. We arrived on Valentine's Day; and, to celebrate, I managed to carry a chocolate cake on the bus all the way for Bud. It remained in good condition. I had packed it in cornflakes.

We thought our stay in Gainesville would be two weeks, but it lasted six weeks. Then the day that Helene and I dreaded arrived. Bud left for overseas and Helene and I took the bus back home. I blubbered all across the panhandle of Texas and into Colorado.

When we arrived in Durango, Dad, Mother and Jerry met the bus. I was so happy to see them, especially my sweet little boy. I hurried off the bus and reached for Jerry. He would have nothing to do with me. He had

Taken in Pittsburg, California, July 1944, when Jerry was 5½ months old.

forgotten me. He began crying and so did I. It was a darn soggy, bitter-sweet homecoming. It took a day or two for him to accept me again.

Helene went on to Silverton and I settled into a routine with my folks at Ft. Lewis. I guess I was the usual serviceman's left-at-home wife. I wasn't a "Rosy the Riveter" with a factory job since I had a baby to take care of. I had Bud's service pay that he sent home every month. Jerry and I were fortunate to be living with my folks, so we had it pretty easy for those days. Of course, I worried about Bud. By now, it was toward the end of the war, but there was still some heavy fighting going on, with casualties from Colorado printed regularly in the local papers.

I wrote to Bud every day. He had a New York APO address so that put him in the European Theater somewhere. He did not have as much opportunity to write as I, but no letters before or since have been awaited with as much anticipation as those from him. Eventually Bud was allowed to let me know he was billeted in Germany. He got in on some of the last fighting of that conflict and some of the mopping-up jobs.

Jerry's second Christmas and birthday were spent again at Ft. Lewis—without his father. The last of January, Bud wrote that he would soon be sailing home. He gave some possible dates and times for landing Stateside, so my anticipation mounted. When he debarked on the East Coast, he telephoned, saying he would arrive February 17 at four P.M. in Durango. The year was 1946.

Mother went with me to meet the train. I was so excited watching the train pull in. We checked everyone getting off until no passengers were left — no Bud. Mother suggested that, though it was a longer route, he might have had to take the bus in Alamosa, Colorado. When the bus arrived, we were there to meet it. We watched each passenger debark. There were quite a few servicemen, but not my Bud.

I was upset. I could not imagine why he had not made either connection. He had been very specific about the day and time of arrival. Mother and I decided our only recourse was to go back to the Durango house. Maybe Bud had missed connections someplace and we would get a call.

I walked in, feeling tired and defeated — and there was Bud! He had caught a ride in Alamosa. A man and his soldier son were traveling to Dolores, a town about fifty miles west of Durango, and had dropped him off at the house. To say that I was glad to see Bud is an understatement of large proportions. Jerry, however, was not at all pleased with this strange man hugging and kissing his mother and trying to pick him up. He let out an uproar and took some while to placate. It was several days before he could finally accept his father as "dad-dee."

We waffled around several weeks getting acquainted again as a family. Bud was unsure of what he wanted to do, but he knew he wanted to return to Silverton. Eventually we bought our own house in Silverton, jokingly called "the Little House on the Prairie," since it sat by itself out on a flat area on the edge of town. I went back to teaching after we had added another boy and two girls to the family. Bud worked in all of the hard rock mills in San Juan County. He passed away in December, 1983.

Not Much of a Letter Writer

Marjorie Chapman Joslin

My first contact with the military was in early 1942. I had passed a federal civil service examination which qualified me for a position with Uncle Sam. I went to work at Mather Air Force Base, a navigator training school east of Sacramento, California. I was a clerical person in the "Sick and Wounded Office," in later years known as the Medical Records Department, in the base's Station Hospital. Initially, my duties were more or less clerical in nature—preparation of reports, hospital census statistics, etc. As I became acquainted with medical staff members—psychiatrists, surgeons, internists, orthopedists—they became aware that I knew shorthand and could take their dictation. Thus, I graduated from clerk to medical transcriptionist, recording their statements into personal medical records. At the time, I lived with my sister and my dad in a home the three of us shared in Sacramento.

Memory fails me—I'm not sure how I happened to attend a picnic at McClellan Air Force Base, located in the north area of Sacramento, in the spring. That is where I met Sgt. William Chapman, who was in medical supply at that base. The first time I laid eyes on him, he was wearing white swim trunks and heading for the pool. I thought he was handsome. Attraction seemed to be mutual, both of us outgoing and *young*. Little did I know he would be my future husband!

The summer flew by—lots of dates and fun times with Bill. Summer months were great for swimming, picnics and joy-riding. A buddy of Bill's, also stationed at McClellan Field, owned a convertible and frequently loaned it to Bill for a few hours. Most enlisted men didn't have such an advantage.

Came July, he received orders for overseas duty, to report initially to some Air Force base in Boise, Idaho. Calamity! August was a blur — togetherness and discussions. Supposedly, the plan of the time was overseas duty for one year, then replacement with troops from stateside. Bill's assignment was England. Favorite tune: "Goodby, dear — I'll be back in a year."

Upshot of our discussions: I would join Bill in Boise and we would marry. My sister Wilma and a friend accompanied me to Boise and witnessed our "wedding" on August 29, 1942. No flower girl, no ring bearer, no bridesmaids. Ten days' honeymoon in a Boise motel, Bill off to the base each day. On or about September 8, 1942, we said goodbye, with hope of a maximum absence of a year. I returned to my job at Mather.

East St. Louis, Illinois, was Bill's home town. Lots of family there — mom and dad, five sisters and one brother. Since there had been no opportunity for them to meet me, I decided to take some time off from the job and make a trip to East St. Louis. I had communicated with my new in-laws and settled on a rather extended stay — six weeks. Travel in those times was hectic, with troop movements and dependents of military changing locations.

Being young and healthy, I decided to go by train without sleeping accommodations. After three days and two nights of jammed rail cars, I was not in very good shape to meet a horde of new relatives who didn't know what I looked like. Their key to my identification when I left the train: look for a short, rather chunky blonde wearing a moss-green suit. The plan worked. We were soon greeting each other and were at ease at once. My time with them was long enough that I was able to get acquainted with all the family. They were most hospitable, and they made me feel welcome. We maintained good contact in the ensuing months and years.

I returned home and began a projected one-year wait for Bill's return. One year stretched to two; two stretched to three. It was difficult to understand why the one year thing did not materialize. There I was, working in a military hospital staffed with enlisted personnel in the same field as Bill was. These same troops, with few exceptions, were still there when the war ended — a matter of three-plus years later — with never a thought of overseas duty.

My friend Betty and I socialized with the non-coms [non-commissioned officers]. There was a non-com club in downtown Sacramento. I'm not sure how that worked — maybe the military paid the rent. The club consisted of a sit-down area for visiting, a bar and a jukebox for dancing. The medics were a close knit group. One segment formed the "24-44" Club

Marjorie "Midge" Chapman Joslin, 1942.

(24 guys in the year '44). After the war, the group carried on, getting together in different areas of the country every few years. My socializing information was not shared with Bill, just as his socializing was not shared with me — a source of concern post war.

V-mail was the choice of letters. I wrote many of them. Correspondence from England was infrequent. Bill was not much of a letter writer. In fact, on one occasion, after his mother had not had mail from him for a few months, she called the Red Cross. This agency contacted Bill's commanding officer, who called him on the carpet for failing to write.

Bill's assignment included many flights to Europe to return sick and wounded to England — stressful and shocking, I am sure. However, he did make a number of friends and realized some social life. Likewise, I did my job, and also enjoyed some social life with co-workers, including the enlisted personnel. Such extended duty in England plus few letters left many blanks on both sides.

I remained with my sister and my dad during Bill's stay in England. My sis was single. Since I had daily contact with eligible single males, I tried test runs, inviting one or another home for dinner, with the idea of finding the right one for Wilma. She didn't show a lot of interest. Then I invited "Wag." Good thinking! M/Sgt. Lambert Wagner was a great guy — friendly, full of humor, easygoing and pleasant to work with. He made the grade. Wag and Wilma were married April 8, 1945, in the base chapel.

Bill was honorably discharged at Fort Sheridan, Illinois, September 11, 1945, almost three years to the day after his departure for England. After a brief period of rest and recreation, he secured employment in Sacramento with a surgical supply company. I left my job at Mather, but stayed in the medical field, working for a doctor as receptionist/secretary.

Post-war adjustments were many and disturbing. Our lack of ongoing communication during the three years we were apart had a lot to do with our troubles, actually. I don't think I could say either of us changed much—the "old feeling" was there, but filling in the gaps was not easy. I felt I "filled in" more than he did. I made him aware that I hadn't become a couch potato. I never did get much detail from the England side. My socializing activities during Bill's absence didn't set well with him and he wanted that connection broken ASAP. That is why I left my job at Mather. The three-year separation complicated matters for sure, but we managed to work through it and start our new life.

Sleeping in a Woodshed

Jeanne L. Roberts

World War II was the traumatizing experience for my generation. Men and women reacted to it in a multitude of ways, but all were affected by it. When I returned to college for my sophomore year, Germany had invaded Poland, and I knew about it through the newspapers and news magazines. I really tried to ignore it and lived my college life as if nothing were happening outside of Corvallis, Oregon. With Pearl Harbor this all changed because of the proximity of Hawaii and the President's declaration of war.

I learned of the bombing of Pearl Harbor as I ate dinner with my family while we were in Portland for a wedding. We were eating Sunday dinner to the accompaniment of a broadcast of the New York Philharmonic Orchestra, the only program my father would tolerate while we were eating. Suddenly, at the close of one of the numbers, an announcer came on the air with the news that Japanese planes had bombed the harbor in Hawaii. We felt threatened, but we finished dinner and then went to the wedding.

When I returned to the sorority house that night, the atmosphere had already changed. The groom at the wedding we had attended had been in Army uniform, and on campus all ROTC (Reserve Officer Training Corps) members appeared in their uniforms. Our spring vacation was canceled and we started the third academic quarter without a break. The administration was trying to help those male students who wanted to finish their college courses before being drafted or volunteering for service.

I was one of those who participated in the graduation ceremony in the college gymnasium. Art, my fiancé, did not graduate because of the time he spent working to be able to support himself in college. But when recruiters came on campus, he was interviewed by them as if he had his degree. He signed up with Alcoa (Aluminum Company of America) in their Vernon, California, plant where he would work as an industrial engineer, helping in the manufacture of aluminum for airplane bodies.

After a stint as a housemother for a group of 4-H girls, I headed for my parents' home where I planned to live while teaching nursery school in the Portland schools. I said "good bye" to Art in the train station in Albany, where he boarded a train for Los Angeles and employment with Alcoa.

We each followed our career plans for the next nine months, then were married at my church as soon as school was out and I finished teaching. We had a short honeymoon at Cannon Beach, then returned to Portland, packed our wedding gifts and headed for Los Angeles where Art was still working for Alcoa. We had a year of being newlyweds. Art's military deferment was still in effect but would be eliminated by spring. He knew he would be drafted, so again we packed our belongings from our little apartment and returned to Portland so that he could enlist in the Navy.

I settled into the room Art built in my parents' attic while he waited to report to duty. He left for the naval training base in Farragut, Idaho. He spent July and August there, experiencing the misery of the lowest rank of the Navy. After training, he was advanced to the rank of ensign, junior grade. He then was sent to Tucson, Arizona, where the last class of officers were being trained at the University of Arizona.

I spent a month filling in as a kindergarten teacher in Portland, at the school where my father was principal. His regular teacher quit to join her husband at some Army camp, and there were no more kindergarten teachers available. With my previous school experience, I did pretty well, even holding a parents' meeting during the four weeks I was there.

Art found a place for me to live in Tucson not far from the university—a kind of communal arrangement—so I quit being a kindergarten teacher. By that time, another teacher had become available for my father's school, so I was free to leave.

This large house in Tucson was the place where I coined the phrase "instant intimacy," for the women told each other the stories of their lives, but forgot them the moment they parted company. We each had our own room but the bathroom was down the hall. The kitchen was large and an alcove off it had been sectioned off so that each woman had a few square inches of space for a few foods. The refrigerator was sectioned off too, so we could fix a few simple meals for ourselves. There were other inhabitants in the kitchen. This was my first experience with cockroaches, and these were frightening as they scuttled around the floors and shelves.

Jeanne and Art Roberts, 1944.

Art was able to get leave on the weekends, but I had to amuse myself most of the time. There were some bridge players who provided a distraction each day, and I wrote letters and read. In my trunk I had some unfinished sewing projects, so I found a Singer sewing store where machines could be used at an hourly rate. I completed a green dress for myself and a plaid sport shirt for my father for a Christmas gift. I bought gray yarn and knitting needles and started a vest for Art to be worn with his gray uniform. The Navy wives went together to a restaurant for a Thanksgiving dinner.

At the close of Art's classes he was sent to Coronado Amphibious Training Base in California. Christmas was two days away and he had to report in by December 28. We had been in touch with our friends Jack and Rhea and arranged to meet them in Los Angeles. One of us remembered the large vertical sign at the corner of 7th and Broadway — LANKERSHIM HOTEL — and it wasn't too far from Los Angeles' gorgeous Spanish-style train station. We struggled with our belongings to the hotel and checked in.

It was Christmas Eve and we settled into our room. The only place we could think of to eat was one of Clifton's Cafeterias, with its organ music and fake palm trees. Neither of us had eaten in many restaurants, so this seemed like quite a treat. We didn't miss the hassle of the big family dinners at home where we had to choose which family to eat with. My mother sent us small red socks with white satin borders at the top. We hung them on the dresser drawer knobs before we went to bed Christmas Eve. When we awoke on Christmas Day, we opened the small gifts our families had sent. (We still use the sterling napkin rings included in these gifts.) Our friends took us to visit their friends and to dinner with Rhea's family in Beverly Hills.

The next day we headed for Coronado Training Base, for Art had to report in by January 3 and I needed a place to live. We checked into the U.S. Grant Hotel, but we could only stay three days—hotel policy since so many service-connected people needed a place to stay. After our three days, we headed for Coronado Island, taking the ferry which connected San Diego to the island. We read ads in the paper for rentals and contacted two people we thought could help us, but couldn't.

Somehow we found an unoccupied wood shed which was being rented. It was painted white and inside was a double bed and a cupboard. The owner in the big house in front of it said one of the rooms in the house would be vacated the following week. So we took the wood shed with the understanding that we would move into the house when available. Water was from an outdoor faucet by the back door of the house in front, and toilet facilities were inside the house.

My trunk was still in the storage room of the San Diego train station, so we had the option of sleeping in the used sheets and blanket on the bed, or not sleeping. We silenced our squeamishness and slept in the used sheets until we could retrieve my trunk. We did move into the second floor unheated room a week later. Our next expedition was to go to San Diego on the ferry to a hardware store and buy a kerosene heater to take the January chill off the air. I wrote all these details to my family and was immediately advised by return mail from my mother that we were now in danger of asphyxiating ourselves with the fumes from the heater. So we heeded her warning and left one of the windows ajar whenever we lit the heater. We also heated soup on the top of it.

We lived like this for six weeks, with Art at the amphibious base during the day and returning to our "home" for dinner and the night. I spent my time knitting, sewing, reading and attending a bridge group of officers' wives.

The end of February brought forth rumors that Art's group would be leaving, so I prepared myself for a return to Portland and the refuge of my parents' home. Art accompanied me to the train station the first of March and we had a tearful farewell. We knew where I was going, but Art's future was unknown. Later I learned he went to Hawaii on an LST (Landing Ship Tank) and was deathly seasick.

When I changed trains in Sacramento, I had breakfast at the station meal counter and ordered cream of wheat, which I thought my queasy stomach would accept. This was the first indication I had that I was pregnant. I had decided that I would have a baby while Art was gone, sticking to the schedule we would have followed if there hadn't been a war on. I had an unrealistic view of what my life would be like if Art didn't return. I hadn't given a thought to how I would support myself and raise a child on my own. When I told my family, my mother was shocked for she had assumed I would wait until Art's return. My grandmother sang her usual tune of "What a pity to bring another child into this wicked world." My father thought it a fine idea and my sisters were delighted since they thought it would be fun to be aunts. These reactions didn't faze me.

The next eight months I lived with my parents. My mother took me to Emanuel Hospital when it was time for my baby to arrive, and I stayed in the hospital for ten days, the acceptable time for post-partem hospital stays. Mother called the Red Cross with the baby news, to be sent to wherever Art was in the Pacific Ocean. He never got the news, so he learned of Danny's arrival when he called from Seattle to say he was on his way home. By that time, my father had died unexpectedly, so Art came home to a changed family.

My experience of World War II was minimal in comparison to that of many women and especially men and families. My husband's older brother died at a training camp so I never knew him. I was so horrified by the entire process of what was going on that I read nothing of it in the newspapers. Twenty-five years ago I finally decided I could read some of the books without falling apart, so I read quite a few. I mourned again the deaths of high school and college classmates.

My Wartime Marriage

Joyce Moredock

I had three or four boyfriends through high school but only one was serious. Both my parents objected so when I went off to college and to nursing school, the relationship pretty much dissolved.

Then one morning in July of 1941, I was home from training at Merritt Hospital in Oakland, California. "Probies" (probationers) got weekends off. I had gone to church with my mom and as we were leaving, she looked over my shoulder and said, "There is a nice looking young Navy officer over there. Why don't you invite him home for dinner?" When I turned around he recognized me. (Husband's note: My ship had come into Mare Island Navy Yard the previous summer to have her bottom scraped, and there in Vallejo, California, I met Joyce when she worked at the Peter Pan ice cream shop.) So I felt I could easily ask him to dinner. He had a tennis challenge that afternoon but he said he could come around five o'clock. When I checked with Mom, she said the meal could wait. So Stewart agreed to meet us at our house at five o'clock. For dessert, Mom served a cherry pie and that pleased Stewart a lot! He asked to ride back to the hospital when my folks drove me back to school and that was the beginning of it all.

I had picked up some complimentary tickets to the circus and asked if he'd like to go with me. We set a date for the following week. He was so handsome, and he looked so nice in uniform. I subsequently found out that he was a Naval Academy graduate from Annapolis in the class of '39. I think we had one more date in San Francisco at the Opera House. I was so impressed. He not only exchanged my circus tickets for much better ones but when we went to the opera we had very good seats right in the center downstairs.

The next thing I knew, his ship was ready to depart. All I remember of that last dinner was that it was in a nice restaurant near Lake Merritt in Oakland and he took me for a rowboat ride on the lake.

Then we began exchanging letters via military mail. His had to be censored by a shipmate and mine was also subject to censorship. I got a letter once a week on that system. As you can imagine, they were not the typical mushy teen-age love letters. The five year age difference between us may have had something to do with our restraint, too. But I learned a lot about his family and doings of a social nature.

Then came Pearl Harbor on December 7, 1941. From then on it was pretty sad. The letters stopped and I began to worry. Not knowing is always the hardest.

The next event was December 23, 1942, when a whole bunch of letters arrived from Stew. My roommates strung all of them from the chandelier to my dresser. As I was trying to pull them down, I got a phone call from a corpsman at Oak Knoll Naval Hospital just outside of Oakland. He said that Stew had arrived there and was not expected to live.

[Ed. note: Stewart's ship, the *Atlanta,* was in the Friday the 13th naval battle in the Pacific. He was on the bridge with Admiral Scott when the ship was hit. Admiral Scott was killed instantly and Stewart, wounded and unconscious, fell into a pile of dead sailors on the deck below. Fortunately someone saw him move as they were abandoning the sinking ship and he was transferred to a destroyer and taken to hospital.]

Needless to say, I was on my way. My roommates each put in whatever cash they had and it was enough to get me a cab to Oak Knoll. I wore part of everyone's clothes, a blouse from one, a skirt and shoes and jacket from another. When I got to the hospital, the guards wouldn't let me in because I was not a relative. I was too stupid to lie about it and say I was his fiancée. Nothing had ever been said about that.

The next day Stewart was helped to the phone and called me to say my name was cleared for the following afternoon. As soon as I was off duty I hopped a bus and was out of there P.D.Q.

It was obvious he wasn't that bad off. He certainly had serious injuries to his right arm and leg and the gangrene smell was awful. Fortunately penicillin had been discovered and I knew from my hospital experiences that it really worked well. So I could reassure him that his chances were good.

Then began the long process of surgeries that brought him to the best recovery possible. They set his leg and, with a cast, he was soon able to walk. After that, the equally long process of rebuilding his shattered right hand began. To replace his right thumb they made a pedicle graft tube on his abdomen and used his left floating rib for a bone to hold it in shape. This was grafted onto his hand. When all was completed he had a usable hand that is strong enough to hold a cocktail glass.

During all of this time I was able to talk to him by phone and on my days off I visited him at Oak Knoll. We went to the base movies and out to dinner there. Later, when he could manage the bus, he came to Merritt Hospital to pick me up. We would go out for dinner or to see plays and musical events.

I'll never forget one incident when we went by bus to the San Francisco Opera House. We were standing across the street from the Opera House, Stew with both his right arm and left leg in casts, looking helplessly at six lanes of very busy traffic. A policeman saw our plight. He blew his whistle and stopped traffic in all directions, then led us carefully across to the Opera House.

Slowly things kept getting better, but we never had much time totally alone. In April of '43 we were talking in the lobby of the nurses' home and he somehow got around to asking me if I liked kids. Without thinking seriously I said, "Yes." He then asked if I would like a miniature of his academy ring as an engagement ring. I said "Yes," because his gold ring with a blue sapphire looked so beautiful. After a while he brought one with him and asked if we could make it official. I was so happy.

We were not supposed to wear rings on duty at the hospital because of contamination. By that time, I had advanced in the training program enough that I was working the PM shift (3:00 to 11:00). I could not resist showing the ring to one of my classmates. It was my job to pass out medicines on the maternity ward that evening. Everything went well and I was showing off the ring the first half of the evening — no problem. After passing the little cups of milk of magnesia, I spilled one of them on the tray. When I took it to the sink to wash it, I wiped my hands on a paper towel. As I threw the towel in the waste basket I noticed my ring looked silver. I was crushed, thinking that the gold had washed off.

As I went off duty, I told one of my roommates about it. She was a smart Cal student and she thought for a moment. She took me to the scrub room where there was some chlorine bleach. Lo and behold, the magnesium came off but so did the black enamel that highlighted the engraving. So, from that time on, I have had a very shiny gold engagement ring. On our 50th wedding anniversary, Stewart gave me a gold band with little diamonds circling the big diamond in the center, but I will always treasure my shiny gold ring.

Joyce and Stewart Moredock, June '43.

When Stewart was O.K.'d to travel by plane, he wanted to go home to his family in Indiana. My parents were recently divorced so it seemed right for me to go with him and be married in Indiana. When Stew presented the idea to me, I had to say that I didn't think I could get my hospital's nursing school to say yes. The school's policy was absolutely no married nurses in the school. Finally I suggested that maybe we would have better luck if Stew also went to the director and asked her himself. He is a courageous man — so I have found out over and over.

After he talked to the director, she called me in and asked if I would agree not to get pregnant before completing the program and to live off campus. That was no problem, so she gave her consent. She gave me two weeks off and we flew to Indianapolis. We were married in Sheridan in his church next door to his home on June 13, 1943. We were feted by his family and his friends. The local car dealer managed to get us a beautiful new blue Chevrolet (an almost impossible feat during the war) and I managed to get a driver's license.

We drove back to California to live in our apartment in Oakland. After completing my nurse's training, I graduated in August, 1944. Stew found us a great apartment near the top of the hill at U.C. Berkeley where he was completing his Ph.D. and I my B.S. in nursing.

Our marriage has been as difficult and as good as most marriages. We were brought together by the war from very different backgrounds and tastes, but we have compromised and talked things out as calmly as possible. Now that we're retired we even take turns arranging dinner. One day I prepare the meal at home. The next day he takes us out. O.K.? We women have our rights!

Voices from
Daily Life

Behind the Combat

Mary L. Appling

Had I known that these remembrances would be of interest to anyone at a later date, I would have recorded them at a time when they were clearer in my mind. As it is, now that I am 81, what I recall as the "war-impacted" life of one young, single American woman in the U.S. during World War II may, when added to accounts of others, give some idea of the diversity of women's experiences on the home front.

In May 1940, I graduated from the University of California at Berkeley with a B.A. in English. Then I did graduate work there and at U.C., Los Angeles. By May of 1942, I possessed a secondary teaching credential and a certificate of librarianship. At the age of 22, I was ready to start my career!

In the meantime, on the morning of Sunday, December 7, 1941, word reached me over the radio in my room at International House, a dorm for graduate students, at U.C. Berkeley, that Pearl Harbor in the Hawaiian Islands had been attacked and bombed by the Japanese. The news was a great shock since we had just been hearing on the radio, and reading in the newspapers (no TV yet) that Japanese diplomats were in Washington, D.C., for peaceful discussions with our government.

I have always felt both guilty and fortunate that I had so few personal involvements in the combat side of WW II and therefore was spared that constant worry felt by those who had relatives and close friends in great danger in the military forces. The fact that I was totally untraveled, except for having gone, at the age of nine, by car from California to North Carolina, probably contributed to my feeling of insulation and safety. Also, my knowledge of things political was not particularly well developed and

Mary L. Appling, between 20 and 21 years old, 1940–1941.

at that time I had isolationist leanings. No wonder I was able to harbor that feeling of uninvolvement.

My career choice was to go to Oakdale, California, in the central San Joaquin Valley about 90 miles east of San Francisco to be the sole librarian in the Oakdale Joint Union High School. This school drew its approximately 500 students from the surrounding countryside and small towns, as well as from the local schools. Oakdale was then a town of about 2000 people.

For five years, September 1942 through June 1947, I gave my best effort to bringing better order out of and to building up the book and magazine collection that had evolved without much professional direction. We used the Dewey Decimal System for classifying books. We maintained a card catalogue and accession book, and I succeeded in turning the library from a noisy lunch room and gathering place into a realm of relative quiet for reading and study.

A car was not part of my equipment; therefore, I suffered no hardship from the rationing of gasoline. On a rare outing a group of us teachers and friends, all traveling by bus, train, or carpool, would head for San Francisco for a weekend to sightsee or see a stage play or musical. "Lady in the Dark," starring the English actress Gertrude Lawrence, was one such musical. Its song about "Poor Jennie, bright as a penny," still brings to mind those trips during which we were always aware of the uniformed service people around us in the streets and were reminded that a war was on.

My parents, as did most of the people in the U.S., willingly and generously made what contributions they could to the national war effort, beginning with the regular purchasing of war bonds. Everyone who could was urged to create a "victory" garden and my parents did just that, to give practical support to the domestic food supply. Their garden was carved out of pasture land, a patch possibly 40 × 50 feet in area.

Mother did quantities of knitting for the American Red Cross—socks, sweaters, scarves, helmet liners—whatever was needed for the troops. She joined legions of other women doing the same thing. I, her not-so-handy daughter, volunteered at the Oakdale Red Cross to knit the long, heavy wool socks. I learned to turn the heel nicely, but I was not a speedy knitter. Almost always before I could produce an entire pair, the Red Cross would call and gently suggest that I return the unknitted yarn and allow someone else to complete the project before the war was over.

The collecting for reuse of used cooking grease and of "tinfoil" from candy and gum wrappers, cigarette packs, etc. became second nature. I can remember the huge ball of tinfoil that my dad added to daily. The grease was taken regularly to the meat counter or the butcher shop to be used, we were told, in the manufacture of munitions. Used motor oil was collected and returned to service stations and garages for recycling.

Mother also shared her home cooking a number of times with North Carolina soldier relatives who found themselves stationed at nearby Camp Beale, home of the 13th Armored Division. The news that the visitors brought of North Caroline "kinfolk" was most welcome and added to my parents' pleasure in entertaining.

Not only older people and students changed the direction of their lives. At least one of our teachers worked in an aircraft factory in the Los Angeles area. She was a tall, lanky, intellectual type who was head of the English and drama department. She felt strongly that she should do her "bit" and thus spent several summers climbing around in airplanes with her checklists and her keen attention to supervisory detail. We younger faculty were duly impressed by these activities of such an "old" person—she was at least 52!

The young and beautiful Spanish teacher, two years into the war joined either the USO or the Red Cross and went off to seek overseas adventure. I was giving some thought to joining the Women Marines, but the war ended in 1945 before that happened. Only one woman I ever knew at that time joined a service.

There were other signs that a war was on. US War Bonds were on sale regularly at the high school. After several years I had amassed $1500 worth of $25 bonds, at $18.50 per purchase. That was not a lot, but my salary was only about $1900 yearly during that time. We all did what we could. Physical changes also abounded in the landscape. A munitions plant sprang up in Riverbank, California, five miles from Oakdale. A huge military installation of some sort, complete with chain link fences and guard posts, arose near Livermore, California.

The personnel at Camp Beale made their way into Marysville and Yuba City, twin cities about 12 -15 miles west of the camp. Each town had about 6,000 population in normal times but swelled with people during the war. Business undoubtedly increased as the servicemen spent a great deal of their pay checks there. The presence of so many uniforms on the streets gave an entirely different appearance to the towns, usually quiet centers of an agricultural area.

Word began to filter back concerning the young men who had gone into the services. One Hammonton boy was killed in an airplane training accident not far from home. Another was soon a second lieutenant in the Air Force. Two brothers from my high school class lost their lives, one as a naval aviator in the Pacific and the other in a munitions explosion on the docks in Richmond, California. A boy I had dated in junior college made it to England in the army and was killed in a Jeep accident. After the war, I finally learned of the fates and experiences of a number of my acquaintances, some very sad, some heroic.

In Oakdale, as the students became older, some of them enlisted, some were drafted. One quiet boy volunteered for submarine duty. He returned once to school to visit, looking handsome in his uniform. The next we knew his boat had been destroyed at sea. A tear was always shed at such times and thanks given for the sacrifice of another young person. Many students served their country and returned safely. We were grateful to them too.

With many agricultural workers in the armed forces or essential industry, local farmers had difficulty getting their crops harvested. Several times a group of the faculty volunteered time and labor in the tomato fields. My first sight ever of a huge, juicy green tomato worm was rather jolting. On the job, I wore a red and green plaid long-sleeved shirt, not as camouflage but as protection against the sun and scratches. By the end of the day, however, I was covered with tomato plant green fuzz and itched all over!

Airplane spotting was a volunteer endeavor which I pursued. Rodene MacAuley was my "watching" partner. Once a week in late afternoon, we drove in her car (I had only a bicycle) out of town a mile or two to a small shed by the side of a country lane. The shed housed a telephone on which we called in our reports of airplane activity during our shift of four or five hours. Little training was required to do the spotting. We were given sheets of labeled airplane silhouettes (both US and foreign) to help us identify any planes we might see flying overhead. As long as there was daylight, we were expected to give the identity, if possible, of the plane or planes, the number flying, and the direction of the flight. After dark, we reported the number as "single" or "multiple" and gave the flying direction.

This watching program was probably set up by the Air Force or civilian defense (memory fails) as a warning system in the event of an aerial attack from the north and west, i.e., from the Pacific Ocean and Japan. At one time a report or rumor reached us that balloons, supposedly loaded with explosives, had been sighted floating in from the ocean over the northern coastal mountains of Oregon and California. Such reports were never proved, but they definitely were a spur to our diligence in observing.

All ages participated in this spotting, even if only in an auxiliary capacity. Rodene and I often had the company of six-year-old Herbie Royce, the son of the high school principal. These important missions were a thrill for him. The horses, cows, birds and rabbits we encountered also entertained him. When things were dull, we read many pages of "Winnie the Pooh." Some nights we delivered him back home fast asleep. My youngest daughter remembers her grandmother speaking of the "Coast Watch."

One domestic war-related event remains clearly in my mind. On April 12, 1945, word came on someone's radio at school that President Roosevelt had died. I immediately hand printed (no computer) a large sign with the news and tacked it to the front door of the library to help spread the word. There was much grief and shock expressed as well as speculation and doubt concerning the capability of Harry Truman to be President. Fortunately, Mr. Truman rose to his position of leadership and guided the country well.

We got our war news through radio, newsreels, magazines, books, and personal letters. The telephone, telegraph and word of mouth also served to spread the news farther. Oddly, I do not remember having my ear glued to newscasts on the radio, but radio was surely the main source of information that reached us most quickly. My parents frequently mentioned what H. V. Kaltenborn and Walter Cronkite had said on their nightly broadcasts. Newsreels shown in the movies before every feature film gave us "action" photos and informational comments but they didn't reach the numbers of people that radio and the newspapers did. Magazines such as the weekly *Time* and *Newsweek* supplied news that was a few days old, some pictures and broader views of the world developments. *Life* emphasized pictures as the medium for news.

Newspapers, like radio, were available everywhere. In our area of central California, the largest daily newspapers were the *San Francisco Chronicle* and the *San Francisco Examiner*. Lesser dailies were the *Sacramento Bee*, the *Modesto Bee*, and the *Stockton Record*. The small, weekly *Oakdale Leader* featured news of local boys in the service.

No matter what its size, each newspaper considered the war "big news" and covered it accordingly as best it could. Reporters and photographers risked their lives as near to the front lines as they could go to get the news back NOW to the U.S. The names of Ernie Pyle, who wrote human interest stories from among the troops, and Bill Mauldin, who drew cartoons featuring the G.I. Joes, became well known. There were many others who made their reputations as serious war correspondents by keeping the country well informed if we but bothered to read or to listen to their words.

The continuing war information and vivid descriptions soon began to appear in a sturdier form — books. Our high school students read them avidly.

Personal letters formed another body of war news, one full of intimate details of interest primarily to individuals, not to the country in general. Yet the thoughts and feelings revealed in these letters from both those in combat and those on stateside posts no doubt influenced the solid decision of the American people to give whole-hearted support to the waging of the war and to be determined to win.

Eventually, V-E. Day (Victory in Europe) was proclaimed on May 8, 1945, and there was much rejoicing. Oddly I can remember nothing specific about that day.

The following summer was full of speculation concerning the remaining war in the Pacific. In early August, the U.S. dropped two atomic bombs on Japan which caused catastrophic destruction and great loss of life. A few days later, on August 14, I was vacationing at Lake Tahoe, California, with a friend and her family. From the radio on our picnic table came the announcement that Japan was going to surrender. Again great jubilation! War's end at last.

Life did not suddenly return to pre-war norm. The war had to be wound down and the troops had to be brought home. It all took a good deal of time.

In December, 1945, Hugh G. Appling, only son of the Oakdale postmaster, returned home from his wartime service. Hugh had enlisted soon after Pearl Harbor and served in military intelligence with the 9th Infantry Division in Europe. After being discharged in early 1946, he appeared at the Oakdale High School seeking employment. He was hired at once as a teacher because substitutes were few and far between. He came into the library to get the textbooks he needed for his classes and that circumstance accounted for our first meeting. As I turned to go after the books, I stumbled over a newly arrived box of books destined for the library and fell almost flat! No comment. Hugh and I became better acquainted from that point on. We were married in March 1947. An impact of the war?

Hugh attended Stanford University in Palo Alto, California, for the school year 1946-47, and having been influenced by his war experiences, he procured his M.A. in international affairs. The idea of entering the Foreign Service of the U.S. (the diplomatic service under the aegis of the State Department) began to interest him. In the spring of 1947, he took the oral and written examinations required for entry and succeeded in passing both.

Cars at that time were still not plentiful and the choices of color and style were not many, but my parents had presented us with a black Chevrolet sedan (only $1500!) as a wedding present. In that we drove across the U.S. to Washington, D.C., where Hugh was indoctrinated in the diplomatic service by attending the Foreign Service Institute for about eight weeks. I was invited to attend the lectures and to participate in language training. Couples were encouraged to perform as a "team" whenever possible as we represented the U.S. abroad in its relations with foreign countries. Hugh and I had that wonderful privilege for 29 years as we had posts in Vienna, London, Paris, Bonn, Damascus, Manila, Canberra, Vietnam (war again) and Washington, D.C. We retired from the Foreign Service in the spring of 1976, feeling, with pride, that we had "done what we could" to make the world a better place.

Lillian Addis— Volunteer Personified

Sara Mae Wiedmaier,
as told to Pauline E. Parker
and from The Oregonian,
October 4, 1942

In October, 1941, when the stirrings of possible war spread through the country, the Aircraft Warning Service was established in Oregon. About 500 observation posts were set up throughout the state. It took as many as 200 workers to man one post 24 hours a day, seven days a week, and over 60 per cent of these observers were women.

My mother, Lillian Crawford Addis, joined the first training class in Portland for Area IV. Area IV headquarters were located in the basement of the Masonic lodge. One section was called the Portland Information Center. Here notations of flights throughout Oregon reported by observers were printed on markers and shoved about with long-handled pushers on a large, sectioned off map called a grid. In another area, the Filter Board, volunteers sat in a balcony high over the filter center map. They were connected by telephone with the control center board and relayed the position of the aircraft as shown on the filter board grid to the state control board. In this manner, the State of Oregon patrolled its airways during World War II.

My mother worked in both sections. I have her award pins showing 1750 hours of work at the Filter Center. It wasn't unusual for her to work all night when she took someone else's shift.

I was a teenager and did not understand all of this at the time, but I did understand the excitement at home when an article appeared in the *Oregonian*, a Portland newspaper, describing the operation, displaying pictures, and carrying interviews with Mother and several other volunteers. The reporter wondered how these women budgeted their time so they could give six or 12 or 24 or 30 hours each busy week to do volunteer work. She had a fixed set of questions which are reflected in my mother's answers.

> "'I wash on Saturdays these days instead of Mondays; I iron on Mondays instead of Tuesdays; I clean on Fridays." She mentions, quite casually, that she has three children, 14, 17, and 19, that she does all the work of a four-bedroom house, the sewing for her two daughters, that she sews one day each week for her church's war relief work. "Certainly, it has meant readjusting my household schedule," she says, "but I can't go out to work — this is my way of helping."*

In each interview, the reporter recorded the number of children and the number of bedrooms in the home, indicating the amount of responsibility the home-maker carried and how busy her life was. I wonder what she would select as the criteria for judging the responsibilities of volunteers today.

My mother was born in Michigan in 1900, one of five children. When her father deserted the family, her mother traveled west with her children until her money ran out, which happened to be in Mullen, Idaho. There my grandmother scrubbed floors and did the chores that lone women in her situation did to provide for her family.

Mother didn't finish high school, so she was very young when she went to Seattle to live with relatives and find employment. She remembered going to lots of dances. She found work clerking in the china department of a large Seattle store. And there she met the boss's nephew, Judd Addis. She talked of missing dancing because he didn't dance. Some Army buddy tried to teach him when he was in France, during the first World War and said he was unteachable. Of course, they were wearing Army boots in some barn with bad floors. We tried to convince him he could do it, but he never would try again.

Mother was twenty-one when she and Judd were married in Tacoma. When I was clearing out the family home in the 1990's after all those 60 plus years she had lived there, I found a letter from Lillian to Judd which said, "I can hardly wait. We are going to be married in five days, I really think you should tell your mother." Sometime later they transferred to Portland. I was the youngest of their three children.

SAY AGAIN ITEM

Lillian Addis (right) with two unidentified companions.

People were always coming to Mother for help. Eventually, to be better prepared to help them, she became a Christian Science practitioner. She was always concerned about the welfare of other people and during the Depression, brought home strays to feed. She was an excellent gardener, providing food for whoever sat at her table or came to her door. Her Victory garden each year of World War II was a significant source of vegetables for the family table. She canned lots of her bounty. She also worked on a neighborhood garden that covered many blocks.

To further help the war effort, Mother began donating blood when the first drive started and she continued long after the war was over — until she was too old to give any more. She had pins that showed the many gallons she gave.

The war touched all of our family, as it did most families. One of Mother's brothers became a mining engineer. He was working in the Philippine Islands early in the 1940's when the Japanese came. He, his wife and three young children spent the first year in the hills hiding from the occupation forces. When they could find no more food, they had to turn themselves in to the Japanese in Manila, and the family spent the remainder of the war in Santa Tomas, a girls' school turned into a prison. The prison guards let Uncle Paul slip back to the hills because they knew he would be back, since his family was there. They would torture him each time he returned, to try to get information as to where the fighters in the hills were hiding.

My brother Myron came home from the South Pacific where he had served with the Navy. My sister Joyce had traveled by herself to Alabama to marry her college sweetheart in December, 1943. He was in the Army and after a few months he was sent to Europe. He was in on liberating one of the Jewish concentration camps.

I always thought my mother was next to God. She was one of the thousands of women who dealt with their personal anxiety over their loved ones in the military by answering the call to volunteer their services in the many projects necessary to carry on the war effort. I, too, have been a professional volunteer — no money — just many, many, volunteer jobs through the years. I have been on counting boards and church activities and library work in my four children's schools and the Vancouver Library, a UNICEF Christmas card seller for years, Campfire leader, PTA participant and a member of parents' clubs. Lillian Crawford Addis set a clear example for me to live by.

Voices from Abroad

From Prewar London to Postwar Paris: An American in Europe

Mary E. Hawkins

Mary Hawkins gave up a position on a New York magazine staff to move to London for a supposedly three-year assignment with her journalist husband. She lived in nine countries of Europe for seven years during World War II.

Barely had we set up housekeeping in a flat in London when the blackout curtains appeared, as did huge balloons over Hyde Park, and we were issued gas masks. It was summer, 1939. Though there was yet no war, the British were preparing for what would surely come. Blackout was to hide the city after dark and the balloons were to keep enemy planes away. The balloons were a doubtful endeavor.

Little news was breaking in Britain, so the news agencies began to scatter their correspondents to other transmission centers. Many agencies had bureaus in the larger cities and used "stringers" (local correspondents) elsewhere. Most managed some sort of wireless communication to the United States throughout the war. Tom, my husband, drew Amsterdam. This was one of the rare times we traveled by air, trains being the usual mode of transportation in those days. As we landed, the stewardess told us that, while we were in the air, England had declared war on Germany, September 3, 1939.

Nevertheless, we expected to stay in Amsterdam and immediately found an apartment to sublet and "settled in," getting acquainted with the city, taking many photographs and generally waiting for something to happen. Actually, little did happen those first few months of what was called the "phony war."

Then came a spell in Copenhagen, also with the expectation of staying. We were no more than settled into a charming apartment, with meal service, when it was on to Stockholm where it seemed that a news center could operate. Having come from other cities in Europe that were then more in the danger zone of war, we thought Stockholm seemed brightly lighted and warmly housed. It boasted the first automobile salesrooms I'd seen for months.

In a month or so, Tom was assigned to cover the "winter war" (the Russian attack on Finland) and I was left alone to move into a pension (boarding house) in a city where I knew no one and couldn't read or understand the language.

Even in peace time, a foreigner who wishes to "live" rather than just stay in a country must learn many new things. During war time, those things become more numerous and more imperative. Most terrifying is the language. Ordinarily one might learn only a few shopping and politeness words and get along with German or English in such a small country. During the war, however, one needed to know Swedish in order to be able to read the newspapers. British papers were available but they said little, while American papers were many weeks late. Going through the newspapers in the dictionary stage was such hard work that by the time I looked up a dozen words, all meaning "shot," "dead," "injured," or "powerful attack," the day seemed ruined. But to try a new Swedish phrase on a friend and find she understood gave me such utter, childish joy that the lessons continued.

The Swedes whom I met in the pension or through the stringer very quickly helped out with friendship, as well as language lessons. They also taught me how to ski. The skiing never let up during the war. Three-year-olds learned the art on one side of a hill in the park while the other side of the hill was being dug out for a public air raid shelter.

Occasionally I wrote stories for the press back in America. One I remember said that there were no bystanders in Europe. Everyone was somehow involved in doing something concerning the war. No one could be so close to Finland without feeling that one must do something for the refugees who poured into Sweden. They were welcomed as guests and no one could do too much for their comfort.

In Stockholm, the Singer Sewing Machine Company made a room and machines available for sewing clothes for the Finnish war refugees. I joined the group, for sewing was one thing I could do. My companions looked so exactly like the committee members one would see working for any big church affair or welfare project in a Midwest city in America that I felt quite at home. At first I was assigned to make one type of clothing — mostly, I think, because it was one way they could avoid having to explain things to me in either language! Finally I said, "Look, I think I've made bloomers for every little girl in Finland. May I make something else now?" I think I was allowed to make coats then.

Eventually, the "phony" war and the "winter war" ended. My husband returned to Stockholm — a different city from the one he had left. Christmas had come and gone. When the holiday packages of perfume and shaving soaps came out of the parfumerie windows, first aid kits and gas masks took their places. Snow came, but skis and snow shovels shared window space with food boxes and battery-operated lights for air raid shelters. Normally food stores were stocked with American canned goods and people wore clothes of British wool and British and American cotton. Rationing of many items ensued. The city was battening down for what was going to be a very difficult position.

After the war really began in the spring and the Germans occupied Denmark and Norway, Sweden's neutrality was even more "iffy." One couldn't even go into the train station without a ticket. The country managed to remain neutral, but allowed Germans on home leave to cross its territory from Norway after that country fell.

There was little news into, or the possibility of sending much news out of, Sweden. It seemed that the next "theater of war" might be the Balkans, where the Italians were in trouble in Greece and the Germans might go in to help. So — off we went. First, a few days in Berlin, where I experienced my first air raid, huddled in a hotel basement and thinking how it would be to be killed by an American bomb dropped from a British plane in a German city.

Then came a week or so in Budapest, including Christmas, a dreary day in a beautiful hotel while my husband worked. Christmas all over Europe during those years held little joy in the tired brains of many millions. There was little to celebrate and less to celebrate with.

Then on to Sofia, Bulgaria, to see whether the Bulgarians would allow the Germans to cross their territory. We stayed in a hotel where one morning German officers appeared, hanging their guns on the dining room coat rack. I remember a sad evening at the British legation where the British minister folded the British flag and gave it to the still neutral American minister for safe keeping. The next day, all of the British subjects left Bulgaria.

And the Germans did come in. The Bulgarians and I stood on street corners and watched the Wehrmacht tanks sweep through the city — and we smelled the gasoline! It was the first we had smelled for ages. In Sweden, cars still on the road were fitted with some device that burned wood, providing "gen-gas" for fuel. While still debating about transit rights, the Bulgarians called up their army, but they soon "allowed" the Germans passage across their territory with no resistance and the crisis was averted.

Shortly there was no news in the Balkans, so off we went to Switzerland, still a neutral country with news transmission facilities available. It looked as though we would be there for a long stay, so, again, I found an apartment and language schools, and we enjoyed the country's attractions and possibilities. Switzerland, like Sweden, had restrictions for foreigners, and, in fact, for most civilians, as to where people could go and what they could do. Consequently our photo albums are overweighted with pictures of parks and zoos.

Then in December, 1941, America came into the war, and there was no more moving around for us. I suffered a sharp attack of homesickness to be with my parents, but one couldn't even telephone at that time. Switzerland was surrounded by belligerents. And there we stayed until V-J Day.

Again I found people who wanted to exchange conversation, for they felt terribly shut-in and unable to travel or visit relatives in France or other countries. I also made friends with several Swiss people — one a young woman executive who took me to some meetings on behalf of women's rights, especially the right to vote. If I recall correctly, Swiss women finally got the right to vote in 1971.

The ability to read the German and French language newspapers came in handy, for Switzerland is a four-language country. For one year, I worked at the US Office of War Information (OWI). The overseas branch provided information and propaganda during World War II. (OWI was abolished in 1945.) Often stringers in Basle or elsewhere would find items of interest in the local papers and call our office. I would take their German or French dictated stories and transcribe them directly into English. I stayed at OWI until France fell [to the Allies] and Americans could come from the United States.

Many US pilots who ran bombing raids on Germany and couldn't make it back to England landed and were interned in Switzerland. In fact, I saw my first American uniform on one of these men!

A particularly strong memory of those early Switzerland years was listening to a Hitler broadcast from Germany in which he announced that the Germans were attacking Russia. "Fine," I thought, "let them kill each other off and leave us alone." It didn't work out quite that way.

Eventually, World War II ended and "home leave" plans took over. That meant a stay in Paris while awaiting transportation for the few women wanting to go to America. That was the time of "Get the boys home by Christmas" and anyone else desiring transportation was made to feel very unwanted. The men went on ahead on troop ships. But women had to wait for refurbished old luxury liners that had facilities for women. The Associated Press housed me in a hotel near their office while I waited for transport. We women left behind "enjoyed" or, at least, got acquainted with, a Paris filled with soldiers. Sometimes, we who were on local rations envied their chocolate bars, but we were on our way home!

We finally left France at Le Havre for a ten-day trip. We landed in Boston — finally home from the war — seven years and nine countries from that summer day in 1939.

Wartime in Cairo, Revolution in Athens

Ellen F. Broom

When I was accepted into the State Department Foreign Service in October 1943, I was thrilled. I was assigned to Cairo, Egypt, where the U. S. Embassy was marking time while awaiting the liberation of Greece. I left Washington, D. C., on a MATS (Military Air Transport Service) flight and, after many stops, arrived in Cairo on 2 January, 1944.

The following day I reported to the embassy. There were only four officers and one girl there — and the girl told me that I was to be Ambassador Lincoln MacVeagh's secretary. I felt I was very lucky. Lincoln MacVeagh later became our ambassador in Athens and then in Lisbon.

The next day I went over to JICAME (I think it stood for Joint Intelligence for Cairo, Africa and Middle East) with a letter of introduction to the head of JICAME. The Navy captain, Thomas Thornton, and several of his staff were from Philadelphia — my home town. Right away they took me under their wings and I was never alone after that.

The captain felt that, since I was secretary to the ambassador, I should move to Shepheard's Hotel (long known as the finest hotel in Cairo), where he and some of his staff lived. He arranged everything and I moved in. There were several Red Cross girls in the hotel too. One would never know a war was going on — we dressed for dinner every night, went dancing, went to parties, and just had a good time with the military types.

One met all the rich and famous Cairenes—including King Farouk. He was a real character—always going to the Red Cross Club for coffee in his fire-engine red Jeep. But he never carried money with him. His personal aide was always there to pay. Occasionally the King would have a "picnic" in the countryside and invite most of the top brass. The tablecloth was lovely white damask and there were silver candelabras on the table. This was roughing it! No ants either.

I remember George Papandreou, who was to become Prime Minister of Greece later. He used to hound me in Cairo because he knew I was secretary to the American ambassador, and he tried to get information from me. The Navy captain knew what Mr. Papandreou was trying to do and always stepped in at social events to rescue me.

At the embassy we worked quite hard, and, if I had to work on a Sunday, the ambassador and his wife would invite me for lunch at the Mena House, out near the Pyramids, where Roosevelt and Churchill had met in November 1943, then we might go to a concert or just drive out into the desert.

Captain Thornton took me—and several others—up to the battlefield at El Alamein. The second battle of Alamein was a turning point in the war (October 1942), the beginning of Rommel's retreat and the expulsion of the Axis forces from North Africa. I was told I was the first American girl there and I had to be very careful that I didn't step on a mine.

In late November, 1944, after the German withdrawal from Greece, the embassy staff flew to Athens. It was raining when we arrived, so we three girls walked down the street with our faces up so the rain could fall on them. It was the first rain we had seen in eight or nine months. We were given quarters at Loring Hall, part of the American School of Classical Studies. The ambassador's house was just across from the hall.

More damage was done to the city during the civil war going on in Athens than had been done by the Germans before they left. The civil war was between British forces and Greeks loyal to the monarchy, on the one hand, and guerrilla fighters in the communist-dominated National Liberation Army, on the other. Shelling lasted for days on end in December and we all had to be very careful; we were for a time confined to quarters. The ambassador would come to my bedroom to dictate to me, but my hands were so cold and full of chillblains that I could hardly hold a pen. Then I would race across the lawn to the ambassador's residence to deliver the dictation. It was very scary. One girl was very lucky. She was in the bathroom brushing her teeth, leaning over the sink, when a bullet came through the window, just over her head.

The buildings in the downtown area were riddled with bullet holes, and so many soldiers were killed that a trench was built on the main street just near the embassy and they threw all the bodies in the grave. It was horrible. I can still see those bodies. We had lots of British soldiers come to the hall for safety. They had no place to live, so we put them in the basement.

We had no running water — only well water. That was doled out every day to each embassy employee and that was all we had to wash our teeth, our face and body. I didn't have my hair washed for eight weeks so it looked just like greased string. It was so cold in the building that each morning we would go down to the living room and have a brandy to warm up.

Excerpts from my war-time diary kept during those days give some indication of how we lived during that chaotic time.

Sunday, December 3, 1944

Had bacon and eggs for breakfast — also a marvelous hot bath. Then down to the office, as usual, at 10 A.M. Just Walworth Barbour, Ambassador MacVeagh, Harry Hill and me. At about 10:30, we could tell that something was brewing. The parade of EAMites [members of the communist-dominated National Liberation Front] and KKE's [Greek Communist Party members] marched down the street across from the Embassy and just as they turned onto Queen Sofia Boulevard, the police started open firing, which sent them crouching behind the stone wall. The group was composed mainly of women and young girls and men. They were all carrying banners and the females were fearless, baring their bosoms and saying, "Go ahead and shoot me." The police were only shooting up in the air at first but occasionally into the crowd. Two people were killed outside the office, cars were stopped, the police were rushed and clubbed by the paraders and the streets were free of passers-by. One young girl was killed by the paraders and three wounded in nearby Constitution Square. There were thousands of people in the Square and a couple of thousand people (peaceful) outside the Embassy. Mr. Parsons and Capt. McNeill [William H. McNeill, who was to become a highly regarded historian] walked down to the Great Bretagne Hotel and on their way back were fired on by someone from the Prime Minister's office — so they took refuge in the British Embassy. We all closed down about 1:00 — and went home for lunch.

Meanwhile, this morning at about 8:45 the electricity went off due to a general strike. I am writing this report by candle light and the city is in total darkness. Curfew was called for 7 P.M. but we were advised about the time it had been lifted. The radio transmitter in the office was not working, so all messages had to be sent either by ATC or 3rd Corps.-Signals Office [British]. I went back to the office this afternoon at 3 P.M. and the Ambassador came in about 4 — wrote a telegram to the Department of State on the situation, but we just couldn't see to encode it.

Monday, December 4, 1944

Well, as we expected, no water at all today, and also no electricity or telephone service. During the morning, things were fairly quiet. There was a large funeral in Constitution Square for the victims of yesterday's activities and a long procession of mourners. In Omonia Square, there was quite a lot of shooting and in Piraeus [the seaport for Athens] the Naval Cadet School was besieged for about three hours and the police stations were surrounded and captured.

General Scobie [British Allied Commander in Greece] issued an order saying everyone must be off the streets by 7:00 P.M. until 6 A.M. If official business took you out by car or on foot, a special permit was required. So, having no electricity, we closed the office at 5:30 and all went home. We had 15 extra for dinner — all the Embassy local personnel who were unable to get home because of the situation

Tuesday, December 5, 1944

This morning, I was up at 6:30 and heard several shots then. We had news that Papandreou resigned, then about noon, we heard he had withdrawn his resignation. There was a bit of shooting all day long, and armed trucks and jeeps were posted at strategic points throughout the city and urban areas. The curfew was posted again for 7:00 P.M. but early this afternoon, as the civil war progressed, the curfew was put back to 5:30. In view of the seriousness and proximity of the situation, all the girls in the Embassy were sent home at 3:45 and the rest of us left at 4:00. The shooting was becoming louder and louder and it looked like a real fight. As I write this now at 5:00 o'clock, guns are going off within the immediate area of Loring Hall and loud shots can be heard some distance away, so heavy that they shake the building. And truly, I have never seen a more beautiful sky at dusk as there is tonight. Planes are zooming low overhead constantly but there is no plane traffic in or out — no courier service.

Wednesday, December 6, 1944

Conditions were such that it was impossible and impractical to go to the office. There was gun fire all day long, as well as cannons and heavy guns going off. It was a lovely day outside, as far as the weather went, but the atmosphere was heavy with smoke from the shooting. We had lunch about 1:00 and after lunch we all went over to Mr. Barbour's to play the piano and sing and dance. During the late afternoon the battles became violent and the Greek "Spitfires" zoomed low overhead and let go their guns in the valley. As a matter of fact, yesterday morning, a bullet went through the dining room window and hit the back wall. We had dinner early, about 7:00, and afterwards all sat around the living room fire, some read and some played cards and we popped corn. I went to bed early, but the very, very bright flares kept me awake. They are as bright as the huge arc lights. That went on up until midnight — the hour for ELAS [National Liberation Army] to surrender, or else the Greek Air Force would begin firing on them. Exactly at midnight, the bombs and guns started and kept up all night long. We sent bottles and other containers to the Embassy to fill them up with water for drinking purposes and for washing our teeth.

Thursday, December 7, 1944

I didn't sleep well last night because of the noise of the guns and air-planes. Unconsciously, we are all nervous and under a terrific strain — so I stayed in bed until 8:15. Today, the fighting is the worst so far, and even those in houses are not safe, because the snipers are apt to put a bullet through the window at any time.

Oh joy, six pouches came in today and even in the midst of this war we had Christmas at Loring Hall, at least for the afternoon. Some got letters and some got packages — lucky me, I received 4 packages. It was great fun opening them and oh-ing and ah-ing and seeing what everybody got. But I didn't open all of mine. I'll save two for Christmas. That night I didn't sleep a wink I was so scared. (I'm ashamed to admit it but I was.) Machine guns were shooting off right outside my window and I guess I just let my nerves get the best of me.

Saturday, December 9, 1944

There have been rumors around about the girls being sent back to Cairo until this all blows over (due to the fact that the OWI [Office of War Information] girls went back on Saturday), but as for me, I rather doubt it, much as I would like it. Last night after dinner, the planes dropped lots of flares right close to the School, and we were told to put our coats, shoes and flashlights right by our beds in case we suddenly had to go downstairs for refuge. There were several times during the night when I was tempted to go down and sleep by the fire, but changed my mind.

Wednesday, December 13, 1944

This morning we were all awakened by the planes firing directly over-head, and I was never more scared in my life. It gave me indigestion. Caroline Miller and I picked up 2 bullets from outside our windows.

Monday, December 18, 1944

We moved the Code Room downstairs to the dining room because there were many bullets flying around and coming in the direction of the Code Room. After lunch I worked until 3:45 — then went over to the Ambassador's with a telegram. While there, the planes started strafing in the section behind the Embassy. You could actually see the rocket bombs leave the plane and then hear them hit, and finally see the turmoil caused by it. It is a horrible sight to see those planes diving down on their target.

Sunday, December 24, 1944

Worked all morning in the Code Room. I just about lost patience with the attitude of the girls in there — they complain constantly. I really don't know why they ever came abroad. I can't stand this upset atmosphere all the time. And now, the sun is shining and it is raining. Crazy weather too.

Monday, December 25, 1944

Up at 8:15 and had a hot sponge bath — felt much better after yesterday's rumpus. Had a good breakfast and went over to wish the MacVeaghs a Merry Christmas. Took a short walk in the cold, windy air and felt marvelous. Then at 4 P.M. we had about 10 ATC officers in for tea — also the Navy boys — that ended about 6 P.M. then we sat around the fire. Dinner was served at about 7:20. It was a very nice Christmas for us.

Friday, December 29, 1944

I was awakened about 6:45 by the terrific amount of shooting and planes flying overhead. It got worse as the morning progressed. I was busy again all day. After lunch, there was a huge fire down past Kephissia Boulevard.

Saturday, December 30, 1944

I went over to the Ambassador's for 9 o'clock dictation. Two U. S. Urgent telegrams came in that had to be decoded. So I did them both. But while I was doing them, all the shooting was taking place and I didn't have a chance to actually see what was going on. I was very upset by the rioting and the mobs, but the shooting made me very nervous. It was the first time in my life that I have actually been so close to such a demonstration, and realize, to a small degree, just what these people have [sic] to go through during the occupation. Of course, we Americans always feel that "nothing will happen to me;" but, after today, I'm not so sure. Several windows were broken in the penthouse of the Embassy building from the guns fired by the police at random. It would really be dreadful to have to live for any length of time under these conditions — total blackouts, guns being fired, people rioting, no water and just general tension all around.

In time things settled down. The Greeks were kind to us. They hadn't much after the war, but they were willing to share with us. I spent four great years in Athens and enjoyed the experience.

An American Girl in Germany

Dorothie Dale

The following is a digest of several papers written by Mrs. Dale as assignments in a writing group in the Nehalem Bay area of Oregon. Mrs. Dale died in the spring of 1997. Her husband, Vernon, has graciously shared her writings with us.

I was one of a group of American civilian workers sent to the European Theatre on a ship to Le Havre in March, 1946, destination Nürnberg. We were men and women of assorted skills, everything from morticians assigned to Graves Registration to clerical workers and court reporters. We were to be a part of the international staff dealing with the Nazi war criminals. I was assigned by the U.S. office of Chief of Counsel for War Crimes to the Palace of Justice. I was a secretary in the office of the director of the Language Division, which provided simultaneous interpreters for the courtroom's four-language system, and translators who rendered documents into English, French, Russian and German.

On my first Friday in Colonel Neave's office, Mrs. Alexander (the Colonel called her Mrs. Alex-ON-der, which appeared to send chills of delight up and down her spine) informed me that, since Bernie and I were lowest on the office totem pole (she didn't put it that way, of course), I had been selected to man the office on my first Saturday morning to answer the telephone and receive callers.

The fact that my lack of knowledge about our mission, my deficiency communicating with German-speaking defense counsel, and the non-existence of any typing or other desk work to be done raised a question in my mind as to why my presence was called for on a Saturday.

So, there I was, all by myself, with nothing to do. The only reading matter in the office was the telephone book. There was no one to call on the telephone; they were all out having fun and/or unpacking and washing dirty clothes.

It was a warm, sunny spring day. I opened a window, sat on the broad sill and looked out. Below me was a courtyard with crisscrossing walks that connected the surrounding buildings. A man was plodding slowly along a path, head down, hands behind his back. As I watched, a movement of white, a military helmet, appeared from the shade of a tree. It was one of the guards, super-crisp and disciplined, who controlled access to the building and to the courtroom and, especially, the prisoners — 19 of them, not counting Martin Bormann, who would have been the twentieth if they could have found him.

The guard looked up at me. In the last few days, I had grown used to soldiers looking at me. I was an American girl. G.I.s would look us up and down, noticing nylons, American clothing — sweaters and skirts — casual things, casually worn. Then they would listen to hear us speak. Then, unbelieving, "You're American!" We were still rarities in Germany, especially to men who came from units stationed in the countryside and were newly posted to the courthouse.

The guard advanced several steps, still looking up at me intently. No smile. I smiled down at him. He looked very earnest, very young. Cute. He raised his arm and waved it in my direction. Well! Still no greeting? A gentleman, though; serious and sweet. I was impressed. This window sill was turning out to be a good place to meet people. He raised his arm again, looking even more serious, and — he was waving me back?

Another uniform stepped into my line of vision, raised his arm and waved me back. Nobody said anything. I slid down from the sill and stood behind the open window, looking down. The second guard raised his arm again, pulled it briskly down until his fist rested on his shoulder. They wanted me to close the window. No doubt about it. So I closed it. What a bunch of sour pickles!

That night at our dinner table at the Grand Hotel, I told my friends about the courtyard and the old men walking around the paths and the less-than-friendly G.I.s. Jeannie, a member of our group from Long Beach, California, was assigned as secretary to Colonel Andrus, the prison commandant. She was practicing to be an old-maid aunt. "You," she snorted, "are lucky you weren't shot! That courtyard you were hanging over was the prison yard. And those old men walking around were the prisoners taking their exercise under guard. It is forbidden even to open windows that face on the yard, much less sit on the windowsill and look out. The orders are to shoot at any suspicious activity. Those prison guards were following strict orders from the colonel."

I didn't remember Mrs. Alex-ON-der saying a word about not hanging out of the windows. And I don't think Jeannie ever mentioned the incident to Colonel Andrus. By that time, she knew he had a choleric disposition and needed to be protected from himself. And I was slowly learning the dos and don'ts of my new life.

Travel was easy in the American sector of occupied Germany after the war. Easy, that is, if you didn't demand indulgences like ice water, dining and sleeping cars, cushioned seats, or glass in every window. For drinking water, there was a Lister bag somewhere down the aisle — an elephantine, dark green canvas bag sagging from a metal tripod and filled with stale water that was rendered supposedly germ-free by the addition of chlorine tablets. Nobody ever drank water from a Lister bag — well, maybe in North Africa on a hot day.

The German trains were clean enough, no dust or litter. The German people were tidy. You will agree with this if you have seen the Army photographs, glossy eight-by-tens, of storehouse rooms filled with leftovers from the human beings processed at Auschwitz, Belsen, Dachau. For instance, there was this photo showing a room filled with neat stacks of babies' chamberpots. And another full of baby shoes, tiny soft shoes whose soles had never touched earth. And on and on, room after room.

But I was talking about travel in the European Theater of Operations. The U. S. Army, of course, had slowed down its operations considerably since the spring of 1945. In 1946, it was running whatever trains it had been able to piece together after the bombing. So our travel was not luxurious, but the price was right. All we had to do to spend a weekend out of Nürnberg was to carry a pass signed by the adjutant and get on any train leaving the Bahnhoff and going in the desired direction. When the conductor came around to ask for our "ticketen," we told him, "Amerikanischer." If he insisted, we told him forcefully, "Raus!" which meant "Get out!" and sent him on his way cursing.

On one of our trips, I met Michel, a Frenchman, and we were friends all of the summer of 1946. That Sunday, the trip was to Dinkelsbuhl, a medieval town southwest of Nürnberg on the Tauber River. We started a conversation at a rest stop along the way and then shared a table with others at lunch in a German village tavern. Army Special Services had arranged ahead for food along the way because the German people were under severe rationing after the war. It was good: country sausage, fried potatoes with plenty of onions, a salad of spring garden vegetables dressed with vinegar, those long, white "icicle" radishes that taverns served with beer, crusty bread the color of molasses. Michel ate with enthusiasm and dispatch. He caught my fleeting glance.

"There were so many times during the war that there was nothing to eat," he said. "Sometimes we would get something, maybe macaroni, and we would eat it so fast. Now, it is a habit to eat fast, while I have food. It is hard for me to get used to always having something to eat." I have never forgotten that.

One morning my friend Bernie came in to work with an announcement to make. She had spent the evening before at the Stork Club. There she had met some G.I.s from the 369th Quartermaster Corps and they had told her that she was the first American girl they had seen since they left the States (outside of nurses and Red Cross girls), and how could they meet some more? Bernie talked a good line and was a real "fixer," and how this exchange ended up was that, if their mess sergeant would cook us a real, old-fashioned, down-home chicken dinner, she would bring her date and several American girls to meet some of the men from the 369th, also a date for the mess sergeant. She told me that if I didn't fulfill her solemn pledge, I would be cheating everybody.

Well, I had been sold down the river: the chicken dinner was Army-style Southern-fried and so was the sergeant, but my future was ordained, although I didn't realize it at the time. The boys from the 369th picked us up to take us to dinner in a two-and-a half ton six-by-six and I rode on the open tailgate with the mess sergeant, who may have learned Southern cooking, but not Southern manners. The upshot of this was that Bernie's date squired both of us and helped us fend off the fighting 369th.

Bernie's date was Staff Sergeant Vern Dale. He worked in the document room, where he shepherded a crew of young German women who were employed to assemble copies of the thousands of documents brought to the courtroom as evidence against the major war criminals in the first war crimes trial. For several months we had lived, unacquainted, next door to each other on Prinzregentenufer, across the street from the Pegnitz River, he in Boys' Town and I in Girls' Town. After the fried-chicken fiasco, we became friends and, eventually, he ended up in my custody for a life sentence, but that came later.

Shortly after the chicken dinner came Thanksgiving. The weekend after Thanksgiving, we were sitting around Moerikestrasse, a large suburban house which belonged to a prosperous German family and had been taken over by the O.C.C. as a billet for War Department civilians. We were talking about holidays at home and what we did and how much we would miss being there with our families. As remembrance piled upon remembrance and our homesickness increased, someone spoke for everyone,

"Why don't we have our own Christmas dinner?" It sounded like one of those movies where the group of young would-be actors and singers and dancers were galvanized into action by Ruby Keeler saying, "Let's fix up this old barn and put on a show!"

From that moment on, we all scrounged. Someone wrote home for olives and pickles and canned delicacies. Another asked for lots of canned shrimp, and still another knew somebody in the Quartermaster Corps who could get hold of a big turkey. The Moerikestrasse girls reserved their big dining room and kitchen; cooks and waiters were recruited from the very willing German employees in billets and offices. The Germans knew they would get leftovers to take home. Excitement rose higher and higher until, at last, the Day arrived.

The dining room at Moerikestrasse was furnished with a ponderous table and throne-like chairs, an elephantine sideboard and a massive, medieval-looking chandelier. It could have been the hall in the fortress of a Teutonic knight. The table was dressed in well-ironed linen, brilliant with borrowed crystal, shining with oddly assorted eating utensils. A side table had been set up as a bar and was presided over by the young German bartender from the illicit Boys' Town. He had come into his own, resplendent in a white jacket, pouring real liquor from bottles of gin, whiskey and rum donated from civilian employees' monthly liquor rations.

The only available liquor that wasn't being poured at the bar was Spanish cognac, which was known locally as "Franco's Revenge" and was always the last strong drink to be served — when they were out of anything else. When you went to the Marble Room at the Grand Hotel, the one-and-only watering hole in Nürnberg for officers and civil service employees and prosecution staff and correspondents and visiting VIP's, and you came to the tail-end of the evening and asked what kind of drink they had left and they told you, "Nothing but Franco's Revenge," you knew it was time to go home. If you could drink Franco's Revenge and appreciate it, the next step for you was the gutter.

So here we were at Moerikestrasse, sitting down to Christmas dinner 1946. The kitchen doors swung open and the waiters entered like spirited two-year-olds champing at the bit for the race to begin, trays loaded with crystal stem glasses filled with our headliner course, our sublime, transcendent, our glorious, exalted and prized shrimp! Expectant quiet, voices stilled as we were served. A clear liquid covered the beautiful pink shellfish — a marinade. We tasted: expressions of surprise, then horror! The cooks had used the donated Spanish cognac to pour over the shrimp. We tried to dig the morsels out of the liquid and drain them against the side of the glass. Nothing worked; they were saturated with the evil brew. Most of that course was returned to the kitchen, to be greeted, no doubt, with quiet joy by the kitchen help.

But the dinner continued with the entrance of the turkey, which drew cheers, and the stuffing and the sweet potatoes and the relishes and, finally and blissfully, the pudding. It was quite a Christmas dinner.

Today, after the last of the family has driven away down towards Oregon's Highway 101, surrounded by remaindered turkey and pie and other rich residue of the celebration, my companion of many years looks back with me at December 25, 1946, the first Christmas that either of us knew that the other existed, and we remember how it was that day at Moerikestrassse.

Lessons from a
New World

Vittoria Mondolfo

In 1932, my family was living on the Adriatic coast, south of Venice, Italy. This was an area of beautiful beaches encompassing Riccione, Rimini and Senigallia. It also was an area of great commercial development. The port of Ancona was, at that time, on a par with Venice in traffic with the East.

My father remained a successful business man, while my future husband's family turned to higher education and also politics. Lucio's (my future husband's) father became professor of Greek philosophy at the University of Bologna and his uncle became senator of Italy, which, following Latin law, is a life position.

Lucio and I met on the tennis courts when I was about 16 and he was 21. One of my strokes sent a ball into the weeds outside the court. I went to search for it and he followed me. I became more and more frustrated when I could not find it, and finally, he confessed that he had found it and put it in his pocket. From then on, he followed me and frequently offered to give me a ride on his bicycle, and the relationship continued to flourish in a very platonic manner.

In the autumn, I went back to Rome where my father had established a successful business conglomerate and Lucio went to Bologna to continue his engineering studies. We met again occasionally when Lucio could come to Rome for a few days. He advised me to skip the next year of the Lyceum so as to save a year and in the fall be able to enter the university. Behaving in the characteristic weak feminine manner of the times, I agreed. Little did I know that this meant embarking on a year of nonstop studying, because I had to master two years of Greek, Latin, advanced math, physics, Italian literature, biology and chemistry. With weekly private lessons in Greek and Latin, I managed. At the end of that year, I had the needed 8/10 (equal to an A-) average to be able to take the university entrance examination. I have to thank my mathematics, physics and chemistry teachers who gave me unheard of grades of 10 (equal to A++) to make up for my deficiency in composition.

I passed the so-called "maturity" exam and I finally had a wonderful summer with Lucio nearby. He should have been busy studying for the six very difficult examinations that he had not taken yet. Instead we spent the summer having a great time.

Then came the year of my 20th birthday. Lucio had finished the 15 months of required military service, acquired his doctorate in engineering and gained employment in Milano at the Isotta Fraschini. This renowned maker of deluxe cars was now beginning a changeover to airplane engines since Mussolini was beginning to envision a future of war and conquest.

At this time, we began to think of getting married, but we had to override the desires of both families. My father could not see his daughter marrying a slave of industry. Lucio's family looked down on commercialism, but nobody could present arguments strong enough to make us desist and in 1936 we won. In a last strong stand I got Lucio to promise that, even after the wedding, I would be allowed to live most of the time in Rome with my family, since he had to stay in Milano and Milano did not offer a degree in chemistry and I had still a year of academic work ahead of me. I had from the start told him that I would not join his family and face my in-laws without a Ph.D.

The next year was probably the deciding factor in our future life. It became evident that Mussolini was more and more thinking to join Hitler to establish a position of parity in dividing the spoils of victory. At that point, we had to come to a very difficult decision. Both my family and that of my husband had strong political beliefs and were committed to the liberal socialist party. My in-laws decided that their best future would be found in South America. Spanish was similar enough to Italian that they were confident they could become proficient in that language in a very short time. Lucio's two brothers were medical doctors and felt they could do very well in any country. Lucio was the only one who did not have very strong bonds with his family and we were both too young to understand how much we would miss the support of the family.

Having definitely decided that all the rest of Europe would be doomed for the next decades, we started gathering information on entering the

United States. We had singular problems: The first one was that I was expecting our first child and Lucio and I had a joint passport. There was no way to add the baby to that document. So we had to leave within the next month, since we certainly did not wish to leave the baby in Italy. We could not obtain an immigrant visa since Lucio was of military age and could be drafted at any time if war was declared.

The second problem was that we had to find a way to transfer some money to the US, which at that time was legally impossible. This was easily overcome by visiting the American consulate in Milano. There we met a very drunk consul who boasted that he had access weekly to the diplomatic pouch, and if we would give him Italian banknotes, he could send them to any address we would furnish and have them exchanged to dollars. We decided to split our bets and gave him half of our money. The other half we gave to an archbishop I knew who, for a certain per cent designated as charity, assured me that the remainder would be transferred to a person we knew. This money was sent as a gift of Italian churches to American missions. As a last resort, we gave a small amount to an uncle of Lucio, who hid it in a very heavily starched shirt collar and took a trip to France. It turned out that our trust was well placed and almost all the money was in the hands of our friends, minus a healthy per cent deducted by the archbishop.

After a week of traveling aboard ship, we arrived in New York, my husband, myself and a future American citizen. As far as career opportunities, there is no doubt that Lucio made the right choice. However, I was much more socially active and leaving so many close friends in Italy was very difficult. I have missed them all the rest of my life. We were entering a foreign country and I have to say we were totally unprepared. Our knowledge of the language was practically zero and we were full of the wrong information. For example, I have an understanding of Chaucer and Shakespearean languages; Lucio can understand all the scientific literature related to aluminum alloys, but neither of us could fathom what to order for a meal or what is appropriate for breakfast.

It was 1939, and at that time a large number of immigrants were coming to the United States trying to escape from an imminent war and the incredible death of millions due to Hitler's ideas. We had a total of $150 and a veritable fortune in diamonds and gold draped around my heavy body. I was expecting my first child and my height of five feet was inadequate for a mother-to-be in her last month of pregnancy. My appearance was what could be called that of the "Madonna di Loreto" (That is one of the richest Madonnas in Italy.)

We had received a thorough indoctrination from the American consul in Milano in what to do immediately upon arrival and what to expect.

He was either completely ignorant or very, very drunk when he received us in his house and served us what now I would call a triple Scotch straight. Refilling his glass, he said, "First thing, throw away the Italian passport, then get a job and forget that you ever were in Italy." He continued pontificating about all the riches of the USA and the unlimited possibilities open to anybody. Luckily we were not as naive as that and started asking whoever came close about employment for Lucio, a doctor for delivering the baby and similar questions. Lesson one I learned: the USA and Italy have definitely the same kind of employees in their official capacity and one should stay clear of them if possible.

With the birth of my baby approaching, we found a very small apartment where we could cook a few simple meals and have room to keep the baby. We rented a third floor walk-up for $55 per month and rescued the $2,000 that Lucio's uncle had taken to France with him, hidden in the well-starched collar, and mailed to a sister of my friend, who at that time was getting a Ph.D. at Johns Hopkins University. Of course, I could not travel in my condition and Lucio went alone to Baltimore to get the money. He said that the first hotel he went to was infested with bedbugs. He had led the manager to the bed; and, lifting the mattresses, showed him the problem and got his money back. We learned the second lesson: The claim of cleanliness is not always true.

Finally, we were solvent and we started our new life: Lucio studying English and I minding the apartment and trying to cook. I can assure you that a Ph.D. in chemistry is no preparation for cooking cheap meals and buying food if you cannot read the cookbook. We survived and the day of the baby's birth arrived. If we were not well prepared, neither was the hospital prepared for us. In desperation, they sent me a young resident who was supposed to be fluent in Spanish. He was not; he was a Pole who had received his degree in Bologna, Italy, in the hospital where my mother-in-law was practicing. When the name rang a bell with him, we proceeded to speak Italian, to become good friends and clear all the nurses' problems. Lesson No. 3: My accent was not the southern Italian accent recognized by the local people.

In August, Lucio's English had improved enough that he got a job in Gary, Indiana, and following our Italian habit to live as close to work as possible, he rented an apartment in a kind of Polish steel workers' ghetto. There the neighbors were very nice and always ready to baby-sit, and a kind lady gave me Lesson No. 4. When you arrive in America you should divorce your husband and marry an American because they are the best husbands. This is a lesson I did not follow and, after 66 years of matrimony, I still am glad I did not.

After a while we became so rich with Lucio's salary of $75 per week

that we could afford to move to Chicago in a better area and to buy a dilap-
idated car. Once, wearing a tight, short skirt, after getting out of the car,
I noticed a nice young fellow. He had been looking at me and seeing that
I had noticed him, became embarrassed and looked at his feet. In Italy, I
would have received applause with whistles to wake up the dead. I have to
confess, I felt quite humiliated at this lack of attention. After all, I was
barely twenty-three years old and my legs were quite good looking,
although not as long as they are preferred in the USA.

Lesson number 5 was that different classes socialize in different ways.
This I learned at the very first social affair we had occasion to join. After a
dinner of unrecognizable vittles, to us, the men retreated to the kitchen,
where they proceeded to drink and discuss sports and such enterprises,
while the ladies were comfortably discussing housekeeping and children in
the living room. In due time, we found educated couples where conversation was general and interesting. Nothing to compare to the salons of
Milano, where my husband's great-aunt, at the age of 101, very properly
had informed me that she "received" on Wednesday between 5:00 P.M. and
7:30 P.M. Carefully dressed and with my best gloves on, I arrived at her
salon and found an amazing crowd of university professors, high government officials and such, all partaking of tea and aperitifs and discussing
topics of world importance.

Lesson number 6 was probably the most traumatic — the food. It
reminds me of the Italian proverb: "The best patriot is the stomach." Truer
words were never printed. In the forties, upon leaving New York City, the
country was a desert of steak and potatoes! Now, of course, it has all
changed.

Our life was proceeding on an even keel. My culinary skills were
improving; we were enjoying making new friends and Lucio's career was
proceeding even better than we had hoped. From Chicago we moved to
Louisville, Kentucky, where Lucio had a position in research with Revere.
The company was in the process of changing production from copper to
light alloys when Pearl Harbor and the entry of the United States into the
war caught us in its grip. Immediately the newspapers and radio started to
publicize the fact that citizens of Germany and Italy were to be considered
enemy aliens. Aliens were prohibited to own short wave radios, cameras
and weapons. If they had any in their possession, they were to be immediately given to the proper authorities. We scoured offices in Louisville without finding anybody who would take our radio and our cameras. In
desperation we gave them to a family living in our building who worried
about how they would find us again to return the items.

Now a very odd period began. Lucio was dismissed by Revere for
undisclosed reasons. We returned to Chicago where he found another

position and three months later he was dismissed again and so it continued. We became familiar with many of the Midwest cities. Eventually one
of his employers told him that the Department of Defense took three
months to investigate a new employee in a defense industry and Lucio was
considered dangerous. Of course this system would have been perfect for
a spy, giving him the possibility to discover the secrets of the various factories.

Quite dismayed, Lucio made his way to Washington and managed to
get an audience with the proper authorities. He learned that the black mark
on his record was due to the fact that he had served in the Italian army as
an officer. When the facts were established that, in Italy, military service
has always been compulsory and that any male who has a college degree is
automatically rated an officer, the case was immediately dismissed. Lucio
was cleared for employment and given a rating for traveling on any flight
such that he could bounce any military person who had a rank below general.

The war ground on and we were cut off from what family was left in
Italy, but we could communicate with South America and by devious ways,
we managed to get some news back and forth. And then the war was over.

After a few years our two daughters were old enough for school or
kindergarten and I was feeling very restless and useless at home. In Italy
anybody who had a university degree hired competent help and started a
career. We were in Chicago a short walk from the University of Chicago.
I decided to apply for a position. When I went to the head of the employment office I was greeted with open arms and offered a position in the biology department. It was for a full time laboratory job. Since I did not feel
that I could leave my girls alone after school I politely declined and was
sent to the head of the libraries.

It seems that my Italian education was a big plus: I knew Latin, Greek,
French and Italian and immediately was sent to the Classics Library. The
hours were very convenient, the pay illusory (85 cents per hour), but I
could walk to the office from our house and I liked the old spinster who
was going to be my immediate superior. What I did not know was that she
would quit in June and I would be promoted from the lowest class of clerk
to head of the Classics and Music Library, which consisted of more than a
million volumes housed in seven floors. I quickly reorganized the whole
operation and my rewards were many: professional grade equal to faculty
status and a salary commensurate to my responsibilities.

After seven years of thinking and yearning to go back to a science
environment, I went to the main office, where they were astounded to see
me. It seemed that they had been searching for a chemist and not had any
luck and they had forgotten my background and degree. Within days I was

transferred and for many years I headed the Chemistry Library. At that time the university followed a most unusual path: the librarians were chosen for their subject knowledge and no library degree was required. This factor was to my great advantage and I remained there for many years, very happy years.

Finally Lucio decided to quit his academic position and accepted one in Clinton, New York, at Revere Brass, and I went to work at Hamilton College as assistant director of the library and part-time Italian teacher. So goodbye to the big city and hello to a village.

In retrospect I have to thank the foresight and timeliness of my husband that enabled all of our family to avoid the chaos of the European war experience.

Hot Tea and
Lemon Drops

Jean Hammond Bradley

The warbling wail of the air-raid siren on top of the building next to the school started 40 small children, ages three and four, on an all-too-familiar routine. Each child slung his gas mask around his neck and, in silence, followed me through the cloakroom, picking up outdoor garments. We walked around the building to the air-raid shelters in the field behind the school. Each class competed with the others to see who got to the shelters first. After a head count, I began to help the children into their outdoor clothes (underground shelters are cold), usually in time for the all clear to sound. Then the whole routine was reversed and activities began again in the classrooms. Several times we had to leave the midday meal, get to the shelters and make a meal of chocolate, hardtack biscuits and water from the emergency rations kept in the shelter. One memorable day, this routine was repeated 24 times during eight hours of school.

The City of Gloucester, England, was designated a "safe area" and received children from east London and port cities, such as Hull, in Yorkshire. These children were official evacuees, and teachers, such as myself, were deputized as billeting officers. Our task was to take these displaced children and put them into homes. Sometimes the homeowners were welcoming and accepted their guests graciously. Sometimes the householder was resentful and could only be persuaded to accept the guest by using authority. Poor lost and lonely children!

The east-enders had come direct from running wild in the hopfields of Kent where their parents made some extra money picking the hops. The Yorkshire children came from urban centers, and with those two different and distinctive speech patterns, the Gloucester children were completely at a loss. I had lived in both London and Yorkshire and was able to act as interpreter.

With eight-hour days of teaching duties, which included feeding the hot midday meal, all elementary school teachers had to perform firewatching duties at the schools. In order for us not to be too bored(?), the school board decided that firewatching duties should be performed at a school different from teaching assignments. In my case, I went about one mile to my firewatch duties. In the winter, this meant that school finished after dark at 4:30 p.m. I got on my trusty bicycle and rode to the other school, taking with me my evening meal.

The teachers' lounge now contained four bunk beds, complete with rough army blankets. As we were expected to be alert for any incidents, we slept in our clothes until we had to man (or woman) the stirrup pumps and sand buckets in the event of an "incident." We had some good fellowship and also some scary times. As soon as daylight arrived, back to our teaching—usually with a quick wash and brush up with cold water. Sometimes we had time for breakfast.

Life during the first weeks after war was declared was planned around our fears of immediate devastation of our cities. We walked out only to buy groceries or to our jobs in sandbagged buildings. When nothing drastic happened in those early days, we began to resume fairly normal lives. Most of the men had been called up and, increasingly, women were seen in new areas of life. Women served as postmen (no feminine movement yet!), police, railway porters, and bus drivers, as well as workers in the munitions and aircraft factories. As a teacher, I was restricted to that job. Until well after the war, no teacher could move into any other work. But I found plenty to do working with youth groups during my free time.

All youths between the ages of 10 and 17 were required by law to affiliate with an organized group. Boy Scouts, Girl Guides and Boys and Girls Life Brigade troops were crowded with these young people. At least two nights a week I was in charge of my church's company of the Girls Life Brigade. All the girls from seven years old to 17 studied first aid, nutrition, home management and nursing and enjoyed physical education. When we camped, we also helped the land girls who worked on the farms—some of the girls learning about the relationship between cows and milk for the first time.

Ration cards for food and clothing were issued to everyone, as were identity cards. The coupons had to be clipped out at every shop where food was purchased. A big blow to English tea drinkers was the four ounces per person for a week. Since coffee was not rationed, a number of people began the day with coffee instead of tea. One drawback was that previously coffee was made half and half with hot milk. As milk was rationed, that became impractical.

Because butter, margarine, sugar and eggs were rationed, going out for tea entailed carrying a little bag with tea, sugar and margarine to give to one's hostess. Eggs, two to a person each week, caused much discussion in our family. Should we make a cake, scramble the eggs, or have one apiece for tea? Dried egg powder helped somewhat and we all got used to the taste.

Allotment gardens helped to augment the vegetables and berries for the use of families. These gardens were small plots owned by the city and rented to gardeners for a minimal sum. There was great competition among the gardeners—especially in obtaining good manure. I've seen my father, in full clerical dress, rush out with bucket and shovel as the delivery man's horse-drawn cart went by!

Since fuel to heat the homes and food to warm the body were both in short supply, clothing became very important. Everything from socks and handkerchiefs to coats, shoes, and dresses—all required coupons. After the first few years, the big question was, "Can we buy a coat, or shirt—and, if so, will we have enough coupons for any other clothing this year?"

In our house, with four women, we had one good set of lingerie by the end of the war—everything else was, as my mother put it, "more holey than righteous." The "good" set was used by the one with the doctor's appointment or a special social event. Hats were not rationed and proved an emotional lift for many women.

Margaret, my sister, went to work for the match factory as a social worker, and through her work we were allotted a truckload of logs each six months. These were the root ends of trees which would not go through the machines which cut the wood into match sticks. We really appreciated the logs, but my father spent a lot of time and energy chopping them to fireplace size.

Newspapers, the main source of information, soon became one page of heavily censored news. Most people relied on radios for more detailed accounts of the wartime activities. The shortage of newspaper itself was a great loss. Not only was it almost impossible to light a coal fire without newspaper to start the kindling, but with no paper bags or wrapping paper, newspaper became the wrapping for any purchase. Everything from items of clothes to fish and chips needed newspaper. One day, we saw my father coming up the road from town carrying a whole salmon by its tail. He had forgotten to put a string bag or newspaper in his pocket to wrap unexpected items! Since salmon was caught in the Severn and Wye rivers and was not rationed, we enjoyed the feast and the fun of such *infra dig.* behavior on the part of Father.

Gloucester was not subject to many concentrated raids, but it was situated on the bombing routes to Swansea, in South Wales and Birmingham and Coventry in the Midlands. Usually one or two planes would be left behind during raids on these cities, mostly to harass the firefighters and gunnery enclaves.

One afternoon, Father came running in from the garden shouting, "One for the station, one for the gas works, one for the hospital, and one for us." He had seen a lone plane (no warning siren) drop four bombs. He was not quite accurate. They all missed, doing little damage, but we did lose all the windows in the house and church next door; the house moved off its foundations by inches and a block of granite paving stone flew over the house across the street and landed in our back bedroom.

In between such exciting (?) events, women had to spend many hours of wearisome queuing for various food items. Everyone shared news of items just delivered to a store. Such things as liver caused the whole neighborhood of women to descend on the butcher's shop (it was not rationed) but the butcher said that cows were now bred without any insides and pigs without feet and tails. The truth was that these items were largely reserved for hospitals. Cooking became a test of ingenuity with low gas pressure, small coal fires and lack of ingredients. Such things as potato skins, thinly sliced, were served for a filling meal when roasted.

It was the small things that caused a lot of trouble. Bobby pins to keep hair in place were to be found rarely; needles could be bought only one at a time and safety pins almost vanished. Soap, either for personal cleansing or for laundry, was scarce. The laundry soap deteriorated in quality and clothes soon became a uniform dove grey. Thank goodness, the hand soap was hard-milled and lasted a long time.

Some of our most companionable times were shared by a log fire, reading a book and gobbling up in one evening our month's supply of candy (all four ounces for each of us). One friend of ours always used her ration to buy lemon drops—that way she could have lemon *and* sugar in her tea by melting the candy in her teapot.

The blackout was very real and immediate. Half an hour each night could be spent in making the house light-proof. No street lamps were lit, so when we went outdoors, we took a torch (flashlight) but that was blacked out with tape so only a pinpoint of light showed. Even after we had waited for two minutes outside the door to accustom our eyes to the darkness, we often found ourselves embracing strangers in the street who were also having trouble with the dark.

One of the good things to come out of the war was the opportunity to meet with people from different lands and cultures. There were camps of Poles, Free French, Belgians and, later, Americans all around Gloucester.

Inviting these people into our homes gave us a wonderful opportunity to learn about them and their lives.

Among those who visited our home was a soldier who came from a town he called "Vayeho." Since none of us spoke Spanish, we had a hard time translating this to Vallejo. After several visits, we began to invite him to tea anytime he was in Gloucester. It turned out he visited frequently! His interest, he said, was in visiting the secret monk's passage in one of the town hostelries. We soon found out he was more interested in the young women of the family. My mother persuaded him that he should be most interested in the girl who liked cooking — which turned out to have serious consequences.

Every Sunday afternoon, we stationed my youngest brother at the bay window which looked down the street. His job was to count the number of service people accompanying Father. These, mostly young, men found that, having been bused to town, there were no cafes or restaurants and no picture houses open on Sunday. Father collected them up if they accepted his invitation to tea. When we knew that 10 or 12 visitors were on the way, Mother and I began scrambling around to find enough to feed them. But we enjoyed these visits. One Christmas week, we had as house guests five servicemen whose homes were in the north of England and their families (a wife and two children for each). What a squash! But we had a wonderful Christmas — even turkey!

Train travel was quite an adventure. All railway station signs were removed to confuse enemy paratroopers (not to mention legitimate travelers) and city signs and direction sign posts were removed. Especially at night, arriving at the proper destination could be quite difficult. Few people were willing to give strangers directions. The trains were always crowded and I remember one journey from Gloucester to Edinburgh (about 350 miles) made sitting on the floor of the train corridor back to back with a serviceman — a complete stranger until then. English reserve began to break down as we all shared scary and difficult journeys together.

The end of the war saw my brother and the wife he married in Cairo, Egypt, return on V-E Day. My youngest sister went off to college in North Wales. My father took the newspapers out of his Homburg hat — that was his protection when visiting shelters during air raids. Margaret went to work in London and Douglas finished school. Mother, who had spent most of her time and energy keeping the family fed, clothed and comforted, went on doing the same things. She had some extra time to spend on choral society and drama classes — her great joy. I went to Lancashire and Yorkshire as a national youth organizer for the Girls Life Brigade.

The American soldier who visited so frequently was transferred to the south of France, then to the Philippines. We continued a correspondence begun soon after he left Gloucester. One day a letter arrived from the Philippines proposing marriage. After some consideration I wrote accepting his proposal. However, I wanted to think the matter over for a few days. As I was leaving to conduct a training session, I left the letter, sealed but not stamped, on the mantelpiece. When I returned two days later, I found that my friend with whom I was sharing the flat-let had stamped and mailed the letter! I was committed!

Several weeks later a bank draft arrived with a note asking me to buy an engagement ring. My father went with me to pick it out. Eventually I crossed the Atlantic to California and Gene Bradley and I were married in the First Christian Church of Vallejo on February 9, 1947. Here we have remained ever since.

A Swiss Girl
in Egypt

Cecile Briar

I was born to Swiss parents in 1926 in the eastern part of Switzerland, the Rhine valley. I was one of a set of fraternal twins. When I was two and a half years old, my mother, brother and an older "sister" moved to Egypt. My father had become part of a group of Swiss launching a Portland cement factory about 15 miles south of Cairo. Egypt was at that time a British protectorate.

As the factory neared completion in 1931 we moved into a "compound" abandoned by Belgians whose company had gone belly up. Because of the factory's need for lime we were located on the edge of the desert by the Mokkatham Hills and the Nile. The limestone was brought from the quarries on little trolleys. As children, we enjoyed the wild outdoors; we were not troubled by the faulty provision of electricity (initially provided by a generator) or the distance of stores and restaurants. A "buyer" went into Cairo twice a day and bought all the provisions. Since ours was a gated community, which over the years provided more and more amenities, e.g., pool, tennis courts, bowling alley, the "isolation" did not seem to be a handicap. We went to school in Cairo, a half hour train ride from home, and enjoyed the international flavor of Cairo. French, German, Arabic, Italian and the Swiss dialect spoken at home rolled off our tongues with ease. We were children of the world even though our parents restricted their social and other activities to the Swiss Club and the Swiss colony. We took our vacations in Switzerland.

In 1938, when I was 12, Hitler marched into the Sudetenland just north of Austria. I saw my first English lorries, became aware of British troops and heard English spoken. The British military explored the caves in the nearby Mokkatham Hills. They made preparations to bring ammunition into the caves, which had been created by the stones carved out for the pyramids long ago. Soon the clubhouse and other empty buildings in the compound were taken over by the soldiers in uniform. By the summer of 1939, we were all just waiting for hostilities to break out.

At the end of August my father was called to active service and my "sister" turned out to have a German passport. I learned that she had been adopted by a maternal great aunt and uncle of mine in Switzerland. When they died, my father became her guardian and she became part of our family. Apparently no one had given a thought to her passport. (The natural mother was German living in Switzerland and the father was Swiss.) Rumors had it that the Germans were to be interned in Egyptian jails. This frightened her and she decided to leave with the German colony and go to Germany, to a country she had never been and where she knew no one. She was about 20 years old at that time.

My family was in crisis. My "sister" had left, my father was mobilized and my mother was sick. That same weekend she left, my brother and I were playing when an English soldier, telegram in hand, told us "We are at war." Though we only spoke a few words of English, we understood those words. It was about 1 PM Sunday, September 3, 1939, Egyptian time. Soon we were surrounded by a sea of military from all over the British Empire as well as allies from all over the world.

I was 13 years old and took over the running of the household even though I was still climbing trees and playing hide and seek. I was placing the food orders, cooking, cleaning on weekends and attending a new and far more demanding school. Our servants had gone to work for the army and it took time to recruit others. Cairo was so full of troops that I often wondered where the civilians had gone.

Initially, my family crisis, the loss of childhood friends who were caught in Europe and could not return and the increased violence around me was bewildering. Troops, drunk or otherwise, would get into terrible fights with each other as well as the local population. It seemed that much of what was familiar to me had vanished and the waters I had to learn to navigate were at times dangerous and challenging. I was also learning to master English in a new school and cope with mountains of homework and a six day school week. All this while Cairo became less and less safe for a teenage girl which meant being on the alert all the time. So I experienced the war up to early 1942 mostly in terms of troops, lack of safety, poor food, little reading material and increased responsibilities at home.

Incidents like the following were not uncommon. I was in my Girl Scout uniform, which was navy blue. The Girl Scout uniform had the same hat as the New Zealand uniform and had a big leather belt. I was at the train station on my way home looking at schedules. Suddenly I found myself being picked up about two feet off the ground by a huge, very drunk, New Zealander. He had grabbed the back of my belt and lifted me up like a rat. Two other men immediately came up and said, "Drop that girl, drop that girl." He finally did, but he was extremely belligerent. I think the color of our uniforms must have attracted him.

I was not aware of South Africa and the racial problems they had, except that I knew that the Cape Town blacks were not asked to fight. They built trenches and set up tents, but it was only the whites that carried arms and fought. I can remember being opposite one, again on a train, and he was yelling at me that someday white people would come crawling to him. He was really in a rage and I did not have the vaguest notion of what he was talking about, because where I grew up, anybody could go anywhere if you had the money to purchase whatever you desired, so this apartheid was completely unknown to me.

On the other hand the New Zealanders had no racial problems. The Maoris, who were the native New Zealanders, and the white New Zealanders, always got along beautifully. I never saw a fight between the two of them. What you did see among a lot of New Zealanders and South Africans was shell-shocked people. When there were certain noises, they would absolutely fall apart. That was very painful to see.

After obtaining my German High School diploma at age 15, I enrolled in an English speaking convent school (the American University would not consider me because of my age) whose mother superior was American. I was a boarder but came home weekends and on vacations.

My home had become a receiving center for troops. My parents spoke almost no English, but my mother fed the soldiers and on weekends I was the main entertainer and "guest receiver." At times I resented this avalanche of visitors but mother always said, "Someday you'll be away from home and you'll know what it means to have a place to go to." It was as a result of my mother's hospitality that I became the advisor and mother confessor to many an upset, confused, hurt and lonely serviceman. As England was bombed, a lot of troops lost a mother, a father, child or wife and that was difficult. By the same token, a lot of the troops went out and formed alliances with different women and that created problems at home. I was a young woman and not military and a sympathetic ear. I think that helped them. As a result, I also developed a lot of pen pals all over the world.

Besides being an advisor I sometimes played nurse. The New Zealand base, with close to a million men, was about six miles north of us and the

South African base was about six miles south of us. Troops were like ants, every place. A lot of the New Zealanders were massacred in Crete and the wounded came back in cattle and freight trains lying on the floor. They were brought to a big New Zealand receiving hospital just a few miles from home. Sometimes the patients were allowed to leave the hospital and they would have to have the bandages changed once or twice a day. Many came to our house. Mother always baked cookies and brewed tea for the men. I remember one soldier, a New Zealander who was married to a Maori, a native New Zealand lady, used to come to the house. It was really touch and go for him for quite a while. If bandages needed to be changed, I would change them. I am sure there were others that were wounded, but I just remember the New Zealanders were hit very, very hard in Crete.

During the summer of 1942, Rommel was outside El Alamein, North Africa, which is just outside Alexandria. I was ready to take the junior Oxford test, which was postponed. From our house, up to where the Mokkatham Hills were, as far as the eye could see, the area was covered with trucks, evacuating the ammunition. I don't know where they took it. Every day the asphalt road that led up to the camp was covered with sand so that the airplanes—and there were a few air raids—would not spot it. But of course they could spot it, because there was a railroad and there was the Nile.

During that crisis my mother bought huge blocks of ice daily. They were chopped up and put in the canteens of the ammunition drivers so they had cool water as they returned either to the front or another destination.

We had a number of air raids during 1942 and 1943 because our compound had become a military base. One of the memories that I recall very vividly was that the air raid sirens had sounded and I was on the balcony. The plane came down for a dive and I could see the shadow of the wing. Then we went into the shelter, an old cement oven 12 feet underground that had been furnished with bunks and toilets. There was a tremendous explosion and I thought the plane had crashed, but we were very lucky. A land mine had been dropped attached to a beautiful pale blue silk parachute which landed maybe 100 yards from our entrance. It was caught in a big eucalyptus tree and did not go off. Several more land mines had also been parachuted. The troops went out and collected them and detonated them.

I remember the anti-air craft going on at night. Next to the air raid shelter was a billet (lodging) for troops and they would sit outside making music with spoons, two spoons clacking together. I don't think the seriousness of the situation really hit us. I think we were young. Air raids were an annoyance which interrupted sleep sometimes two or three times a night.

Being a military compound, we had guards and a password every night. The compound had always been a walled, locked community, but now the military controlled the internal movements of the civilians. When Rommel was outside Alexandria, security became tighter and there was talk of evacuation. One night we got orders to stand by for departure. With the certainty only a 16 year old could muster, I told the guard we were not leaving. I did not think it advisable or safe to go to some camp further in the desert. Within hours the Germans started to retreat and the imminent danger seemed over.

I took my exam in August and returned to boarding school in September 1942. The air raids I experienced in boarding school in Heliopolis were very different from the ones I experienced at home. Heliopolis is near an airport and the school was close to the airport. I remember several times we were ushered into the basement; there was no air raid shelter and some of the kids became hysterical because the nuns started reciting the prayers of the dead. Some of us managed to keep the group in control. If something had happened, there was no place to go. I don't remember ever experiencing any particular anxiety or any particular fear. I guess being a teenager, too, I thought nothing was ever going to happen to me.

My interactions with troops so far had been restricted to British men and women. I had had no contact with Americans. (The American troops were segregated at that time. I had seen the American military police throw American black soldiers off a dance floor some place, but I had never really realized what it was all about. I just thought they had misbehaved.) There was always a great interest in the American troops because they had more money than the British; their pay was better. Many women, young women, wanted to marry Americans because they thought they would be better off coming to America, which of course didn't always materialize.

When I was in boarding school, the nuns used to entertain the troops for tea in the afternoon. One day the mother superior asked my girlfriend and me to deliver a message to a Sergeant Chester. Still in our school uniforms, we left the school area and went into Heliopolis to look for a Sergeant Chester. We entered a building with a large winding staircase. Halfway up was a landing with a desk. It looked just like out of the movies. There was a guy sitting there, sort of reddish blond with freckles, smoking a cigar, with his feet on the desk. As my girlfriend and I approached him, we said we were looking for Sergeant Chester. He identified himself as Sergeant Chester. He had to repeat it three times because I could not understand what he was saying. We remained standing, silent, holding onto the note for him. "Come on, what is it, what is it that you want?" I had never spoken to a man while he remained sitting. I was waiting for Sergeant Chester to get up! He obviously was not going to, so I silently handed him the note. He read it and then decided that two people should walk us back to school. Well, my girlfriend was Egyptian, and her father had the psychiatric hospital. As we were walking on the sidewalks which were very wide, at least 10 feet or more, the guys while talking kept slapping us on the back. We in turn moved further and further away from them. We were practically in the street. I can't remember what the discussion was, but I remember one of those men saying to my girlfriend, "You can take the girl out of Egypt, but you can't take the Egyptian out of the girl." I just nearly died at that comment. When we got back to school, the school secretary said, "What do you think of the Americans?" My response was, "If that's what they're like, you can keep them," being still a little bit shocked by the rudeness I had just experienced.

I had no further contact with Americans until I went to college — the American University in Cairo. It was at that point that I learned to appreciate their more casual life style, greater openness and informality. My teachers were American as well as Belgian and Near Easterners.

On campus I became acquainted with men from all over the Near and Middle East, many of whom were unfamiliar with appropriate social interaction with women, let alone western women. Some had lived in households where the sexes were segregated. All of us benefited from our multicultural, multiethnic experience.

As the war headed into the home stretch in late 1944–1945, some things changed in my immediate environment. We now had German POW's guarding the compound, and Cairo was loaded not only with British and American troops, but with free Poles, the free French, the free Italians, Greeks, you name it, they were there. My mother continued to fix tea and sandwiches for the guards, just as she had for the British. Two POWs I remember distinctly. One was an Italian. His mother had been Swiss, and he spoke Swiss like a Swiss. He had been Rommel's Italian interpreter. That man was about 45. Another young guy, in his late 20's, I don't remember his name, was Rommel's English interpreter. The ages of the POWs, particularly from 1944 on, were from 16 to 65 years.

Gradually troops dispersed out of Egypt after the war though it took more than a year. The city was racked with demonstrations which frequently turned violent. The people of Egypt wanted their independence from Britain. They would set everything on fire — streetcars, buses, street lights — and turn over cars. The era of foreigners living securely and comfortably seemed to be waning. Eventually, my father lost everything after the departure of King Farouk in the 60's. They confiscated all foreign industries and business.

Unlike prewar, the English language was everywhere, French was vanishing and with the understandable growing sense of national pride, foreigners had to pass all-Arabic tests prior to receiving a college diploma.

In 1947, it was time for me to leave Egypt to further my education in social work in the United States. Looking back, I realize that the war years had posed a far lesser threat to my safety than the many violent demonstrations I had witnessed during all my years of living in the land of pharaohs.

Mother always said to us, "You only have today. What you learn, nobody can take away from you. You need to have a trade or a profession so that you can stand on your own two feet." I landed in New York on my way to graduate school in Chapel Hill, North Carolina. My mother's words "Some day you'll be away from home and happy to have a place to go to" often rang in my ears as I

Cecile Briar, 1947, age 20— upon graduating from American University, Cairo, Egypt.

enjoyed the warm hospitality extended to me by the families of my classmates and friends. "What goes around comes around" and I had come full circle in my life.

The Path to
Gold Mountain

by Ellen Ong, as told to Barbara Sloan

The Japanese invaded China around 1934 or 1935. It was pretty bad by 1937. That's when I first noticed — when I was about seven. They started coming in from the north, from Mongolia, Tingen, a big port city. They did not come into my town in the beginning, only in the north. We were far in the south. Fighting against Chiang Kai Shek, they took over one state at a time. They came down to the south when I was maybe 12 or 13 — troops in our town. Their planes flew over. This was not a military area, just a normal area where people lived, mostly farmers. They flew over the city and they bombed the city. Outside town, they used machine guns and killed lots of people. My aunt was shopping in town and she got killed. My mother was in town too that day, but she was lucky. She was OK. We kids were at home with our grandmother.

They flew over our village and we all ran and hid in the bushes. We were so dumb! We didn't think the guns would shoot through the bushes. We just wanted to have something over our heads. We went wherever we could find anything we could go under — under a bed, a chair, or some-thing.

Pretty soon the Japanese came in with the horses. They came through town; they raped women and they took our food. They went through the house and took everything, because they eat rice just like Chinese people do. They came through our house. They ate, then they went to a different town. They just went through everywhere. They tortured people.

256

My mother sent my sister and me to some relatives. She stayed with my grandmother. My grandmother had bound feet, she couldn't go anywhere. She walked tip-toe. My mother couldn't leave her by herself, so she stayed and sent us to relatives. We were safe there, the Japanese didn't come to where we were.

Dr. Sun Yat Sen was the father of the new China. All the Chinese emperors controlled the country for so many generations, many hundred years, and everyone got so sick and tired of it. The emperor controlled the whole country, controlled who people married, everything, the old-fashioned way. Dr. Sun Yat Sen wanted to change the whole country. He overthrew the Ching dynasty, that was the last one, the last emperor. The Japanese came in and took advantage of the disorder and confusion. Dr. Sun Yat Sen died and Chiang Kai Shek became the President of China and started fighting with the Japanese, but they took over one state at a time, and our town eventually was bombed.

I was born in 1930 in southern China, near Canton, in a village called Taishan. The village had no hospital. We had five in our family: my mother, my grandmother, and my brother, my sister, and me. My brother is a year older, my sister is two years younger. My grandfather was over here in America, and my father was in Beijing. My father was teaching school; he was a professor. He wanted my mother to go join him to live there, where he worked, but my mother couldn't leave my grandmother at home. The grandmother was her mother-in-law, my father's mother. Traditionally, in China the daughter-in-law is expected to care for and be responsible to her mother-in-law.

My mother was the kind of woman who wanted to do everything herself. But my grandmother couldn't do much because of her bound feet. Her father was an old-fashioned teacher in a village. She was supposedly from a high-class family. If you are poor, the parents expect the kids to help out and work. If the family could afford it, they made the girls have small feet. If you have small feet, how can you help out? When a little girl was five or six, they would wrap her feet with strips of cloth very tight so her feet wouldn't grow bigger and continue to wrap them until she was grown. It was very painful. In time her legs were like stumps with tiny feet shaped like a V. Their families wouldn't let them marry a farmer, not a lower class man. Only rich people can have girls' feet bound. That way the daughters can marry into a better family and they don't have to work.

My mother was from a different generation. My grandmother's generation had long hair that they put up in a bun. Before they got married, their long hair hung down in a braid. My mother's generation cut their hair off, just after Dr. Sun Yat Sen overthrew the dynasties. Things changed. After my grandmother's generation, nobody bound feet anymore. The students came out to fight and said the girls didn't have to bind their feet. The girls could do anything they wanted. If they don't want to do anything, that's OK too. They just didn't have to have small feet. I'm glad I didn't have to do it. My grandmother went through a lot.

My grandfather came over to the United States at the end of the 1800s and he always sent money home so my grandmother didn't have to work. She had a servant because she couldn't walk.

We depended on my grandfather to send money home. He had a restaurant here, in Red Bluff [California]. But all of the Chinese people with relatives in the United States were cut off from their support because of the Japanese invasion after Pearl Harbor. We didn't have any money for living, because we had no men in the house to do any farming. My grandfather was over here in California, my father was up north in China. So there were just the two ladies and us, the three kids.

We lived in southern China. Our house had two bedrooms and a big living room and two kitchens. Some people had an upstairs; we didn't, we just had the ground floor. We had a vegetable garden. We had no sewers and no running water in the house. We had to go to an outhouse to relieve ourselves. We didn't have electricity. We had a public well. Everyone went to the same well to get water. My job in my house with my mother and grandmother was to go get the water. We had a big barrel, about three feet high, and I had to go bring water and fill up this thing every day. I had two wooden buckets with a stick over my shoulders. I haven't done it in so long, I'm not sure I can do it anymore. I always had to help my mother carry water to water our garden. We didn't have a hose; we carried the water by bucket. We had long-handled scoopers to scoop water into the bucket from the stream and then we carried it to the garden. When I first came over here, sometimes I would dream the barrel was low and I had to go get water.

We had a big tank for the rice, too. We had to polish the rice. We didn't eat it like here, the brown rice. That isn't polished. Chinese people don't like to eat rice that is not polished. Rich people could buy rice already polished. We were poor, so we had to polish our own rice, using manpower. Every household had a granite rock, a big bowl. When you build a house, you build one in. The bottom is smaller, the top is open. We had a 4 × 4 piece of hardwood. At one end it had a granite rock about eight inches around, built into the wood. A person stood on one end of the 4 × 4 piece of wood to raise it up, then let the end with the rock fall into the rice. The rock falling through the rice took all the rough skin off without crushing the rice. We had to do this about once a month. Then we would store it in a big container.

We had a stove, built with bricks, and a big wok. When we harvested, we brought rice straw home and dried it. We fed it into the stove to cook the rice. When we cooked rice, we put the meat or vegetables on top of the rice on a bamboo rack.

When we wanted to get something, like some meat, we had to go to a little town near us. We had to walk maybe three or four miles, kind of a long way. People had no cars, no bus, no bicycle; everybody walked. We didn't have meat too often. Here, chicken is so cheap, we eat chicken any time, but in China, we had to wait until a holiday to eat chicken. We could go buy them, but we had no money. We had a mother hen and raised our own. Here people eat two, three eggs at a sitting, for breakfast. We would put two eggs in a bowl, add some water, and steam them and they would come out all set like a pudding. We would add some onion tops and we had some rice and we each would get some to eat on the rice. When I came here, I was surprised to see two or three eggs for one person.

Here people have one piece of meat for one person. We would have maybe a half piece of meat, sliced into small pieces and cooked with vegetables. The whole family would share. We would put it in the middle of the table. You would get a bowl of rice and get some meat and vegetables to eat with your rice. The only time we wouldn't mix everything together was the holidays. You need a whole chicken to put in front of your ancestors as an offering. That was the only time we had a whole chicken. After that, we would chop up the chicken and put it in one dish and everyone would get some chicken to dip in soy sauce and eat with rice and vegetables. That was a special time.

We had eggplant, tomato, broccoli, cabbage, Chinese bok choy, snow peas, potatoes, peanuts. We grew our own potatoes, we grew our own peanuts. We grew all kinds of things — eggplant, pumpkins. We didn't have white potatoes, only sweet potatoes. We didn't have a pig or cow.

My brother and sister and I played in the grass in the woods. I knew what kinds of leaves we could eat, they grew wild out there. We were skinny, but we were healthy. The most fun was to catch fish. The farmers would have a cow to pull the plow. That was how they prepared the muddy field to plant the rice. They let the older adults and the kids go in and fish. We would take a little basket or a net to catch the fish. When the farmers stir up the mud, the fish need air, so they come up to the surface. You can see the fish and scoop them up. They are all small fish, as big as my finger. We ate them fresh and we ate them later. We'd clean them up and fry them, then we'd put them out in the sun and sun dry them and put them inside a big container, so we could eat all winter. We'd use a little bit of fish, with soy sauce on top and soybeans, and cook it to eat with the rice. It was really good. Gives you lots of protein, too. Sometimes in the summer when we got a heavy rain, we would get flooded around where we lived. We would all sit around and put a line in the water. We would catch fish maybe nine inches long.

The war years were the worst. We just ate whatever we could find. We had rice, but not a lot to cook. We cooked it with lots of water to make it like a porridge, kind of thin. So you eat a whole big bowl, but you still feel hungry a little bit later. When we didn't have enough vegetables, we would go out on the farm. If you live there long enough, you know what you can eat and what you cannot eat. We'd pick stuff and go cook it and eat it.

My sister and I were with my relatives for three weeks when the Japanese came. I didn't have real rice once! Every day we had rice soup and soybeans to go with the soup. After I came home, I was real sick. My mother thought that I was going to die because I looked real pale and couldn't walk too much. She said it was because I ate too much rice soup, no rice, and just a bit of soybeans.

My mother suffered a lot. She did all kinds of things to save a little money. We made all our own clothes, we grew our own vegetables, we raised our own chickens. My mother went to town to buy old sweaters. She would bring them home, and my grandmother would sit there and pull the yarns apart and wash them and straighten them out. We all sat around and knit sweaters. We took them into town to sell. We made a little bit of money.

When we kids played, we played with rocks. We picked up some rocks, like people here play jacks. You go to the store and buy these things. We just would find five rocks or six rocks and play a game. We would pick some big leaves and use some pine needles. That's how I learned to sew when I was little. I remember I used pine needles to sew the leaves together.

My mother let me go to school. Lots of times families didn't let girls go to school, only boys, but I got to go to high school. We didn't have money to pay for tuition. The principal was nice, though. He said if you don't have money but you have rice, you can pay with rice. We had a little bit of rice left, so my mother took the rice to school and paid for my tuition.

During the war, we had no new clothing. We just wore the same thing over and over. We had to wear a uniform to school. Some mothers of other kids would go to the store and buy new material and have somebody make a uniform. But my mother took one of my father's long sleeved shirts and cut it down to make a shirt for me. She went to the back of the village where all kinds of bushes and trees grew. She got some kind of little fruit from the trees and used it to dye the shirt in hot water. Then she used some other material, like denim, from my grandmother's weaving. She used that to make a skirt for me. I felt embarrassed because my clothes didn't look like other kids' clothes, but that's what I had. We didn't have money to buy new shoes. I had to wear shoes when I went to school. Whenever it rained, when I walked home I had to take off my shoes, so I wouldn't get them wet. If my feet got wet, I'm OK — I can go home and wash them! But if shoes get wet, it's going to ruin them. I put my shoes inside my raincoat.

My father was in the north. He didn't get to come home. At the same time the Japanese got into China, the Communists were inside also. They wanted to take over the country. So it was double, double trouble. He couldn't leave, they didn't want any people who had any education to go back to the old way of living. They wanted to keep those people separated. He wasn't in prison, but they kept watching and everybody watched each other. In the 1960s he was imprisoned for six years. He was born in 1908, so he was in his 60s. They let him out later. He died four–five years ago from heart trouble, in China.

Toward the end of 1947, I met Bing, my husband. He was born in China, but he came over when he was young. His family came right before the war started. They lived in Marysville, California. He got out of the Air Force in the United States and went home to visit his relatives in China. His mother didn't want him to marry a girl who was born here in the U.S. The girl might do things different from her, so she sent him home to look for a wife. And that is how we met.

I knew him a little bit, but not too long. We got married in his village, in the next county from mine, not too far. We had a traditional wedding. Four boys from my village carried me in a chair three or four miles to Bing's village, so my shoes wouldn't get dirty.

After we were married, we went to Canton, the big city. They had a Western restaurant, real nice, in the hotel. They had steaks and chops! We never ate meat like that; we always had meat cut into little pieces and sautéed with vegetables, to eat with rice. I'd never had Western food before. They served a whole piece of meat for one person. Bing said he would order a New York steak, a whole piece of meat. I saw this waiter wearing a white uniform. He walked around with this cart with desserts in it, with the glass cover. Bing wanted to know whether I wanted to order a piece of meat. I said, "I want some of those."

He said "Those are not the dinner. Those are for after the dinner."

The waiter was pushing the cart around for the people who had finished dinner already, so they could choose a dessert. I said, "I don't want any dinner. I just want this." We signaled the guy to come over and I got six pieces of dessert. That was all I ate. Bing thought I was a crazy lady.

We went to Hong Kong to get some papers for me to come over here. I was a G.I.'s wife, so it was supposed to be real easy and simple. But they said I wasn't qualified because I didn't have a marriage certificate. So we had to get married again and get a marriage certificate.

I came over in March 24, 1948, by ship to San Francisco, 18 days on the troop ship, the *General Gordon*. It had bunk beds, metal bunks hanging from chains. That was where I slept. I saw some Japanese people on the ship too, and I was afraid of them. Bing said these people are just like you; they are going over to America or over to some other country. They are not the ones who went into China and killed all the people.

The main Chinese name for the United States is Gum Shan, Gold Mountain. In the mid 1880's, lots of people came over to dig for gold. The Forty Niners all dug for gold, so Chinese people called this Gum Shan because of the gold. So I thought it was really a rich country.

I always knew my grandfather was here. My grandfather came home to China a couple of times. He took a Montgomery Ward catalog or a Sears catalog home to show us what they had here and how people did things here. Everybody was interested in looking at the catalog, to see the different faces, different from Chinese people. I thought America was so clean, so good. In the catalog you didn't see kids with bare feet like me. They all wore nice dresses, no wrinkles. The women all wore high heels and sometimes they had hats. I didn't wear a dress when I arrived. I wore Chinese clothes, a pair of pants and a top, what people here call pajamas.

When we came to Marysville, I was really surprised. I expected Gold Mountain, with every building nice, straight up, tall and clean looking. I didn't know some buildings would be low and old. I was still thinking like a kid, even though I was married. I didn't even know we have dirt here! I thought everybody was so clean, always with the shoes. I was used to running around in the muddy water. We wore shoes only when we went someplace. My grandmother used to yell at me, "I told you not to go into the water to catch fish!" I would clean my legs a little bit with water, then next day I would go in again. My mother didn't care, because she liked to go out and do things, too. But my grandmother, she had old-fashioned thinking. She told me, "If you keep going out like that, pretty soon, your skin is going to be so tough, nobody is going to marry you. You will be an old maid all your life."

Bing and I lived in Chinatown in Marysville, on C Street. His father and mother had just started a restaurant, the Lotus Inn. He has worked there all the time since we came here. We have five children and they all had to work in the restaurant. My mother-in-law and my father-in-law worked in the restaurant. Bing's two sisters finished high school in Marysville and went to college. They didn't work in the restaurant. They were both born here.

The United States was all cement, with no gardens around. People's clothes were always so neat and clean. When I first came here, I would still go barefoot when I worked in the garden. I couldn't get over people wearing shoes all the time.

I returned to my town in China early in 2001. The house I once lived in is occupied by a cousin's family. They have running water but still have the outhouse. Things have changed, but they still go barefoot a lot.

Born into War

by "Annaliese," as told
to Carol Ditter Waters

War is indiscriminate. Children must carry its effects in mind and memory — in health and in heart — for the remainder of their lives. The following interview is anonymous. "Annaliese" was fearful — even
today — of the prejudice she might incur from her tale — a tale from what
was then Hitler's country.

Her experiences took place in a small village in Germany, close to what
was then the Czechoslovakian border, when she was a small child. It was
mainly a farming town except for a few factories. It was a quiet place,
until those days of war.

Each day of the interviews, Annaliese sat in her chair with her plump
white poodle wedged in beside her. The shades in the room were half-
drawn against the hot Arizona summer sunlight. We sat in the gloom,
this woman with the heavy German accent and I, while she returned in
memory to Wunsiedel, Germany — reluctantly returning to her World
War II experiences.

Carol Waters

The bombings! They are one of my earliest childhood memories. These
air strikes came often to the small town of Wunsiedel, Germany, where I
was born and where I grew up during the Second World War. When they
came, our warning was from the loud, dull, buzzing sound of an air-raid
siren. We children learned the routine. We would run around the neighbor's farmhouse to a door to their cellar. Once there, in the bitter cold, we
clung together both for warmth and for comfort, and prayed. We prayed
many, many rosaries for our safety in that dirt-floored dungeon of fear. We

could hear the explosions in the distance. At first, we had a few candles with which to break the darkness. Later there were none. We had no light, only black, scary darkness which made the waiting worse.

During the first air raids, our mother sometimes brought small pieces of dried fruit to give us while we waited. We could concentrate on eating these bits of food instead of what was happening outside. Later there were no more morsels of fruit. Often we remained there in the dirt and stone cellar for long hours until we heard with relief the "all clear" signal. We sighed then. We were free and alive — worry was gone for a while.

Herds of refugees were seen about our town and the surrounding countryside. People from neighboring countries such as Hungary and Czechoslovakia, as well as the gypsies, were seen in clusters everywhere. They clutched to themselves their meager belongings. One-room shelters often housed seven or eight people.

My father was away at war from as early as I can remember. In the beginning, he came home for a few furloughs. Then that ceased. Our mother was the sole supporter and caregiver of us four children. We had little food during these days. Our diet was mostly of potatoes — often only one a day. Sometimes we had a bit of meat; this was greatly prized. At these times, we would take a piece of potato and rub it on the meat and then suck it so that we could savor the flavor of this treat and make it last a little longer.

My brother would go to the nearby river with his fishing pole and catch fish. We would gather by the window sometimes when we were expecting him to return. Once in a while he came back smiling. He had been lucky! When our mother cooked the fish, she figured out how to conserve every edible morsel. All of it was precious. Hunger puts value on what is waste in better times.

My mother would make wheat cakes. She would roast some wheat, then grind it up and add a little of whatever we might have in order to bind it. They were very gritty, but good — when you were starving.

There were rationing stamps, but of little good were they to us. There was never enough of them. We stood in lines for hours and hours. Finally we would arrive at the counter. "It is all gone!" they would say. There was never enough.

Over time we were without shoes. They either had worn out or we had outgrown them. The winters were especially bad. It was not only hard to get about with no shoes; our feet were cold, really freezing, as we walked around in only stockings and whatever we could find, like bits of plastic or heavy paper, to wrap around our feet. It is bad enough to have nothing in your belly and the fear — always the fear — but to have the cold, too…

One day someone arrived to tell my mother that our father was dead.

She tried to get more information, but the man could tell her no more. There was nothing else to believe. We heard her sobbing in the night. There could be no funeral, of course, because there was no body to put into the ground. Our mother lived with this grief along with all her other trials of the war.

Work! That's all our poor, tired mother did. For some time she worked in a small factory that made scrub brushes. Also, she bought and sold animals. She and her sister would go about and purchase any animal they could get, even horses, and resell them for a profit. If it was a pig or a cow, they would take it to the local slaughter house and try to get a good price.

Fearing that her money in the bank would lose its value, my mother turned all her assets into currency. She told us, "I want us to eat, to have something. If it stays in the bank, it will be gone." She ended up with great bundles of it which she hid away in suitcases. Unfortunately, when the war was over, all this hoarded money was rendered valueless. The money left in banks held a portion of its value, but Mother had none in the banks. She lost it all. My sister and I tried to reassure her that we would get along, but she was devastated. There would be no relief to our poverty.

After many years, the war's end came. It was not a day of joy. We were the defeated. Fright clung to us as we listened to the roar of the trucks and the clatter of the tanks' treads on the cobblestones. A soldier stood tall in the middle of each tank and the trucks were filled with smiling, victorious men. They were heroes to their own. What would happen to us, we wondered. They had won. We knew we were at their mercy.

They were throwing something at us. We jumped back and covered our faces. Some of the people ran before we realized it was candy. Candy flew through the air, not bullets. However, we did not claim them, for we did not know if it was all right to eat. It might be poison. Was this a gesture of friendship or one of harm from the enemy — the same ones who had come to bomb us those many times. The candy lay there at our feet. It looked good, very good to us starving children, but we dared not touch it. Of course we had no trust. We knew Germany was responsible for the war. We fled terrified.

In the days of occupation which followed, one thing I remember was that piles of dirty laundry and brown soap appeared on our doorstep and on all the doorsteps throughout the town. My mother told us, "We must do their laundry now. You must all help." The locals were expected to wash the clothes of the American Army. Not much was said about this, we just did it. We had known worse. We were the conquered. But, as it turned out, there was one good thing about it. We were allowed to keep the left-over soap for ourselves! You don't know what this meant. When you are without it, you and your clothes — nothing can come clean. You live with grime on everything. We had had no soap for years. It came now with the army's wash.

Then after a while — surprise! We found hidden amid the dirty clothes an occasional can of ham and a can of beans. Ham! Beans! We hadn't had the likes of this. We hardly knew of their existence anymore.

Unfortunately, this was not without a price. For the American soldiers had pitched their tents in the surrounding fields and we would suddenly smell the delicious odor of roasting chicken — our chickens! Those poor hens from which we gathered a few precious eggs. The soldiers had traded their canned rations for our fresh poultry meat. It does not seem so important now, but then...

Another thing they took from us: we could not attend school after the Americans came since they took over the school building and made it their headquarters.

And then too, what comes with conquering armies? Rape. The women lived in total fear. All the women in town made sure that they did not venture out alone after dark. Yet, soon to the war widows and single women of this place which had few German men anymore, there began to appear small babies that had been fathered by the men who had conquered us. Thus was life.

One day, years after the war — in fact, it was in 1955 — a big man appeared at our door. He was a stranger to us young people who were now teenagers or older. He asked to be let in. We would not let him in. Our mother had instructed us not to let anyone we did not know into the house. He repeated, "Let me in." We again declined. He said he was our father. We didn't believe him. Our father was dead. His words went from German to another tongue — Russian — although we did not recognize the language. We were frightened, but remained firm. Finally, we told him where he could find our mother. She would handle this. Our mother returned home shortly with this man. He *was* our father!

He had been a prisoner in a Russian concentration camp for years and then finally had been freed. Of course, there had been no transportation home for soldiers from defeated armies. But by foot, and by hook or by crook, he had made his way back to be met at his own door by his children who did not know him. We did not know what to say to this man. He, too, looked at us as if we were strangers.

Our mother was joyous at this turn of events, but, as with most things connected with war, this returning soldier brought no happiness, only more sadness and distress. He was not the man our mother had known and loved. In his place now reigned a maniacal, mentally disturbed man. Apparently, his intense suffering in battle, his starvation and mistreatment in a prisoner-of-war camp had robbed him of himself.

He soon began beating all of us, his children and our mother. I have scars on my neck and my hand, where he cut me when he tried to kill me. He beat our mother repeatedly. My brother, Ludwig, one time suffered a horrible battering when he put himself between my father and my mother while he was attacking her. I think my father was acting out the treatment that he had experienced.

The drinking began. At night, for great distances, you could hear my father's drunken shouting with the anguished roars of other drunk veterans in the streets during the nights, trying to forget. I can still hear them in my head, mad cries of the physically and mentally wounded. He remained as drunk as possible whenever he could find the money. He sold whatever possessions we had in order to buy alcohol. He didn't care if they were needed or precious to us. All he thought about was drinking. This and his brutality made life almost unbearable for us. All we could think was that in his mind, we were enemy soldiers. He thought he was in battle.

There were not enough facilities to care for these defeated German soldiers. We were mostly good people who were caught in a web that Adolf Hitler had woven, that had brought destruction, sorrow and grief to everyone throughout the world.

Our aunt came to us one day and told us we must move away from our father and that she would help us find a place and help us pay for it. She told us, "No one should have to live with beating, especially after all you have been through." We found an apartment and moved when he was out. Because it did not belong to my father, he was not allowed to enter the apartment. After a while he wandered off to a fate we never really learned about. We attended his funeral years later. We were there to honor the man who once was.

All through those awful days of what must be the world's largest and most extensive conflict, our mother kept her faith in God — a strong, staunch, surviving faith. She stood by her four children, caring for us, sacrificing for us, showing us a brave example in the face of it all. She was our war hero.

In time, I wanted to get out of Germany, get away from all the bad memories, and begin a new life. I thought, maybe, in America, I could put all the bad times behind me. So I began to save my money. This took some time. When I had saved enough, my mother contacted a friend who was living in Massachusetts. The woman and her husband had an only daughter who had recently entered a convent. They were willing to take me in and help me start a new life in the United States. I obtained a visa for entry into the country and a green card so that I could work.

Then, a dream realized! I traveled to this country. My mother's friends picked me up at the airport. They had never seen me — only a picture of me. They took me in as a daughter and let me stay as long as I wished. I found work, and later I found a husband in America.

For the most part, all went well; however, I met with some prejudice here since, of course, our countries had been enemies. An example: a woman came up to me and said, "I don't like you. You are a German and the Germans killed my father in World War II. I don't like you."

People tend to hold you personally responsible for the consequences of war if you happen to be on the other side, even if you were a small, completely innocent child at the time of the battles and the killings. Prejudice is not based on reason, but on blind emotion. It is an iron wall with no windows.

God does not judge us by our race or our nationality, but as individuals. Why can't people do the same and eliminate the prejudice which instigated that war?

The plump, white poodle was sound asleep beside her, as Annaliese returned to the present. "Don't ask me any more questions. Do what you want with this, but don't ask me to go over it again. Reliving the past has brought back the old nightmares and I don't want them. I don't want to be there again in any way. "

I thanked her as she sat there in the gloom. Then I walked out into the brilliant sunshine. I was overwhelmed by the intensity of her grim memories. Over sixty years have passed and her childhood is as real to her today as when she experienced it. For her to share that portion of her life with me took real courage.

A Refugee's Tale

*by "Hedwig," as told
to Carol Ditter Waters*

> *Those in their elder years sometimes return in thought to the events of
> their youth. Most of us can do this freely, but for one whose early years
> were of trauma and tragedy, horror and hunger, revisiting that time in
> memory is to again face the fright and suffer the sorrow of those days.
> The following story was related to me at the expense of recurring night-
> mares by just such a teller. She re-experienced things mentally suppressed,
> events too much for the mind and emotions to bear at the time of hap-
> pening.*
>
> *Carol Waters*

I was a refugee in my youth, during the Second World War. It is the
closest thing to living like a wild animal; a homeless scavenger on the run,
scrounging for food. My siblings and my mother and I slept in the woods,
beside roads, in barns or in empty freight cars. Cold, afraid and desperate,
we moved ahead of the advancing Russian army.

Before the war, and during the first years of the war, my family — parents, my sister, my seven stepbrothers and stepsisters — lived on my father's
ancestral farm in Prussia, near where the Gdansk shipyards are at present.
It was a big farm, one that had food at the start of the war. My father was
gone. He had refused to join the Nazi Party so they took him away and made
him dig trenches for the German army. He was subjected to this hard labor
for some time. And his large family, who needed him, were left without
him.

In 1944, we were forced off our land. Word came that the Russian army was advancing and we were in its path. The women and children left by themselves. Packing what we could, we began our journey, sometimes by train and sometimes on foot. Once we missed the last train out and were greatly saddened. We learned later that it had been bombed. We took the train to the town of Thürnsdorf, close to Dresden on the Elbe River. Our luggage never arrived, so we had nothing. We moved into a one-room shelter, all that we could find.

We saw the bombing of Dresden, times when the whole sky was red with the fire of exploding bombs and burning buildings. The fire could be seen from hundreds of miles around the city and people could hear it as well. The explosions echoed loudly into the distance. War is described as hell. This was part of the hellish inferno.

A very beautiful old church was partially destroyed in Dresden. This ruin was never repaired. The people have left it as a reminder of the destruction of war, of how it is a crime against God as well as man.

Food was scarce. We had to eat whatever we could find. The American bombs would explode in the River Elbe. This killed the fish and they floated to the surface. We grabbed them from the river as they floated by.

And, alas! In the middle of all this, my only pair of shoes were stolen from me. I had them hidden behind a stone, thinking they would be safe, but someone managed to find them. I did not know how I was going to tell my mother of this loss.

Our father learned where we were and joined us there in Thürnsdorf. One day, we could not find the key to the room in which we were living. While we were locked out, a Russian soldier came along, grabbed my father, and held a knife to his throat. "Find me a woman before dark," the soldier commanded, "or I will kill you." My father did not know what to do. He had no solution to this threat. Fortunately, we found the key to our housing and were able to hide before the Russian soldier returned.

Our father had raised stallions on our farm in Prussia. They were beautiful animals and he managed to take one horse with him when we were forced to leave. This horse he prized. He kept it in a barn in Thürnsdorf. But the Russians found out about it and took the stallion from him. If you resisted in such a situation, they would kill you.

My father's brother, who was married to a Jewish woman, had a prosperous business in Berlin before the war. In 1932 or '33, it became very apparent that the Nazi Party was going to sacrifice the Jewish people in Germany. My uncle made the decision to move his family to Johannesburg, South Africa, and thus, avoided the holocaust. A Nazi moved into his house in Berlin after he and his wife departed.

Just before the war was over, we were compelled to move on again, forced to keep ahead of the advancing army. We were stalked by the Russian army, pushing further and further into German territory. We walked for days and had nothing to eat. Homeless, hungry, we crossed ice-covered rivers, slept in barns, and walked through the snow. Terror was everywhere. Women hid on the roof tops, hiding from the raping Russian soldiers. These men raped the Polish women, as well as the German women.

When we were out in the open, the enemy planes would suddenly appear and swoop low. We had no shelter, so we would lie flat on the ground as the machine gun fire ripped across the ground, aimed to hit us. These were extremely frightening times. The bullets came so close. We knew we could die at any moment.

Among the horrors of war is the fact that you lose so many people you were close to. You never even learn the fate of some. One was my half-brother. He remained behind with our grandparents when the family was forced to leave the farm. We do not know if the Russians sent him to Siberia or whether they hanged him from a tree as they did with many young men. When we were traveling on foot as refugees, we often saw this sight in the woods—the body of a young man dangling from the limb of a tree. It was horrible.

I was ten years old on V-E Day. After the war, we were forced to take either Russian or Polish citizenship. During this time, we were met with strong prejudice wherever we went. No one wanted us. Even our relatives with whom we sought refuge thought of us as useless, wandering beggars, and did not want anything to do with us. Refugees have no status. They are poor, stray, and mostly without an immediate future. Once, when my family was staying with relatives, the Red Cross gave me a doll. That was my only doll. My cousin threw it into a pond, reflecting his family's resentment of us as a burden.

At the end of the war, our family's ancestral farm was given to the Communists. The Communists took everything they could from the people. They claimed they needed it to pay for the war. Everything went to Russia. All the good Meissen china from the factories was sent off to Russia along with money, food, whatever.

I had a recurring dream in my youth. I dreamt that I was attempting to cross a body of water. I would start out, but then plunge down in the middle of it. I continually failed to make it to the opposite shore. I had the same dream for many, many years. In reality, I met a G.I. of German descent in Stuttgart when I was adult. We fell in love and I left East Germany and came to the United States in 1955. I never had this dream again after I came to the United States. My brother and sister who remained behind never got out. The Wall went up and they were held captives of the Communist regime from that day forward.

Prejudice came to me, too, at the time of my wedding. The mother of my husband-to-be did not want him to marry me. There was no nice wedding, no church service, no flowers, no wedding cake. We were married by a justice of the peace, and had a piece of coffee cake in celebration. And never did her prejudice die. She always thought of me as the enemy.

Many do not seem to realize that it was the leaders of some countries that sought this war. It was their thirst for power and desire to conquer that brought it on. Prejudice towards the common peoples of these countries should not endlessly persist.

I want to say that I do not blame anyone for this war. But I have to ask, why wasn't man more civilized? And aren't we supposed to love one another?

*A Lonely
Voice for
Peace*

Peace Workers: "Marginal to Society"

Elisabeth D. Dodds

That war is the worst way to go about solving geopolitical problems has been my firm conviction for more than 60 years. Though it was very, very hard to take that stand, my husband chose to be a conscientious objector in the Second World War. Sociologists have a term to describe people who are on the fringes of the rest of humanity: they are "marginal to the host society." Though we detested fascism and grieved about the Holocaust, we thought that there could be other, more lastingly effective ways to change the course of history. To spend the war years isolated from the rest of society was a very lonely choice.

A major influence on my own life had been my merry, pink-cheeked Quaker grandmother, who had never lost the lilting Irish brogue that came with her from Ulster when she moved to America in the 1870s. Her father had read in a friend's newspaper about a peace community being settled in Kansas. (It turned out to be a scam by the Santa Fe Railroad, which wanted to sell off land and create customers for the new cross-country rail system.) She stuck it out and stayed here, and she never abandoned the reason she had come to this country.

While at College of Wooster in Ohio, I had become interested in the Fellowship of Reconciliation, an international peace group. My family was supportive of my interest in the peace movement. Also at college, before

Pearl Harbor, I won a *Vogue* contest. The usual prize was a job in their Paris office, but because of the war in Europe, I ended up instead as an editorial assistant in New York. This was a fun place to work and a lovely life. New York was fun to be in, in those days. I went out to concerts in the evening and never thought to worry.

I heard about Pearl Harbor when I was on the train returning from visiting Bob Dodds, a man whom I was seeing. On that train ride, on Monday after the attack, I saw servicemen in uniform boarding the train. I felt as if I'd caught a medicine ball, something heavy and unwieldy weighting me down. Even then I was skeptical of what my government told me and I believe still that Roosevelt was delighted to get the United States into the war.

Bob, for his part, had learned through a group of Yale friends about Thoreau, Gandhi, satyagraha (soul force) and social change. Though he was 6'6" tall and technically too tall to pass the physical requirements of the armed services, Bob became a conscientious objector and I visited him several times at the camp where he was housed. Bob's draft board in Montclair, N.J., had sent him to a former CCC (Civilian Conservation Corps) camp in Maryland. The camp was administered by kindly, well-meaning, but squelched Quakers representing the American Field Service (AFS). In their charge were roughly 100 highly educated idealists who longed to be useful, yet were told to dig ditches and do pointless repetitive tasks.

Many of this group had studied or traveled abroad. They were in close contact with Quakers who already were hard at work trying to mitigate the horrors being directed at the Jews. At that time, the American press was silent about the Holocaust. So was the U.S. Department of State. Many foreign service personnel came out of Princeton and at that time there was a degree of anti-Semitism we can hardly imagine now.

Conscientious objectors were in a variety of situations. Some went to jail, some helped with refugees in France, some went to C.O. camps, some were trained in public administration to help rebuild Europe after the war, some went to seminary school. C.O.s volunteered for starvation studies in Minnesota. Some served as attendants at Massachusetts General Hospital on the mental ward. Their assignments were luck of the draw, depending on the attitude of their draft board. These boards were civilian volunteers; some were punitive, some were flexible. Some men chose to go to jail as the most extreme form of protest.

Bob's camp was a very depressing collection of bedraggled shacks. The men had to pay room and board, or I guess they went to jail. I stayed with the dietician, the only other woman in the camp. When I visited Bob, we were so chaste, we wouldn't think of doing anything improper. One night he had fire tower duty and I spent the night in the tower with him. I didn't want to walk back to sleep on the floor of a shack. I felt such a guilt, however, for having spent the night with a man! You can't imagine what a difference the pill made, later.

Some draft boards in the U.S. were more flexible than Bob's had been. One of my brothers was allowed by his board in New York state to take a leave of absence from Princeton to drive an ambulance with the British 14th Army in Burma. He was in the siege of Imphal, worked valiantly, and was awarded the British Empire Medal. He returned to graduate. His efforts were under the AFS and like Bob, he was not paid for his work.

The men who were rotting in the CCC Camp in Patapsco, Maryland, longed to be allowed to join the Quakers' efforts to save and relocate Jews. Many of them had met Dietric Bonhoeffer, when he was a student in New York City's Union Theological Seminary. Bonhoeffer had returned to Germany to work with a group of "good Germans" who were planning to challenge Hitler from within his own country. Bonhoeffer was caught and killed.

The C.O.s also knew of the courageous Huguenot pastor in Le Chambon, in the French Alps, who had rallied a whole town to take in Jewish refugees. Not one person had squealed, and many refugees were saved. The C.O.s would gladly have joined in that kind of effort. We bombed everything but never bombed the train tracks leading to the death camps.

I had met Bob at College of Wooster and we had a stormy courtship. I was enjoying dating lots of people. One guy I dated was in the peace movement. His father was treasurer of Gulf Oil and was mortified that his son was involved. That boy, a sweet, artistic man, became a conscientious objector and went to jail, where he was raped. People paid heavy prices for peace involvement.

We were sitting on the steps of a Methodist church in Baltimore when Bob asked me to marry him. I thought, I really have to back him up; I can't give him one more blow. I was confused on every level; I was only 22 years old. It was a very immature decision. We had a nice wedding in Greenwich Village in New York, May of 1942. We spent three days at the Jersey shore in a cottage loaned to us by a kindly Quaker lady. Then Bob returned to C.O. camp and I went back to my job at *Vogue* magazine.

I was a lowly editorial assistant in the features department, but I was treated with the greatest courtesy by the magazine. The editor in chief, Edna Woolman Chase, took pride in her ancestor, the Quaker mystic John Woolman. She was the first elderly woman I'd ever seen with blue hair, and when I tremblingly explained that, in conscience, I could not buy war bonds, Mrs. Chase smiled benignly and excused me. Businesses were under a lot of pressure to sell war bonds to 100 percent of their staff, but the magazine staff were very nice to me. I contributed to the AFS work in Germany and France instead.

Bob and Elisabeth Dodds on the roof garden at 123 W. 13th Street, New York City, May 23, 1942. The photograph was a gift from Lisa Rothschild, Vogue *staff photographer, who went on to become an award-winnig photographer for* Life, *until her sad, too-early death. Lisa was a refugee from Nazi Germany.*

I met Millicent Fenwick while at *Vogue*. She was the congresswoman who was the model for the character "Lacey Davenport" in the *Doonesbury* comic strip. When I knew her, she was the society editor and a very warm and nurturing person, just like the *Doonesbury* character. She called me "the little girl from Wooster." She never could remember my name. She was very tall and had to get a special dispensation from the government to be allowed to buy clothes under the rationing system. She told us she was in a special category under the Office of Price Administration, for "corpses, monstrosities, and brides"!

By 1942, there were two million young men in uniform in the United States. It was dicey for a man in civilian clothes to walk on a city street. One middle-aged woman who looked respectable walked up to Bob and spit at him.

I went to the Friends (Quaker) meetings at Grammarcy Park for support. I found that friends in the peace community meant a great deal to me. I made more lasting friendships than at any other time in my life. I did not have to justify my position to them.

One of the main activities of the peace community was resettling Jews in the upper west side of New York. The "Fellowship" newsletter would have notices asking for help with housing and jobs and for cash contributions. The Jews escaping at that time were people with skills. They added a great deal to New York life. One woman from Austria was a photographer at *Vogue*. We became good friends. We also did intercessory prayer for refugees, those in death camps, and others who were suffering. We didn't dare have protest parades. We kept our heads down and held study groups instead. Politically, it was a minefield. The United States was aligned with Russia, so ironic to be on the same side as Stalin. In the peace community were people I found very attractive who turned out to be Active communists. It was years later, however, that I figured this out.

Bob's guardian uncle, who was president of Princeton for 26 years, had been chairman of the infamous "Bermuda Conference" in 1943. It had been convened by President Roosevelt to decide what to do with a boatload of Jewish refugees who were asking asylum in America. They were all sent back to Europe, to their deaths. I never forgot Bob's row with his uncle about that decision.

The whole idea at Bob's camp was to not make it comfortable, because the C.O.s were slackers. So sad, such a waste of these well-meaning men. The crew leader at the C.O. camp, one humid summer day, ordered the C.O.s to dig a ditch. The next day they were told to fill it in. Bob's savings were hemorrhaging as he paid out each month for his upkeep in camp. He cracked with a nervous breakdown. When he was discharged from a hospital, we were helped by friends who had a splendid country place near Buffalo, N.Y. They offered us a gardener's cottage and scenery that soothes the soul. Bob was to tend a population of ornery turkeys while he pulled his life together. I left *Vogue* and joined him there.

During these painful months, we were marvelously befriended. Like passengers stranded together on a life boat, we isolated peace people became peculiarly bonded. I was sustained by some friends who still are primary in my life. Amusingly, one of the most significant friendships was with a couple who, like us, were great embarrassments to a prominent family. Henry Stimson Harvey was named for a relative whose power in Washington was beyond measure. With Henry and Marge Harvey we had much in common throughout the length of our lives. I could never do justice to the gift of friendships with other people in the peace movement, or thank them adequately.

I found a job as a feature writer for the *Buffalo Evening News.* I was treated with great kindness, but I found one day memorably painful. On D-Day when the Allies invaded Normandy, I was sent out to interview people on the street about how they were feeling. I shared what everyone was feeling that day — immense respect for the daring and complexity of the invasion and concern for the combatants, but I felt excruciatingly unworthy of what was being done for me. It was as if I were trying to shout through a thick pane of glass, a spectator.

In 1946, encouraged by a friend, we moved to Cambridge, Massachusetts, and Bob entered Harvard Divinity School. A grateful Congress was showering the returning G.I.s with thanks: mortgage assistance, college tuition — two inspired acts of social engineering that were to change American culture forever.

The dropping of the A-bomb turned me from a mild apolitical pacifist into a fierce nuclear opponent. During the years in Cambridge, I went to work for the YWCA and the AFSC as a college spokesperson, visiting campuses in the Boston area, talking with students about the kind of world they were building.

Our funds depleted, we were competing for scarce Cambridge housing and field work. It was essential to earn while we learned. Church after church turned us down. They didn't want to be led by someone they considered a "slacker." At last we encountered a cantankerous village which resembled the set of "Brigadoon."

The mid-Cape highway had not yet been built and the Cape [Cape Cod] was a sleepy peninsula which briefly bustled for two summer months. The rest of the months, the village of Dennis dozed. The "natives" were a mix of quirky, cranky, and courageous. They had lived as they pleased for several centuries, often ignoring governmental rules. (During Prohibition, they kept "revenuers" hopping.) The one church in town had for many years been the ruling political entity, the "parish" which was both worship center and town government. This struggling one-room church took a chance on us.

They could pay us only $100 a month, but they had a wonderful snug parsonage with a working fireplace. In the kitchen was a woodstove which I found daunting at first, but in time I grew to love the daily ritual of filling the kitchen with crackling cheer. I liked to walk and was famously frugal, so would pick up for kindling every scrap of wood that I came across, to feed those fires.

We entertained every church board and committee. The church building at that time had no bathroom or heat during the week and parishioners seemed to enjoy meeting in a comfy living room around a fireplace. Those ladies taught me how to keep house, how to listen, how to savor simplicity. (Today that same threadbare church thrums with activities and golf-playing retirees have transformed the Cape into suburbia.) Those were quietly fulfilling years. At last we felt secure enough to start a family.

From those years of zero income, I acquired a lifelong habit of voluntary simplicity. Those afternoons when I would return from my walks, scraping tree branches noisily behind me as I brought home kindling, I evolved a low-maintenance life style modeled on Thoreau, Dorothy Day, and Gandhi. My frugality hasn't always been fun for our children, but I think they acquired some valuable habits—a taste for travel, a curiosity about other cultures, a delight in dinner-table conversation about politics, a reverence for the privilege of voting. Most of all, I think we have passed on to our vivid, useful offspring a capacity to survive change and to march to their own drummer, even if they find themselves a little marginal to society.

Voices
of Grief

Personal Delivery

Evelyn T. Smith

Oak Street was one of the few paved streets in our neighborhood, and, at that, it was only partially blacktopped, so that between pavement and lawns lay a strip of caliche soil. On the rare occasions when it rained in Phoenix, this strip became a quagmire, but most of the year the postman's rackety Model A rolled to a stop beside the mailbox in a cloud of dust. Clem had been our regular postman as long as we had lived there. He suffered from hay fever, and to combat the effects of the dust he wore a white handkerchief tied around his head just below his eyes. The rakish highwayman's air imparted by this bandanna contrasted oddly with his uniform; the eyes peering over the mask were often red-rimmed and watering, but the tears couldn't quench their genial gleam. Until his daily arrival became the hub around which my little world revolved, I gave no more thought to Clem, or to what he looked like, than I did to the car that he drove.

Those first few months in 1945, our lawn must have been freer of weeds than any in the Salt River Valley. Each weekday morning as soon as my housework was done I spread a blanket on the grass for eight-month-old Abby, and while she absorbed her quota of vitamin D, I pulled handfuls of burr clover from the winter-killed Bermuda grass lawn, and together we awaited the postman's arrival. Our vigil began early in January when her daddy was sent overseas from Fort Lewis, Washington, as a replacement officer for the First Cavalry Division, then engaged in the Leyte campaign.

For the first three weeks of that month Clem stopped only to deliver bills, or circulars, or tedious missives (once eagerly welcomed) from family and friends; or some days, stopped not at all, but waved a brown arm out the open window of the Ford as it careened past. Then one day, while my first glimpse of the approaching dust cloud told me Clem's car was still a block away, I heard a raucous honking of the horn in a reckless rat-a-tat that set my heart pounding. The squeal of brakes punctuated the cacophony, and Clem leaned out to hand me two letters. My hands shook as I tore them open. Clem pulled the handkerchief off his face and wiped his forehead while I scanned the transparent sheets.

"The letters were written aboard ship," I told him, "the *Lurline*! Everything is *fine*. He says I should hear from him again soon!"

I leaned against the mailbox and grinned at Clem and Clem grinned at me, looking like a clown, for the skin around his eyes was gray with dust, his forehead was streaked where he'd given it a hasty swipe, and the lower half of his face was still clean.

February was an up and down month, a month of light and shadow, of bright days and gray days. Letters arrived in twos and threes on days when the dust motes danced in the sunlight like bubbles dancing in champagne — letters from New Guinea, from Leyte. Or days passed when no letters came, and though the sun shone with its accustomed brilliance, its warmth failed to reach the icy core of fear inside me.

The month of March started out best of all. By the time Herb's group arrived in Manila at the end of February, organized Japanese resistance had ended. As a part of the 8th Engineer Corps, his unit was assigned to "mopping up" operations and restoration of roads and bridges. Arriving too late to participate in the siege of Manila, A Company still had to cope with the "inconveniences" of booby-traps, land mines and guerrilla snipers as they constructed "Little Burma Road" and "Safari Boulevard." Mail service was miraculously regular, and almost every day Clem heralded his arrival with a series of blasts on the horn that meant "Here comes a letter!"

It rained twice, and in a clean-washed new world, Clem doffed his bandit's mask. Timorous green shoots appeared in the brown Bermuda grass; bolder rosettes of burr clover challenged me to renew the battle I had thought won. Baby Abby, clad now only in a diaper, dazzling white against her papoose-brown body, stood alone, staggered two steps at a time. Days were warmer now, and Clem gratefully drank iced coffee while I stood at the gate reading my letters, the baby balanced on my hip.

Dated March 14, 1945, Herb's latest letter was written from an officers' club in Manila. "We have moved quite a ways," he wrote, "and are back with the squadron in garrison for a few days, resting, repairing equipment, and reorganizing for whatever comes next. It's good to see the tents all set up and to sleep on cots; that foxhole was getting smaller every day. It's quite a long ride into town, but worth it. We've built a bar here in the club, have running water and a *refrigerator*. I'm sipping a Tom Collins while writing this."

Unbelievably, then, for twenty-eight days following that letter there was no news at all. At first, Clem stopped daily, drank coffee, left trivial mail. We reassured each other, confidently at first, then with less optimism as the days dragged by. Those days were a relief when there was no mail at all and the Ford rattled quickly past, Clem's hand raised in a perfunctory wave.

I began to hide from Clem. Abby fretted indoors, missing her sunbaths. I skulked behind the curtains of the living room until Clem had come and gone and I could steal out, unobserved, to open the mailbox, confirm at a glance that the agony of waiting was not ended. From my hiding place I watched Clem, more

Evelyn Smith and Abby.

than once, carefully balance packages atop the fence behind the mailbox rather than sound the horn, and I knew he avoided me, too.

Early on an April morning I stood at the open front door, coffee cup in hand, feeling on my face the sun's tentative warmth and absently assessing the inroads of my late enemies, the weeds. A battered car stopped at the gate, its engine left idling with a tired wheeze. The man who walked across the lawn looked old and tired, too, his shoulders stooped as though under a burden, though he carried only a clipboard and a small sheaf of yellow envelopes. As I stared at the lined face under the Western Union cap, I felt a surge of pity for this ancient messenger of death, so unlike the brash, bicycling boy my tortured imagination had pictured.

It must have been Clem who delivered the adjutant general's confirming letter and the dismaying deluge of official communiqués and messages of sympathy that followed. I did not see Clem, nor was I more than vaguely aware that friends placed the mail on my desk, and helped me cope with replies.

I walked out one day with a letter I had written and was surprised to see Clem walking toward me across the yard. He pulled off his cap and wiped the sweat from his face as we met. We stood for a moment in silence; began to speak at the same time, stopped, embarrassed.

"I don't quite know how to say this, but I felt like I had to stop by. You see, I'm retiring tomorrow, and the wife and I are moving to Riverside to be closer to the kids."

Clem old enough to retire? I stared at him in dismay, noting for the first time that his thinning hair was as gray as the dust that smothered the roadside weeds. We had shared so much, Clem and I, yet never had I thought of him as a person, old or young, married or not; never had asked of his family, or even inquired his full name. My self-reproach deepened as he continued to speak.

"I've been on this route a long time. I remember this house when it was being built, and how your young man put up the mailbox himself, just before you were married and came here to live. You get to know a lot about folks in this job — lots of the good things, and some you'd just as soon not know. And sometimes, there's mail you've got to deliver that, well, it just *hurts*. I couldn't just leave these in the box and have you come out here and find them; not without telling you how sorry I am about the way things have turned out."

He placed a small packet of letters in my hand, then turned quickly away. I must have stammered some words of thanks and farewell as he got into the car and drove away, the familiar outline of the old car soon obscured by the inevitable billows of dust.

The small bundle of letters I held was tied together with a cord. Their edges were frayed, and they bore unidentifiable stains. On each, my name and address appeared in the upper left-hand corner, as I had written them (how long ago?). Below, the name and APO number had been carefully crossed out, and printed above were the words, "DECEASED — RETURN TO SENDER."

A Wife's Premonition

Mary Chance McClain

In the early 1940s, I was known as Mary Detrick — a minister's daughter. I was 22 years old and worked at Thurber's Fine Foods— an all-purpose grocery store at the corner of 9th and Elm in Albany, Oregon. Those were the days when groceries were delivered to the home; sometimes my boss hired his brother, Dick Thurber, to do the delivering. Although I didn't realize it at the time, my boss was soon to become my brother-in-law.

Dick's main interest was airplanes and learning to become a pilot. It evolved as a surprise to the two of us that our chemistry seemed to be magnetic. I was going with a young man, George, from Stayton, but after a few dates with Dick, I realized that he was the one whom I wanted a relationship with. After what seemed to me to be many, many dates, he finally gave me a diamond.

The night before our wedding, Dick had an impacted wisdom tooth removed. The dentist gave him some strong pain medicine so he could sleep. Sunday morning, March 16, 1941, I paced the floor as he overslept and was an hour late to pick me up. I was sure he had gotten cold feet and stood me up. But that man never stood me up. For most of our honeymoon, Dick's jaw was swollen and painful.

Dick's flight training took us to Portland and from there to Albuquerque where he received his Wings and where he and some of his best friends enlisted. While he was in flight school, we lived at the Central Street Motel which provided one room with bath. We had a bed, a table and two chairs, an old-fashioned icebox with ice delivery every other day and a two-burner gas stove with a one foot square oven that could be set over one burner so we could bake. We used the oven every third day since we shared the kitchen with two other Air Force families. We three couples became very good friends.

Each Sunday afternoon we would go to the officers' club to a tea dance and always stayed for dinner in the evening. It was always a formal affair with the officers wearing their dress uniforms and the ladies all dolled up.

Often when pilots were on maneuvers, I would go to the flying fields and watch the planes take off and come in. One day, as I counted, all the planes landed but one. I just knew the missing plane was Dick's. He had to be in trouble. Fire trucks and ambulances were arriving. I can close my eyes today and still hear the deafening sirens. Time and my heart seemed unreal for a few seconds. Then a tiny dot appeared way off in the blue sky. It was Dick's plane, but could it land without crashing? Again it seemed that even the breeze stood still. The plane came down and made a perfect landing. There had been trouble lowering the landing gear and Dick had maneuvered the plane until he had it under control. This was my first experience with what life had in store for me as a wife in World War II.

From Albuquerque the orders were for San Francisco. The men went on the train while we girls drove across the desert. We knew that this was our last time to be with our husbands before they were shipped overseas. When Dick and his friends prepared to leave for the front, we were filled with excitement and patriotism.

I returned to Albany where my brother-in-law needed help. Once again, I went to work at the little store at 9th and Elm. As I was working one afternoon in 1944, about 2:00 p.m., I had an ominous feeling that I must go home. I turned to my brother-in-law and told him I was going home to receive a message. I just knew I had a message at home. As soon as I arrived, Dick's mother called and told me I would be getting a telegram. It arrived, telling me that Dick and his crew in the B-24 had been downed over Formosa. All were lost.

It was August 1949, before those bodies were shipped to St. Louis to be buried in the military cemetery there. Along with Dick's brother and other Thurbers, I attended the ceremony for 13 military servicemen — Jewish, Protestant and Catholic.

After losing one husband in the early part of the war, I married Bud in 1946. On Christmas Day of 1980 we bid Bud good-bye. We had a wonderful, loving marriage and I will always miss him. In 1982, I married James H. McClain, an old friend of Bud and mine. He passed away in 1999. I have had much happiness and sadness, too. I've had a very good life and have many happy memories.

What's a Pearl Harbor, Mommy?

Carol Ditter Waters

It was early afternoon, West Coast time, that infamous winter day. We were eating Sunday dinner. "Quiet!" My father raised his hands and commanded. "Quiet!"

A special news bulletin was coming over the radio. I was the one being hushed. I had turned seven years old on December 5, 1941. It was two days later. Everyone's world had stopped. My father sat by the radio all that afternoon. My mother was somber and withdrawn as she did the dishes. Both parents were absorbed. They remembered World War I.

I did not understand what was happening. I knew who the Japanese were and had a vague notion about bombs—but what was a Pearl Harbor? No one would explain. Children are just "kids-under-foot" at such times.

Then there was a declaration of war. We were far, far from any place that was to see action, but we were touched by a "fallout." Our peace-time childhood was gone. New words, military words, soon crept into our vocabulary: air raid, machine gun, camouflage, blitzkrieg, torpedo—and, much later, atom bomb.

The neighbor boys built wooden B-29 model planes and held mock skirmishes in the vacant lots, using toy guns. Their weapons became more sophisticated as time went on. My sisters and I played "Red Cross." We crayoned a big red cross on a sheet and draped it over branches. It served as a tent for bandaged dolls. We used a wagon for an ambulance.

"Buy war bonds" was heard. We did so at school. There we also heard the war stories of some of our classmates whose fathers or brothers had been called up. "Rationing stamps" were household words when shortages began. We talked of stamping out Hitler and Tojo as our little feet crushed tin cans for scrap metal.

The strains of Glen Miller's music on the radio were preceded and followed by the latest news about London or Leyte, Iwo Jima or Africa, Casino or Corregidor, Sicily, the Solomon Islands, Battles of Britain, the Bulge...

And my grandmother would say, "Wonder if we'll be getting a letter from Ralph? Wonder if we will be hearing from him?" He was her son — my uncle. He was in the Navy. In the Pacific. She wasn't wondering about a letter. She was wondering if he was all right, if he was alive.

When some censored mail arrived, with childish reasoning, I told this uncle's brother that the two of them should have developed a secret code when they were kids. They could use it at a time like this. He didn't say anything. Nobody said anything. They were worried

We had a practice "black-out" or two. I remember standing in a pitch-dark room and peeking out closed blinds to see if any planes were overhead. Thankfully, there weren't.

The words, "Don't you know there's a war on?" were heard frequently. Yes, we did. It was about all that adults talked about. The newspapers and magazines were full of those black and white pictures of soldiers in battle — thousands of pictures, thousands of scenes— killing scenes.

Featured with every movie we attended was a colorful cartoon. Bugs Bunny — Donald Duck — Goofy — and their antics. Fantasy. Then the newsreel. Not colored. Reality. War pictures. Hitler and Mussolini — the other goofies, other craziness.

The newsreels were graphic. They were not toned by the same morale building, flag-waving patriotism and glamour of the war movies put out by Hollywood. We saw those, too. We were drinking it all in.

Gold star service flags began to appear in the front windows of homes. They indicated that a family member had been lost to the war. We would become quiet in the car when we spotted a home with a gold star flag.

Though we children living in the United States were probably the luckiest children on the globe at that time, we felt the war. There was an attitude — an attitude of anxiety and of unhappiness that prevailed for "the duration." And, after a while, what with being so young, we kids forgot what it was like before there was a war on.

But, then, finally, one day it was over.

I was ten and a half years old by then.

We went downtown the afternoon of V-J Day to celebrate. Being August, it was warm and sunny. Men were there in uniform — home on leave. The joy on their faces was indescribable. Joy that must have been felt by servicemen all over the world that day. They had been given back their lives—the living ones, that is—had been given back their lives.

And that particular uncle who saw action in the Pacific did come home. He was one of the lucky ones. Everyone said so. He survived. He lived. He lived, however, only to relive all those horrors over and over, the nightmares and the terrible hauntings, only later to be drowned in alcohol.

Though he spoke little of his experiences, we learned bits of the story from others who had served with him. They had met the enemy. He had seen his buddies burned alive on that ship in those days of fierce fighting.

He died only twelve years after the end of the war. Cause of death: lung cancer. Yes, he had smoked cigarettes. But, he had inhaled, too, the smoke of a burning ship, of fuel on fire and the stench of the burning flesh of his comrades.

The coffin was flag-draped. There was a gun salute at burial and the words, "He served his country" were bandied about in eulogy and in conversation in a hollow way. Words that must have been said in the eulogies of all those men who had died in battle itself.

His wife and children were at the funeral, of course. And so was his mother — my grandmother. They had lost him to the war in another way. He had died of old "war wounds"— emotional war wounds like so many other veterans must have.

Let peace be their memorial.

Index